AUSTRALIAN ARCHITECTURE 1901–51

Sources of Modernism

Frontispiece Preston Shire Hall. Competition entry of H. Desbrowe Annear, architect. 1892.

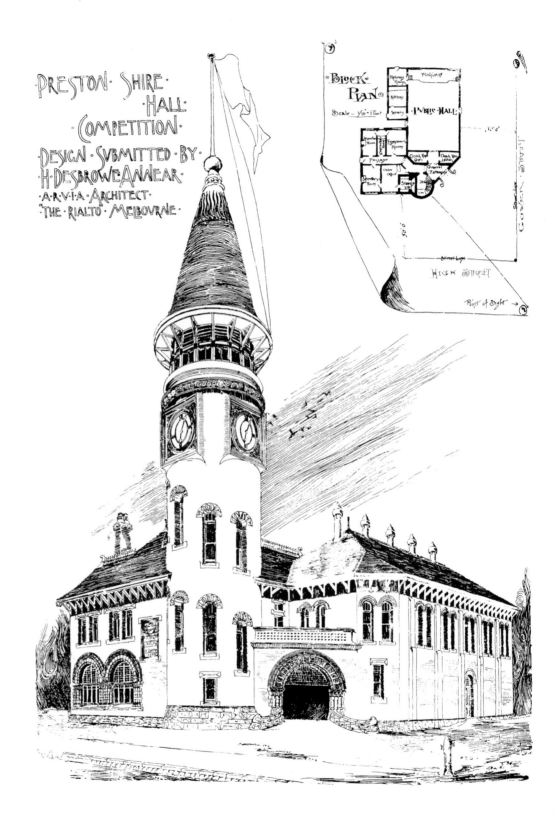

PRESTON·SHIRE·
·HALL·
COMPETITION

DESIGN·SUBMITTED·BY·
H·DESBROWE·ANNEAR·
·A·R·V·I·A·ARCHITECT·
·THE·RIALTO·MELBOURNE·

·BLOCK·
PLAN·

Scale – 1/16 – Foot

AUSTRALIAN ARCHITECTURE 1901-51

Sources of Modernism

DONALD LESLIE JOHNSON

SYDNEY UNIVERSITY PRESS

SYDNEY UNIVERSITY PRESS
Press Building, University of Sydney

UNITED KINGDOM, EUROPE, MIDDLE EAST, AFRICA
Eurospan Limited, 3 Henrietta Street, London WC2E 8LU

NORTH AND SOUTH AMERICA
International Scholarly Book Services, Inc., Forest Grove, Oregon

National Library of Australia Cataloguing-in-Publication data

Johnson, Donald Leslie.
    Australian architecture 1901–51.

    Index
    Bibliography
    ISBN 0 424 00071 7

    1. Architecture—Australia—History. I. Title.

720.9'94

First published 1980
© Donald Leslie Johnson 1980
Printed in Australia by Macarthur Press (Books) Pty Limited, Parramatta

Contents

To Sonya

Preface

This monograph grew out of my studies on the American architect Walter Burley Griffin who lived and practised his art in America, Australia and India. As those studies proceeded two important questions or observations emerged. Why was so little known of this important architect, and why was he not accorded a proper position in the history of architecture, American or Australian? Over succeeding years the first question has been answered by people similarly concerned: Mark L. Peisch, H. Allen Brooks, W. R. Hasbrouck, Paul E. Sprague, D. T. Van Zanten and, more peripherally, others in America. In Australia, first Robin Boyd, then Peter Harrison, Petter Willé and myself have attempted to sort the local history. But the second question has remained unresolved. Perhaps too many comments in the past about Griffin's failures or importance were too personal and/or unsubstantiated guesses without reference to parallel events.

As we will learn, one can come to grips with the architecture of Griffin from his beginning in 1901 and, from 1948 with the designs of the Viennese architect who also immigrated to Australia, Harry Seidler. That period bound by the launching of each man's career, is one of great importance during which an architecture of character emerges, warranting at least international interest. It is undeniable that the two men stand prominent at each end of the time scale as sentinels of architectural quality.

Australia is not an isolated case of a country that has come under the influence of foreign architects. One need only reflect on the sway of Scotsman C. R. MacIntosh on the Viennese, of Bostonian H. H. Richardson on Europe or of the mid-western American Frank Lloyd Wright on Germany and the low countries, or of the Swiss, Le Corbusier, on Germany. Immigration has had a greater success in providing inducements for change, not only as a means of transporting ideas but in easing acceptance by an almost tangible personification. Again, people come to mind: the Frenchman Paul Cret in Philadelphia, the Austrians Richard Neutra and R. M. Schindler in California, the European Serge Chermayeff in London, the Germans Walter Gropius in England (and then at Harvard University) and Mies van der Rohe in Illinois. But is personification the only source for change?

My book, *The Architecture of Walter Burley Griffin* (South

Melbourne 1977), contained only a hint as to Griffin's role in the development of modernism in Australia. It was intended that his influence—or lack—would be knitted with that book but it was limited in words and illustrations. Yet, since its release new information about modernism has come to light, so whatever frustrations one felt, they have partially subsided.

And a final point: there is a rather explicit moral value given to the modern movement which came out of the urban centres of central Europe, to the International style. Suffice it to say I am aware of that value but it was, after all, a judgement made by people in their own time.

In a sense, the essays in this monograph attempt to search out of the recent past a set of pragmatic reasons for change. Also, they attempt to answer an important implication of the discussion above: if there was no internal development of ideas in architecture, why? The discussion, therefore, revolves around the problem of inventiveness and the components of communication in the architectural profession in the first half of this century.

D. L. J.

Kangarilla
1978

POSTSCRIPT

Research for this book was complete in early 1978. Many details have come to light since that date but they do not alter the basic theses. In fact, a colleague in England, Anthony King, wrote me the following information in November 1979 which seems important to convey to readers:

. . . the idea of the Piddington Bungalow of J. H. Hunt is almost certainly taken from the Birchington/Westgate bungalow innovation of John Taylor I mentioned in the 2nd *AAQ* [*Architectural Association Quarterly*] article. . . . It has very many similarities to a number of photos and drawings I have of the Taylor bungalows. More than that is the fact that these Taylor bungalows were first illustrated in the *Building News* in 1873 and 1874 and it would seem more than a coincidence that JHH coined the name and did the design in 1876. . . . This all reinforces your point about the diffusion of ideas thru journals, etc.

Acknowledgements

There are only a few architectural historians in Australia. Anyone attempting to piece together a history owes a great debt to the first, Robin Boyd. This is especially so for his observations on the twentieth century in *Victorian Modern*, *Australia's Home* and to a lesser extent, *The Australian Ugliness*. For the late nineteenth century one's debt is to J. M. Freeland for his book *Architect Extraordinary: ... John Horbury Hunt*. Freeland's survey, *Architecture in Australia: a History* was always helpful. The first serious student and historian of the nineteenth century was Morton Herman and his initial study *The Early Australian Architects and Their Work*, although not critical to this work, was given reflection in the Australian continuum. This was also the case in relation to his more relevant study of Edmund Blacket in *The Blackets, an Era of Australian Architecture*.

Since so much of the research for this book paralleled efforts for the Griffin book, the people mentioned in that book must be acknowledged here. Others to whom I owe a debt of gratitude are: John Kenny, Melbourne; the architects who provided so much time and material—Harry Seidler, Frederick Ballantyne, Edward Billson, Louise Lightfoot, Les Grant, and E. J. Weller; David Gebhard and Gerald Groff, Santa Barbara; Vince Terrini, Auckland; Peter Navaretti, Melbourne; Elmar Zalums; the state libraries of New South Wales, South Australia and especially Victoria; the reference section of the Flinders University Library and Reg Brook and his photographic staff at that university; and my mother Mrs D. M. L. Johnson. My thanks are also due to Mrs Lesley Glaysher of Sydney University Press for editorial guidance and assistance during the production stages of this work.

An outline of the period to 1935 was given as a paper to the Art Association of Australia conference in August 1976 and a revision of that paper was published in the association's *Architectural Papers 1976* (Sydney 1978). I would like to thank the editor of the *Australian Journal of Art* for permission to quote in part from my essay on Harry Seidler that appeared in the first issue (1977) of that new art history journal.

Some people provided photographic material and they are mentioned elsewhere. Most of the extant buildings (and many of the original sites of demolished buildings) in America and Australia

ACKNOWLEDGEMENTS

mentioned in the text were visited by this author. I would like to
thank the people who assisted or opened their doors of hospitality.
The Flinders University Research Committee gave financial
assistance on a number of occasions. Some students offered ideas
and sources of inquiry by providing excellent seminars in courses
and honours topics.

And some were patient: thank you Sonya, Karl and Adam.

Let it not be imagined that building, merely considered as heaping stone upon stone can be of great consequence, or reflect honour either upon nations or individuals. Materials in architecture are like words in phraseology, having separately but little power; and they can be so arranged as to excite ridicule, disgust or even contempt. Yet when combined with skill, and expressed with energy they actuate the mind with unbounded sway.

FRANCIS GREENWAY, quoted in Walter Bunning, 'Fifty Years of Federation', Australian Broadcasting Commission, recorded 9 April 1951

1

1901-13: Attempts at Cultural Redefinition

It is difficult to discern any coherent cultural development or much achievement in the first third of the century.

In fact the period 1900–1940 marks a perpetuation of colonial dependence and curious hesitation in development towards nationhood.

GEOFFREY SERLE, *From Deserts the Prophets Come*, Melbourne 1973

In the 1880s there were serious discussions and many meetings all urging the colonies to federate and form a single nation. There were barely three million people on the Austral continent during that decade and they had been members of the British colonies for slightly more than one hundred years. It was by no means a wealthy group of people (except for the grazier) and the colonies were not the most financially successful (except with wool) nor diverse (ethnically or economically) so the proposition to unite seemed reasonable and relatively easy: and so it proved.

In 1901 the colonies finally achieved federation culminating a fervour of nationalism that dominated the previous two decades. Two important reactions to federation affected the course of Australian architecture. The first was to seek a source of inspiration for the development of the country and the second was to choose or perhaps build a capital city. Both were part of a search for an Australian culture.

The Quest for an Australian Style

One product of that search was an attempt to discover an Australian architecture. The search seemed to concentrate less on product and more on potential and on written discussion. There were no debates as such, just occasional ideas or thoughts. Since the number of professional or semi-professional journals was extremely limited (see Bibliography) British journals were often used. To the casual reader of those journals the discussion might have seemed more of a debate than actually occurred. But the question of what might compose an Australian architecture was fair. In 1890 the architects James Izett[1] and Howard Joseland raised the question, 'What, in the first place, must guide us in the development of an Australian type?' Both believed that climate was the answer.[2] James Green, an Australian writing for the London architectural journal *The Builder*, the most popular of English architectural magazines, agreed that climate was important but also thought that a style must be selected. His choice indicated prevailing attitudes about contemporary building styles: public and urban buildings were seen as one style, domestic architecture as another. Green selected the obvious Roman and Greek precedent, 'the very early Classic for city edifices', as he described them, 'and the Swiss (as seen in the Alpine *chalet*) for residences'.[3] The definition of chalet was not clearly set out, but among his selections of those already built was an unidentified 'Log Cabin for a Country Club' for upstate New York.[4] These American vacation cabins (some were palatial mansions) were part of a growing interest in the bungalow and cottage and Green was quick to identify the type.

There were local more practical attempts to answer the question. In Sydney, for instance, Lucien Henry devised in the 1880s an 'Australian order of Architecture'.[5] He suggested local flora on the traditional Greek orders rather than the acanthus leaf or Ionic volute. But his designs remained paper ideas. More substantial discussion continued in the waning years of the century but soon faded. It was revived in the new century with Robert Haddon's book published in Melbourne in 1908 which expressed a desire for a national architecture. He was an English immigrant aware of modern work in Britain. He became a teacher and architect in Melbourne practising in the contemporary English styles. His book *Australian Architecture* contained few original ideas except for one or two rather novel, if not advanced, aspects of modernism: a little Art Nouveau and a lot of Queen Anne, both to be discussed later. He suggested the student read 'some good standard book upon the history of architecture' but offered no bibliography. He advised the student to draw and measure the 'very best buildings here existent' but none were mentioned. He believed the old, 'conservative' British forms most appropriate for Australia: a popular view. Haddon's ideas are typical of those of the period *c.* 1895–1914. He had little notion of what a new architecture might be or of how to break away from the old styles.

Although Britain and Europe were historically and nostalgically the cultural fountainhead, a more logical choice for emulation was America. Australia saw not only the material and industrial development of the United States, but felt that the two countries shared a similar history, that a latent independence might not adversely affect a comparable development. There was also a similarity of geographic size, if not geography. Because of their

1 'Little Coppice', Bucks., England, C. R. Ashbee, architect, c. 1905.

common language, communications were accomplished with relative ease. Information about the steel skyscrapers was eagerly sought, as well as the architecture of rapidly developing and climatically similar California. Architecture for industry received as much attention as ideas for houses and housing. On appearance it was America that induced change—change for a better life, for efficient industry, for diverse urbanization, or whatever one wished to consider. America was involved with the ideas of change. Change was part of *fin de siècle* concepts. Ideas of and for architecture took on a vitality in the American scene without equal in Europe. Indeed, between 1885 and 1910 the most profound and illuminating architectural achievements were emanating from American architects—pragmatists challenging the new world. It was an infectious atmosphere, seducing not all Australian architects but at least those of similar concern if not persuasion. They were few in number and even fewer of that number were able to cope with the complexities involved.

This does not mean to suggest that the British traditions were immediately dismissed. On the contrary, the changes in America

caused most Australian architects to keep even more tenaciously to the traditional building styles which gave known results as Haddon demonstrated. Nor was Europe cast aside. Two attempts to find a response to the forces for change received attention from Australian artists and architects: the English Arts and Crafts Movement (begun in the 1860s) and the European or Belgian Art Nouveau (begun in 1892).

The Arts and Crafts as promoted by the Englishman William Morris and encouraged by his followers in the last half of the nineteenth century was related not only to the arts and crafts but also to an investigation of medieval ideas of the English cottage life and industry. The movement in Australia had a timid beginning in the late 1880s and remained more of a curiosity for many years. By the 1920s it was purely decorative or absorbed by the ideas and manifestations of the bungalow craze. The first indication of formal interest in the movement was in Melbourne in 1890. The first and apparently only magazine devoted solely to the movement was *Arts and Crafts. An Illustrated Magazine of Arts, Handicrafts and Sanitation*, begun in Melbourne in 1895. Typical of the movement, it was mainly concerned with things for the home—furnishings and the like—not with the house itself (or

2 A house interior, *circa* 1910.

3 'A Suggestion for a "Green" Bedroom', in *Building* magazine, April 1908.

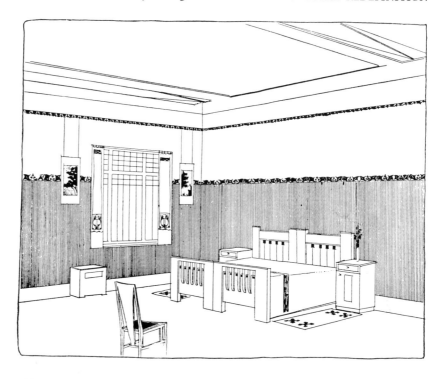

if so, more incidentally). When the Society of Arts and Crafts was founded in Sydney in 1907 it too was interested in the objects within the home, in the promotion and encouragement of 'the use of Australian materials and motif in design'.[6] The idea of using native materials pre-dates, therefore, the introduction of Art Nouveau as does the idea of using native flora and fauna. In fact natural motifs were widely used in the stucco and brick relief sculpture in Romanesque revival buildings in the 1880s and 1890s, particularly in Melbourne. Gum nuts, kangaroos, emu, kookaburra and such, were part of Arts and Crafts decorative design[7] and blossomed profusely during Art Nouveau. But the influence on Australia of William Morris' movement and his followers, such as architect C. R. Ashbee's arguments for a cottage design or style (**1**), was limited more to spiritual resolve than material substance, and to a limited audience. For architecture the potent ideas in England of those supporting the medieval cottage led to more flexible ideas of the bungalow which evolved in England and then matured in America at the turn of the century.

Art Nouveau, on the other hand, offered no direct lineage to the future as did the theoretically stronger Arts and Crafts. Art Nouveau tended to be superficial in its application to architecture. Buildings containing elements of Art Nouveau were usually part of the cottage ideas or the relatively new aberrations of Queen

Anne revival, a rather heavy architecture of many angular roof forms and white posted verandahs. Or, Art Nouveau was applied to a variety of tried and successful architectural styles including the Arts and Crafts cottage. The mix of Arts and Crafts with Art Nouveau, for instance, cannot be too heavily stressed. The pure new art of Belgium and Europe arrived in Australia about 1900 or so, but it was an English derivation organized about cottage and Romanesque ideas and forms. More often than not it was a heavily massed architecture with surfaces of glass or white wood which received a touch of Art Nouveau form, line or colour. This was true of most of Art Nouveau architecture. The very tenuous whipped lines extending into the architecture of Frenchman Hector Guimard's buildings, as exemplified in his designs for the Paris Metro stations, or the full forms and colour of the Spaniard Antoni Gaudi which found a completeness throughout his buildings, in particular the Casa Batlo, Barcelona, have few equals in the rest of Europe and none in Australia. Historian John Freeland's statement that in the hands of Australian follow- ers and imitators 'Art Nouveau was sterilized into utter super- ficiality'[8] was true. The implication was twofold: as a means to a full design there was little in Art Nouveau to offer the architect and those who tried failed the offering.

The paradox of stylistic mix is revealed in two interiors. The first was photographed in 1910 (2). It is the interior of an Australian house showing classical elements (cornice, flower stand and colonettes), Queen Anne chairs, Victorian over-stuffed furniture and furnishings, Arts and Crafts end tables, Edwardian tiles and fireplace and Art Nouveau screen. The other interior was published in Sydney in 1908 and was of a design usually defined as geometric Art Nouveau (3). We have not been able to trace its source, that is if it is an Australian design or from an overseas journal (perhaps English or German), but it is a most unique interior to appear in Australia in that year. Designs of such advanc- ed ideas did not appear again until the 1930s.

The prevalent attitude just after the turn of the century was exemplified in an article in the profession's journal, *The Salon*, where the voices of prophecy, proposal and change were offered a naive reproof so typical of reactions at the time and comparable to comments as late as the mid-1920s.

A day never passes without our hearing our architects called upon to be original, and to invent new style, and an Australian order, to go down to posterity alongside of Gothic, Renaissance, etc., etc.

We want no new style of Architecture. Who wants a new style of painting or sculpture? We want, however, *some* style.[9]

4 House, *c.* 1902–3, Ivanhoe, Victoria. H. Desbrowe Annear, architect. (Courtesy *Architect*)

Three houses by Harold Desbrowe Annear in 1902–3 for a steep site on The Eyrie, Eaglemont, Victoria, were the fullest, most complete Art Nouveau in Australia. They were not the pure English or European variety. They owed a great deal to the traditional nineteenth century, something to Queen Anne, and to Queensland verandah domestic style of a bulk raised on posts ('stumps') with wood dominating structure, surface and ornamentation. Annear's designs had subtle changes in level within, sliding doors to change spatial appearance and size, as well as rather non-traditional plan forms, all suggesting ideas of the open plan. The exterior forms were unpretentious and related to the bungalow by their informal arrangement and materials. Ornamental characteristics of rhythmical verticals in a suggested half-timbering were contrasted by sweeping curves which recalled Art Nouveau and the Queensland precedents. Their overall effect, therefore, was related to Art Nouveau: fluidity of space and form, strong sweeping lines and the whole conceived as a related unit without traditional or formal encumbrances such as ornament or axiality (**4**). But the Annear houses (one was his own) were exceptions. In general, Art Nouveau suffered from the general misconceptions of eclecticism and resulted in another pastiche.

The rather sad results of the English and Belgian movements in Australia were indicative of the reluctance of architects to commit themselves wholly and completely to an idea, to ferret out its complexities in order to gain complete knowledge and thereby gain a freedom of action with understanding. Most of the first third of this century was characterized by this reluctance and by dabblers willing to affect any style on whim or demand. They were symptomatic of architecture's quandary and of Australia's isolation.

One might well ask how the local architects discovered the architecture of the world outside Australia. Quite simply, the architect either saw the original works of art or read about them. Before 1895 probably some 95 per cent of the architects were immigrants and they were from Britain, usually articled to an English architect. Most practised or were assistant architects prior to emigrating and therefore were knowledgeable of English architecture and, perhaps, the architecture of the Continent. Few were concerned or even aware of modern trends, styles or ideas. Around 1900 the picture changed. A few were knowledgeable of both English and Scottish and European modernism. And many who were articled in Australia visited or worked in Britain. After 1900 many also visited or studied or worked in America.

Architect Jack F. Hennessy studied and worked in America. On his return in 1911 he offered his impressions of American architecture in an article for the journal *Art and Architecture*. He devoted a significant proportion to the Chicago area. While the internal Australian magazines often commented on modern trends or ideas and the imported magazines contained information, it still remained that a full and meaningful impression on the Australian architects of overseas work was achieved only if one of their fellows discovered the architectural work and the people concerned, and then related the fact to professional colleagues. Personal experience gave the act an important sense of credibility. Hennessy, therefore, presented his thoughts with some authority, even more notably since he studied at the University of Pennsylvania, one of the leading architecture schools, not only in America, but in the English-speaking world.[10] A large portion of his article was about architectural education in America. Also, from appearances, the various strains of American architecture which were coping with the changes inflicted on the art by technology (and the schools) were seen as one reason for the architect's management of the design and building team. To architects still urging for a professional school in a university, Hennessy's experience was of great interest. He explained at length about Pennsylvania's programme and the influence of the teachers, most of whom were trained at L'École des Beaux-Arts in Paris.

Three portions of Hennessy's observations should be noted. First, he offered a warning about the necessary qualitative development of new Australia, about 'the still-unformed colonial art' being still 'peculiarly susceptible' and urged 'political and commercial independence'. Second, he succinctly stated a view of American architecture that was not prevalent, yet in many ways was nearly a subconscious reality for most keen observers:

America is the only one among the British colonies . . . whose architecture has as yet entered upon an independent course of development, and this is only within a comparatively recent period, nor has even this development produced as yet a wholly independent national style.[11]

However he noted originality of construction techniques, especially the skeletal steel frame. Third, and almost in contradiction to the second, he saw some significant trends. The first was in Chicago where architect 'Louis H. Sullivan has introduced this personal style which illustrates freedom of the art in a land without tradition, and it seems to have obtained a number of followers [the Chicago School]'.[12] The residential work about Chicago received attention as well as derivations in the New England Shingle Style, a wood architecture derived from Romanesque revivalism, as did the Western bungalow. In summary of these trends he stated:

The artlessness of the planning which is arranged to afford the maximum of convenience rather than to conform to any traditional style has been an element of great artistic success. It has resulted in exteriors that are the natural out-growth of the interior arrangements frankly expressed without any affectation of style.[13]

The background and views of Jack Hennessy have been selected for review and comment because in many ways they are typical of much that was said, unpublished or published, before 1913. Hennessy also was a forerunner of the new breed who were to be trained or to study in America, not just pass across the continent from ocean to ocean to have a look-see. In 1911 Hennessy was 'elected' as the Lecturer in architecture in the School of Engineering at Sydney University.[14] The professional journal *Art and*

Architecture noted that Sydney Technical College was 'unfortunately the only school of pure architecture we have, as our [Sydney] University only utilizes architectural lectures to engineering students'.[15]

The period before 1914, therefore, is best described as a time when there was a search for a new or Australian architecture and when aberrant attempts at a non-traditional architecture, conducted by a mere handful of architects, were attempted by a softening of customary styles with stark, simplified presentations. Some of the more interesting work was by the Brisbane architect, Robin S. Dods. He was born in New Zealand, educated in Brisbane and Switzerland, and was articled in Edinburgh and received some training in art. He practised in London until 1896 when he returned to Australia. From 1896 to 1913 he practised in Brisbane, where he 'built up the premier business of the Northern State',[16] with R. Hall. A contemporary of his remarked that Dods found the value 'of simplicity and reticence in the designing of small structures'.[17] In 1913 he moved to Sydney and there continued practice until his death in 1920. His residential work in Queensland was, in isolated cases, a development of the traditional vernacular post or stump architecture to an elegant, simple statement rich with undulating ornamentation and repetitive detail. Yet, there were no successors to Dods' fragile, inventive moment. Dods was aware of contemporary British design[18] for he worked with Aston Webb and became a member of the Arts and Crafts Society in London. But other than fragmentary incidents in his design development, he was an eclectic. Most of his work was characterized by Georgian or Edwardian designs, particularly in Sydney. Exceptions were some rather fine Romanesque revival designs such as the Geelong Church of England Grammar School, awarded first in a 1911 competition.[19] Dods' work tended to exemplify the period.

Generally speaking, work other than of historical modes was extremely difficult to conceive. It was, after all, an age of tired and overworked—if exuberant—eclecticism. And it is within this understanding that we must consider the period about the turn of the century. In Australia it was a time of search; in North America a time of pragmatic resolve; in Europe a beginning of the *avant-garde* and internationalism. In retrospect, it was the death throes of historicism. Revivals were still in chaos and one indicator was Queen Anne. Revived in the 1870s by the English architect Norman Shaw and others, it tenaciously held the architect's attention. It was a design that appealed to the waning taste for high Victorian styles. It was a design carefree in interpretation

5 St Andrew's Presbyterian Church, Brisbane, Queensland. G. D. Payne, architect. 1907.

collecting elements that might be piled on the building by fascination and whim. Yet, Queen Anne had order, symmetry and, most assuredly, it was domestic as the more classical Edwardian (if one might so call the result) was commercial. Each sector of the English-speaking world which used Queen Anne developed peculiar idiosyncrasies. For Australia it was a squat, red, often saw-tooth roofed house with white trim. Because it was born in revivalism and nurtured in eclecticism, it had a certain viability. For the architect there was some freedom, some laxity in organizing forms and motifs. The same argument might be offered for many of the styles of this period, but it seems especially reasonable for

Queen Anne and, later, for the Spanish Colonial, a popular revival in the 1920s. Except in exceptional instances, the Queen Anne Style and other revivals suffered the transitional years badly. Laxity was indeed a key word to the chaotic result.

Perhaps the Style might be called something else[20] but it can never escape its most fundamental historical and architectural aspect: it was English (in fact urban London and country estate) in origin and development. In Sydney or Melbourne or Adelaide it was Australian Queen Anne. It had uniquely Australian characteristics based on historical precedents.[21] Because of its historical base there were limitations to its adaptability. It was not able to accept reduction to simple planes and volumes. There were elemental and idealistic theories other than Queen Anne where the resultant architecture proved to be highly adaptable.

St Andrew's Presbyterian Church, Brisbane, undertaken in 1907 by architect G. D. Payne, was an isolated example (5). A blend of stripped classicism and the Romanesque revival, the traditional form and plan was greatly enhanced by a simplicity of wall and arch in exposed brick.[22] A bold single arch reached full height (recalled on the interior) with minor arches on an inset, convex curve, which suggested a lingering influence of the Romanesque style evolved by the American architect Henry Hobson Richardson in the 1880s. Payne was familiar with the Romanesque. In 1889 he submitted a very competent design for the Melbourne Commercial Bank of Australia competition, which he called 'Romanesque: American'.[23] Again, in 1890 he submitted another Romanesque design in the competition for The City Avenue building[24] for Sydney, although it was rather diluted with Edwardian features.

Interest in the American and more particularly the bold simplicity of the Richardson Romanesque led to what might be termed the warehouse style. Developments of a Romanesque revival began in America in the 1860s but it was the later developments in the 1880s which were of particular interest to Australian architects. A few were taken with the bold and direct style of Richardson. His Marshal Field Wholesale Store in Chicago of 1885–7 and the Ames Memorial Library, North Easton, Massachusetts, of 1877–9 or the superb if diminutive Crane Library of 1880–3 (6) are examples which come to mind. The earliest of the Australian warehouses was probably the John Taylor Warehouse, Pyrmont, New South Wales, of 1893, by the architect Arthur Blacket. From then on a number were built in Pyrmont, around York Street, Sydney, and then in Melbourne, especially on Flinders Lane. More suggestive of the Richardson source was

6 Crane Library, Quincy, Massachusetts. H. H. Richardson, architect. 1880–3. (Photograph permission of the Houghton Library, Harvard University, gift of Henry Richardson Shepley)

E. Jeafferson Jackson's design for Lark Sons and Company, Wynyard Square, Sydney (7), a warehouse first proposed in 1892, or the less effective Alcock's Warehouse, Sydney.[25] In 1904, the architectural press observed of these warehouses:

the façade is worked out in a bold and imposing manner. . . . The piers are simple, massive and unweakened in any way by unnecessary ornamentation. This is a style which is coming into vogue in the construction of simple warehouses. The Americans have taught us what a beauty and grandeur there is in plain simplicity.[26]

The idea of a warehouse style was established. One of the more refined compositions of *c.* 1900 was the 340 Sussex Street building, Sydney, in near mint condition in the 1970s and very suggestive of the American and earlier Australian paradigms. *Building* magazine actually published a series on the new, now acceptable building type during the years 1908 and 1909 titled 'Great Warehouses of the Commonwealth'. It was seen that ornament was not necessary, nor was a logical or traditional use of historicism.

Before the turn of the century the source of Richardson and to a lesser extent of the more flamboyant and decorated American Romanesque was clearly articulated in the designs of Edward Raht,

7 Lark Sons & Company, Sydney, new warehouse proposal. E. Jeafferson Jackson, architect. 1892.

an American sent to Sydney in 1891 to oversee the construction of his design of the Equitable Life Assurance Society of America building (8), completed in 1895[27] and the Society's more reserved Melbourne building, completed in 1896.[28] The Sydney building has a marked resemblance to the Studebaker (Fine Arts) Building, Chicago, of 1884 by S. S. Beman. There was William Kemp's Richardsonian design for the Technical College at Ultimo, New South Wales in 1891.[29] Comparison of the College with the other buildings and projects reveals that Kemp was more interested in the architectonic characteristics of the style. The College is more complete, more wholly conceived as a total building in the style from interior spatial structure to exterior form and detail and use of material. It was in contrast to most of the other work which tended to be façade architecture. Included in this ephemeral category would be the design of E. G. Kilburn for the Commercial Bank in 1890. It was an odd mixture of Queen Anne applied to high-rise design, of Italian Renaissance revival and classicism, with an Anglo-American Romanesque dominating the exterior. Yet, the architectural press was very encouraged: 'the opening of a new style of architecture in this colony, one which—if it be introduced by competent architects—will be a great advancement on the present so-called classic architecture of our city'.[30] Rather

8 Equitable Life Assurance
Society, Sydney. Edward
Raht, architect. 1895.

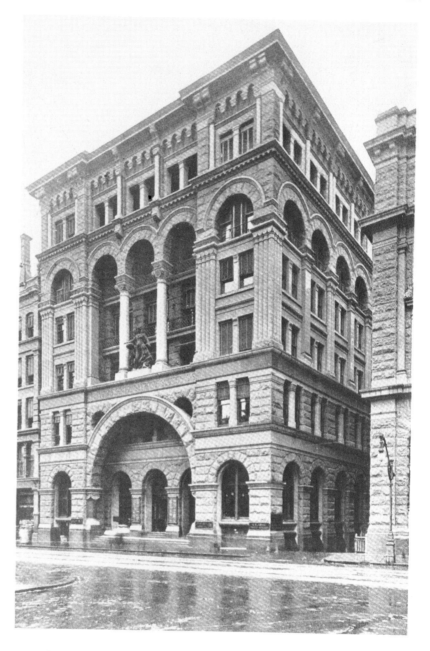

unnoticed were two examples. First, the Dulwich Hill School of
c. 1895 on Herbert Street, Sydney (not far from Burcham Clamp's
Holy Trinity Church of 1915), was a neat Romanesque revival with
Arts and Crafts tiles. Second, was a closer example of Richardson's
influence, in particular of his Ames and Crane libraries. Architects
Walker and Johnson submitted a design for the Williamstown
Town Hall, Victoria, also in 1890 (9). The general massing and

asymmetry, coupled with window detail, a fully arched entry and general proportioning show it to be 'in the Romanesque, as adapted in America'[31] and in particular the Ames precedent.

James Barnet, long-time New South Wales Colonial Architect, observed in 1899:

Recently from the United States has come the Romanesque in an Insurance Office Building [Raht's Equitable Life]; and the same style has been applied to Branch Banks, the Technical College [Ultimo], the Queen Victoria Market Building [Sydney, by George McRae (1893–8)[32]] and no doubt will run its crudities to seed in warehouses, stores and shops.[33]

The seed was sown in these and many other designs, but the evidence indicates that those initial blossoms were unique: that other than similar, less dramatic warehouses, the 'plain simplicity' of the Romanesque of Richardson was not developed in years succeeding 1908. A direct descendant of Richardson's bulky, chunky, massive architecture was The Register building in Adelaide of 1906 by H. L. Jackman of Jackman and Garlick, architects (10). Heavy masonry, narrow windows, simple arches, collected colonettes, and a bold arch at entry combined to present a rugged, individual building.[34] If a string course with dentils

10 Register Building, Adelaide, South Australia. Jackman and Garlick, architects. 1906. Entries remodelled 1931. (Photograph D. L. Johnson)

and two prominent classic balustrades had been absent, the belated design would have been of more than passing interest.

The discussion of Raht's or Payne's work and the urban buildings they designed does raise the more general question of the high-rise. Sydney, Melbourne and the other major cities followed the American example rather than the English or European; that is, they decided to concentrate construction in the high rental areas of the central city and produce the tall building rather than spread commercial construction more evenly throughout a series of juxtaposed districts. The simplicity of the warehouse style carried into the present century but only for the more 'utilitarian' buildings.

11 Anthony Hordern Bulk Stores, Sydney. D. T. Morrow, architect. 1907–8.

Although not structured with a Roman arch, one building of distinction was the Anthony Hordern Bulk Stores addition completed in 1909 to the design of D. T. Morrow (11). It was a very thin, wafer addition on one elevation but a full and complete façade on another elevation. There was a single unadorned base at first floor with high narrow windows inset in the elevation. At the second floor line there was a slight corbel with a series of pilasters extending the corbel. This faded into a further corbel in the final floor and attic. At the attic was the only hint of historicism in a moulding before the parapet. The narrow windows of the main body of the building were single or in sets of two.

In contrast to the simplicity of the Hordern building was Holt House in York Street, Sydney, by architects L. S. Robertson and Marks. Encumbered with a fragile canopy at the entry and

12 Sniders and Abrahams
Warehouse, Melbourne.
H. R. Crawford, engineer.
1909–10.

contrasting heavy Edwardian forms, the façade was dominated
by large areas of glass between structural piers. It was seldom that
glass was given such prominence in those early years of the
century.[35] The building should be compared to the Robertson
and Marks earlier and more robust building, the W. S. Friend
Warehouse,[36] also on York Street, Sydney. It was more refined
in proportion, nearly devoid of historical association yet the
Romanesque was more obvious.

While various structural means were not vigorously explored

before the turn of the century, after 1900 there were a few attempts, particularly with reinforced concrete. For instance, attention was given to the patented Turner Mushroom Principle of reinforced concrete construction. The mushroom column and reinforced slab, eliminating the need for girders and beams, arrived in Australia with the construction of the Sniders and Abrahams Warehouse in Melbourne.[37] The result was not only a major step in revealing structural potential but an interesting design by engineer H. R. Crawford (12). Flat piers rose full height of the building where they were surmounted by enormous Edwardian, stylized capitals. Between the piers, which were structural, were inset alternating areas of solid and glass, while at the top floor some lazy segmental arches stretched between the capitals. Technically and aesthetically, it was a most interesting building for 1908-9.

The E.S.C.A. Warehouse in Brisbane by Hall and Dods in 1908 was a more mature design of a precise geometric formalism of flat piers and glass with no hint of traditional ornament. It suggested an interest in the growing number of factories, especially for cars, and particularly those of Albert Kahn in America.

It should be fairly clear that it was very difficult for architects to accept the new, the obviously peculiar or the subtly different except for some rather fine warehouses. What was necessary was a catalyst, something to cause unity and at the same time to induce action—perhaps an idea or, more pragmatically, something almost tangible which would promote material response and promise things new and real in the Australian context. It is difficult to measure the significance of the proposal to build a capital city. More particularly it is difficult if only architecture is considered in spite of the fact that the profession quite naturally gave its full support to the proposal. Even city or town planning advocates reacted peculiarly during and after the first event which was a design competition.

The Canberra Competition

With Nationhood proclaimed in January 1901, it seemed that a natural course was to select a capital city. The ultimate decision was for the creation of a separate seat of government for parliamentary meetings that was specifically not Sydney or Melbourne. It was to be a new city which would symbolically not only rise above local colour and jealousies and spiritually unite the populace, but announce to the world Australia's newly acquired status. The design of the New Federal Capital City was to be determined by an international competition open to all who wished to participate. It was King O'Malley, an irascible Canadian-American-Australian who, as Minister for Home Affairs, provided impetus and influence which prompted the government to issue the worldwide competition in 1911 and call for submissions to be in Melbourne on or before 31 January 1912.

There were 137 entries received in January 1912. After four months, in May, the Design Board, or jury, reported to King O'Malley, who was responsible for the conduct of the competition, that they were unable to agree. The majority opinion was that 'landscape architect' Walter Burley Griffin of Chicago should be awarded first premium and Eliel Saarinen of Hilsingfors, Finland, second, with the Parisian, D. A. Agache, third. 'O'Malley endorsed this verdict.'[38]

Griffin's winning design was highly praised. Most observers agreed that it was an admirable plan.[39] O'Malley was confident in the majority choice and justly so. 'It is a wonderful design', he said, and he thought it would make Canberra the finest capital in the world. 'What we wanted was the best the world can give us and we have got it. Designs came from everywhere and I am satisfied.'[40] When the Minister was asked if he would proceed with the Griffin plan, 'the best in the world', he said no!

No—we will not be actually restricted to the winning design—we may use all the three designs if necessary to produce the working design on which the Capital will be built. A Park might be taken from one, a boulevard from another, and a public square from another.[41]

In late 1912, members of O'Malley's department put together what is now known as the Departmental Board Plan. It was bits from one design and pieces from another, the result closely resembling the plan of W. Scott Griffiths et al., of the minority report, which did not finally receive mention but which, for some reason, was purchased for £400.[42] Reaction to O'Malley's action and the pathetic Departmental Board Plan was immediate, vigorous, and negative. The Town Planning Review said:

The new plan is evidently the product of a Department whose personnel is utterly untrained in the elements of architectural composition, whose mind is a turmoil of confusion. . . . [It] reminds us of a third-rate Luna Park.[43]

The Review's comments were typical of the condemnation of the Departmental Board Plan from all over the world and internally. Efforts in Australia to save the Griffin plan, or rather to stop the Departmental Plan, were initiated. The architects instituted a circular[44] and the Sydney magazine Building successfully organized a petition by the architects[45] and there were circulars, articles, editorials, and letters indicating general dissatisfaction with the concocted plan. After careful consideration of the public and professional reaction the government invited Griffin to Australia. He arrived at Sydney Quay on 19 August 1913: from a successful architectural practice in the mid-west to the fires of a political arena.

Griffin's arrival in Australia was preceded by normal publicity about the prize-winning designer. Notes about his plan and who he was were made at the time of announcement. *Building* magazine ran what appeared to be a letter Griffin sent to the magazine in June 1912; and in September 1912 it reprinted an article which contained some of his residential architecture.[46] The magazine continued to publish articles by and about Griffin after his arrival up to mid-1914. These few articles proved to be the most comprehensive introduction of Griffin to his professional counterparts in Australia.

During August 1913 Griffin inspected the site and shortly thereafter he and the Departmental Board met to discuss the plan and attempt to sort out differences. The conference extended over some days but arrived at no conclusions.[47] On 13 October, Griffin submitted his rather modestly revised design based on his visits to the site, his discussion with the board, and his interviews. Conferences over this new plan were begun, but the board and Griffin could not reach agreement, let alone an amicable compromise. On 15 October 1913, Kelly thanked the members of the board for their labours and disbanded them. Three days later Griffin was appointed Federal Capital Director of Design and Construction.[48] His contract was renewed in 1916 for another three years and in 1918 he published his final plan for Canberra. But in 1919, the urging for a committee to superintend Canberra was too weighty. The decision was made in 1920 to have a committee and he was asked to be a member and adviser. He argued against the committee concept without success. Finally, in December 1920, his services were excluded.

The Canberra affair from 1913 until 1920 was very complicated and filled with intrigue, cross purposes, petty challenges, infringements on one another's duties, staff-stealing, semantical haggling, confounding administrative details and delays, and on and on. There was also the 1914–18 war; and there was, for instance, to be an international competition for the new Parliament House. Particulars were issued by Griffin in June 1914 and cancelled in September 1914, ostensibly because of the war. With a surge of authority, they were reissued in 1916 by the Works Department, independent of Griffin, and again cancelled. Many people were caught in the emotional waves expected to move throughout a land where people were forming a new nation and building a new capital and fighting a new war. The idea of new capitals and cities was a very much a part of the new century. In fact, there grew a nearly infectious need for 'city plans'. Conventions at Berlin and London, meetings within professions, Daniel Burnham's plans for Chicago and a revitalized Manila, a new capital for Australia, and proposals for a new Delhi and Montevideo are witness. Yet a planning profession was not constituted. A number of men had synthetized some applicable knowledge and practised the art and science of planning. Several books were written on the potential application of this synthetic work but there were no professional bodies of consequence. Both architects and engineers claimed city planning as within their province. The engineers' accomplishments were invariably sterile and devoid of imagination while the architects' dreams were comfortable, if dramatically impractical.

When Walter Burley Griffin entered the Canberra competition he used title 'Landscape Architect'. Undoubtedly he would have preferred the title Land Planner. Succinctly he said:

Land Planning [is] . . . the most fundamental sense of arranging for that use to which the terrain is most suitable. Land in this sense is accorded the respect due to a highly developed and perfected living organism not to be exterminated nor treated as dead material, or as a mere section of the map.[49]

The title Land Planner held little meaning to lay readers or for that matter other professionals: Landscape Architect was a compromise. Still, it recognized his emphasis in planning—the landscape.

Griffin executed a number of strictly landscape designs (that is, essentially gardens) for his own residential clients or other architects' houses or schools in the United States.[50] Since there are one or two rather vague extant plans and the known gardens are not in their original form or intended condition, this portion of the discussion will concentrate on a few of his American community plans. Trier Center Neighbourhood in Winnetka, Illinois, served as his first statement on how to resolve the problem of easy access to private and community space and segregation from vehicular traffic. First planned in 1912 and only partially executed, it was still of great importance. It prefigured the great Radburn principle of Clarence Stein and Henry Wright[51] for their suburb of Radburn, New Jersey. This can be seen in just four of the plan elements. First, the communal space in the centre was surrounded and enclosed by houses. This was accomplished in part by eliminating through traffic on the small nine-acre site. Second, a common driveway provided a shared parking space for two houses in many instances. Third, the living spaces of the houses were oriented to the internal community space. Fourth, the placement of the houses was essential to Griffin's plan:

The houses are so arranged in their pairs as to secure freedom and informality. . . . By spacing the couples alternating across the street as well as back and forth from the street, prospects from each are opened through the grounds and past as many as four houses laterally.[52]

Only the addition of more houses about the common driveway was necessary to define a cul-de-sac more precisely. The first three basic plan elements described above for Trier were to distinguish Radburn as the leading theoretical treatise on residential planning of this century. Radburn was begun fifteen years after Trier Center, in 1927.[53]

One of more interest was the residential community of Rock Crest-Rock Glen,[54] in Mason City, Iowa, on a site which sloped steeply from two high boundaries to the small Willow Creek bisecting the site. On these difficult contours Griffin recognized the value of the steep and wooded slopes. Each building's site was carefully selected for position of trees, potential view and necessary privacy.[55] There were no through roads and all residences, by contract, shared the creek and its proposed park-like shore line. Fitting into the 1912 plan he designed eight houses and five were built to his specifications.[56] Griffin's plan for the Blythe residences indicates the extent to which he desired some communal spaces, gardens (park or vegetable) and courts. Here the houses were to be right to the street edge, allowing more space before the creek. One of the houses was built as the Schneider house under the supervision of Barry Byrne (**13**).

The Clarke Resubdivision in Grinnell, Iowa, was a system to be fully developed and realized in later years, most notably at Castlecrag, north of Sydney. The roads at Clarke were determined by topography for views and drainage; there were open spaces behind houses providing, in Griffin's words, 'a neighborly system of inter-communication';[57] there were staggered set-backs on the roads' edge; there were cul-de-sacs to two houses (shared driveways, more realistically); and the roads were narrowed to lanes, designed it was believed to discourage through traffic.

The very small site for the Community Center on the Caloosahatchi River at Idalia, Florida,[58] was as close as he would come to the formal axiality found in the central portion of the famous

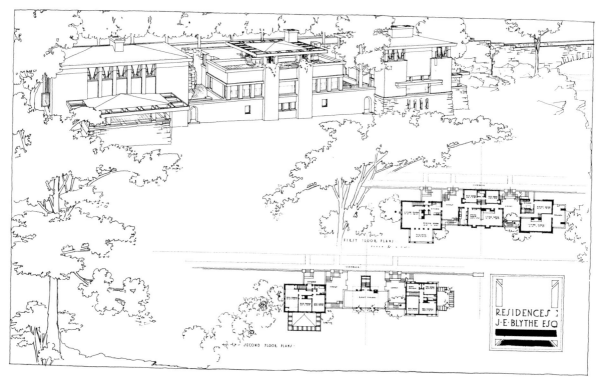

RESIDENCES: J·E·BLYTHE ESQ

13   The Franke, *project*, Gilmore, *project*, and Schneider Houses, Rock Glen, Mason City, Iowa. Walter Burley Griffin, architect. 1913. (Courtesy Northwestern University)

1893 Exposition at Chicago, and characteristic Beaux-Arts. Circumstantial evidence indicates it was designed in 1911.

The competition plans for Canberra had to be in Melbourne before 31 January 1912. Therefore, Canberra was planned before or simultaneously with the works discussed. Only Idalia, Florida, and Emory Hills, a twenty-acre site divided into nine farmlets, may have been designed before 1912. Canberra was the initial, almost spontaneous statement of a young architect and landscape architect on what he thought a new city must be and particularly a new capital city in Australia.

With this background it is not too difficult to look at the hybrid Canberra plan and realize that it was a significant achievement and has proven its stability. Few cities of its size or purpose have been planned or built in this century. There was the reactionary New Delhi which was announced almost simultaneously with Canberra and built during the same period. There was Brasilia in the 1950s, which was conceptually of the Renaissance, and Chandigarh in north central India by the venerable French architect Le Corbusier, also in the 1950s.[59] Other cities have been planned but they did not have to respond to those peculiar ingredients of a capital city—the place of government and the symbol of a nation.

What were the elements of Griffin's plan which made Canberra

25

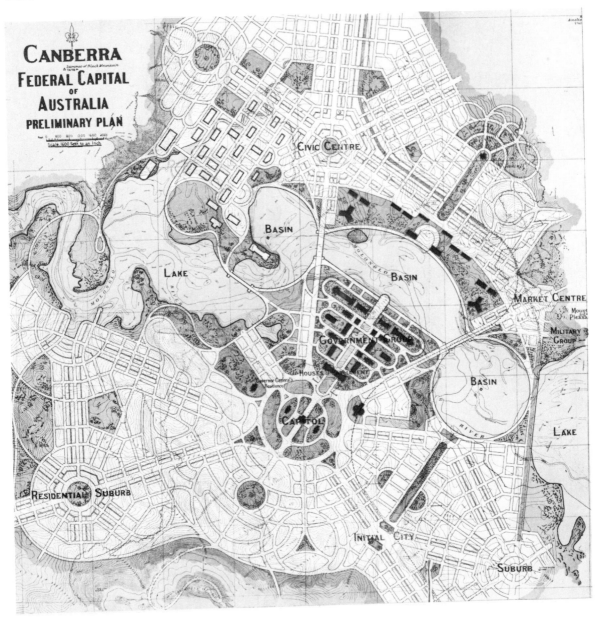

14 Griffin's plan accompanying proposed parliament building competition of 1914 showing proposed disposition of government buildings and parklands.

such an outstanding achievement? First and foremost was his exploitation of the landscape which he analysed as follows:

Taken altogether, the site may be considered as an irregular amphitheatre—with Ainslie at the north-east in the rear, flanked on either side by Black Mountain and Pleasant Hill, all forming the top galleries; with the slopes to the water, the auditorium; with the waterway and flood basin, the arena; with the southern slopes reflected in the basin, the terraced stage and setting of monumental Government structures sharply defined rising tier on tier to the culminating highest internal

15 View from Mount Ainslie, Canberra. Preliminary drawing, 1911. Walter Burley Griffin, architect. (Courtesy Burnham Library, Art Institute of Chicago)

forested hill of the Capitol; and with Mugga Mugga, Red Hill, and the blue distant mountain ranges, sun reflecting, forming the back-scene of the theatrical whole.[60]

Accepted or typical attitudes about city planning placed buildings or statues as nodes or at major intersections. At Canberra it was a hill, a mountain, a valley or a lake. On the main axis, or what Griffin called the Land Axis, the capital and Parliament faced, in sequence, a broad landscaped pool, a lawn, the lake and then Mount Ainslie (**14** and **15**). Radiating from the capital were two major roads: one rode the saddle due north between Mount Ainslie and Black Mountain and the other pointed to Pleasant Hill on the eastern pediment of Ainslie. The termination of the last road was probably the weakest point of the Griffin plan and it remained unresolved. The avenue due north leads to the city's commercial centre which nestles partially obscured behind a hill, subtly defining where the city lies and where government and its attendant pomp reside. Within the triangle created by the two main avenues and the lake was the government precinct resting

27

on the slope from Capitol Hill to the lake and therefore, as clearly described by Griffin in the above quotation, spatially oriented to the water's basin. To the north and beyond the saddle of Ainslie and Black Mountain was the industrial precinct[61] located on a flat plain and isolated from the city and residential areas. Since Sydney was the nearest port this northern location was reasonable. Residential areas were on the plains to the southwest and southeast and on each side of Red Hill and Mount Mugga Mugga. The mountains and hills intentionally remained undeveloped with buildings (vegetation was added) as major, unspoiled elements of the landscape.

The other planning element was function and its vital component, circulation, partially discussed above and both intrinsic to architectural reason. Functions were divided by roads or hills with the exception of the city and community centres and the market and railroad station (at the termination of the northeast avenue). It was believed that people, therefore cars and/or trains, must get to these centres as easily as possible. The space and form of the landscape was used to the fullest degree in defining function, in locating precincts and in determining circulation routes.

One of Griffin's arguments for his plan was an urge to ensure that neither the impractical overly grand ideas (so common) nor the moves toward scientific rationalism were to dominate. He believed the plan must develop a 'more definite and comprehensive organism that will assimilate them. Ours must be the scientific city', he said, and continued, 'quantitative analysis can only effectively succeed through qualitative analysis'.[62] It was an argument that reflected his architectural training, in particular the new notions of rational judgements affecting conceptual and design decisions.

The scale of Canberra is vast. From Capitol Hill to the present War Memorial (a casino in the original plan) is two and one-quarter miles. But the scale of the countryside is also large. The mountains in the immediate vicinity rise 1,000 feet above the ornamental waters. From the mountains and hills one can see mile upon mile of plains, broad prairies and hills. As a backdrop the blue-green Australian Alps (as they are called) rise in the distance. What the other contestants in the competition failed to grasp was the scale, horizontal and vertical, of the land. Their plans were tight, very urban. Their referent was the typical northern industrial city.

After Griffin arrived in Australia he did not alter his scheme and made only minor plan changes. In October 1913 the plan was not measurably altered and in 1918, the second revision contained only minor changes particularly at the difficult northeastern apex of the central triangle.

Decision making and physical development was a slow, plodding process during the ensuing years. In an attempt to ensure that Griffin's plan would be followed, a very rudimentary street layout based on Griffin's 1918 plan was gazetted in 1925.[63] The action meant that any deviation from that gazetted plan had to be by consent of Parliament. And there, for all practical purposes, the growth of Canberra remained—a street plan on a page of Parliamentary documents. Little, very little was done until 1955. During the intervening years only two events of importance occurred. In 1923 there was an Australian competition (not international as drawn up by Griffin in 1914) for the design of a temporary or provisional Parliament House which was won by Sydney architect, G. Sydney Jones, in 1924.[64] Griffin and many others[65] raised voices against the folly of building a temporary structure and disputed its proposed location. The temporary Parliament House was completed, however, in 1927 to a rather typical British colonial style. In May of the same year 'Parliament began to function in the Seat of Government of the Commonwealth'.[66] Slowly, very slowly, Federal offices and people began to move from Melbourne and Sydney to Canberra.

In 1955 Prime Minister Menzies wanted to know what could be done with Canberra. A few streets had been laid out, some surfaced; sheep grazed in paddocks where the lake was to have been; there was a small shopping area; about 35,000 people; and there was a gleaming, white painted, stucco Parliament building facing a war memorial almost two miles distant and across sunburnt pastures. A 'Select Committee' was appointed 'to enquire into and report upon the Development of Canberra', under the capable chairmanship of Senator J. A. McCallum.[67] The result was a lucid and reasonable document. In 1957, Australia again went overseas for guidance and the English architect and planner, William Holford, submitted his *Observations on the Future of Canberra* at the request of the Australian Parliament. In 1963 the ornamental waters were completed by damming the Molongolo River and called Lake Burley Griffin. As Griffin prophesied, the city was not divided but became one. The vistas, avenues and mountains became united by the locus of the lake.

It has been a partial realization of the Australian dream and the Griffin idea. But Canberra up to the 1960s did not rise above local colour and jealousies nor spiritually unite the populace and it rather embarrassingly announced Australia's newly acquired status. The plan was praised, the execution was generally ignored.

NOTES TO CHAPTER ONE

1. James Izett, 'Australasian Architecture', *The Australasian Builder and Contractors' News* (Australia—henceforth A), 6 (4 January 1890), p. 635.

2. 'Australian Domestic Architecture', *The Australasian Builder and Contractors' News* (A), 6 (20 September 1890), p. 217.

3. James Green, 'An Australian Style of Architecture. 3', reprinted in *The Australasian Builder and Contractors' News* (A), 6 (25 October 1890), p. 302. Cf. John Sulman, 'An Australian Style', *The Australasian Builder and Contractors' News* (A), 1 (14 May 1887), p. 1, and continued in subsequent issues.

4. Green, 'An Australian Style', Part 4, p. 361.

5. E. Wilson Dobbs, 'An Australian Style of Architecture', *The Building and Engineering Journal* (A), 15 (21 February 1891), p. 67, see editorial p. 84, and reprinted in pamphlet form as *Theories and Growth of Australian Architecture*, Sydney 1892. Probably Lucien Henry who studied under Viollet-le-Duc and taught drawing at Sydney Technical College. Cf. 'Lyre bird "antefix"', *The Australasian Builder and Contractors' News* (A), 2 (5 May 1888), p. 286.

6. [Florence Sulman], 'Arts and Crafts in the Home', *Architecture* (A), 9 (June 1921), p. 7.

7. Cf. Terance Lane, 'Gum-Nut Art Nouveau', *Art Bulletin of Victoria 1973* (A), pp. 25–34.

8. J. M. Freeland, *Architecture in Australia. A History*, Melbourne 1968, p. 215.

9. [Nichols V. Shiels], 'Originality in Architecture', *The Salon* (A), 1 (July-August 1912), pp. 1–2, emphasis in original.

10. Jack F. Hennessy, 'A Few Impressions of Modern America', *Art and Architecture* (A), 11 (May-June 1912), p. 486.

11. Ibid., p. 481.

12. Ibid., p. 483. Cf. Hugh Morrison, *Louis Sullivan, Prophet of Modern Architecture*, New York 1935.

13. Hennessy, 'A Few Impressions', p. 483.

14. 'Lecturer in Architecture', *Art and Architecture* (A), 9 (May-June 1912), p. 507. Hennessy replaced John Sulman who was appointed in 1887.

15. 'The Teaching of Design', ibid.

16. 'The Late Mr. R. S. Dods', *Architecture* (A), 8 (August 1920), p. 52.

17. Ibid.

18. See Queensland State Chapter, R.A.I.A., *Buildings of Queensland*, Brisbane 1959, pp. 15, 33, 41, 47; and Robin Boyd and Peter Newell, 'St. Lucia. A Housing Revolution is Taking Place in Brisbane', *Architecture* (A), 29 (July 1950), p. 107.

19. 'Geelong Grammar School', *Art and Architecture* (A), 8 (November-December 1911), pp. 395–6.

20. First suggested as uniquely Australian and dubbed Federation Style by David Saunders and Bernard Smith; see David Saunders, 'Domestic Styles of Australia's Federation Period: Queen Anne and the Balcony Style', *Architecture in Australia* (A), 58 (August 1969), p. 662, and Bernard Smith, 'Architecture in Australia', *Historical Studies* (A), 14 (October 1969), pp. 90–1. Neither Saunders nor Smith fully argue the issue of stylistic autonomy. See also Bernard Smith and Kate Smith, *The Architectural Character of Glebe, Sydney*, Sydney 1973, pp. 107–9.

21. Cf. Saunders, 'Domestic Styles of Australia's Federation Period', pp. 655–62.

22. Florence M. Taylor, 'Unconventional Church Architecture in Queensland', *Building* (A), 21 (November 1916), pp. 46, 54, and 'F.R.I.B.A.', 'Modern Church Architecture', *Building* (A), 2 (April 1908), pp. 39–42, referred to as St Ann's.

23. 'Commercial Bank ... Design', *The Building and Engineering Journal* (A), 8 (5 July 1890), p. 232, and plates.
24. 'Sydney "Avenue" Competitions', *The Building and Engineering Journal* (A), 9 (1 November 1890), pp. 385–7, and plates.
25. Freeland, *Architecture in Australia*, p. 217, and Myra Dickman Orth, 'The Influence of the "American Romanesque" in Australia', *Journal of the Society of Architectural Historians* (United States of America—henceforth US), 34 (March 1975), p. 11 (the Alcock building).

  The Lark warehouse was illustrated in 'New Warehouse, Wynyard Square, Sydney', *The Building and Engineering Journal* (A), 9 (10 September 1892), p. 105 and plate. It was later altered by the addition of a floor and published in *Building* (A), 1 (January 1908), p. 62. In reference to the illustration an historical note: Joseph Paxton in his Crystal Palace, London, provided hollow columns for roof drainage. Exterior plumbing is a distracting feature of the Lark building.
26. *Cyclopedia of Victoria*, Vol. 3, Melbourne 1904, p. 77.
27. R. T. Baker, *Building and Ornamental Stones of Australia*, Sydney 1915, p. 54.
28. Ibid., p. 39, and Lloyd Taylor, 'The Architecture of the Colony of Victoria', *Journal of the Royal Institute of British Architects* (Britain—henceforth B), 6 (August 1899), p. 546.
29. Baker, *Building and Ornamental Stones, passim*. Baker was a curator with the Technical College.
30. 'Commercial Bank Designs', *The Building and Engineering Journal* (A), 8 (26 April 1890), pp. 147ff.
31. 'Design for Municipal Buildings, Williamstown', *The Building and Engineering Journal* (A), 9 (25 October 1890), pp. 377ff.
32. Baker, *Building and Ornamental Stones*, p. 111.
33. James Barnett, 'Architectural Work in Sydney, New South Wales', *Journal of the Royal Institute of British Architects* (B), 6 (July 1899), p. 516. The long-time classicist could produce lovely exceptions such as the Court House at Grafton, New South Wales, 1877–80. See 'Country Court Houses', *Building Ideas* (A), 5 (September 1972), pp. 4–5.
34. Florence M. Taylor, 'The Architecture of Adelaide', *Building* (A), 17 (October 1915), p. 72, and *The Register* (Adelaide), 22 June 1908, p. 4.
35. *Building* (A), 3 (October 1909), p. 39.
36. *Building* (A), 1 (January 1908), p. 64.
37. 'Reinforced Concrete', *Building* (A), 3 (June 1910), pp. 57–62.
38. Lionel Wigmore, *The Long View*, Melbourne 1963, pp. 55–6. The report of the 'Designs Board' and illustrations of all entries mentioned in majority and minority reports is contained in Australia, Commonwealth Parliament, *Parliamentary Paper* (henceforth *PP*), 117, Government Printer, Melbourne 1912.
39. See Donald Leslie Johnson, 'Walter Burley Griffin: An Expatriate Planner at Canberra', *Journal of the American Institute of Planners* (US), 39 (September 1973), pp. 326-45.
40. [G. A. Taylor], 'The Federal City', *Building* (A), 10 (June 1912), pp. 53–4.
41. Ibid.
42. *PP*153, 1915.
43. 'Federal Capital City of Australia', *Town Planning Review* (B), 3 (January 1913), p. 222.
44. 'Canberra', *The Salon* (A), 2 (August 1913), pp. 26–7.
45. 'The Creation of Canberra', *Building* (A), 12 (July 1913), pp. 43–50.
46. 'Walter Burley Griffin. His Idea of the Bungalow', *Building* (A), 11 (September 1912), pp. 50–4, a reprint (without acknowledgement) of R. C. Spencer, 'Bungalow Suggestions', *Architectural Record* (US), 15 (July 1912), pp. 37–48.

47. *PP*153, 1915.
48. *PP*378, 1917.
49. Walter B. Griffin, 'Occupational Conservation', *Australian Wild Life* (A), 1 (October 1935), p. 24. W.B.G. was Honorary Treasurer of the Wild Life Preservation Society.
50. E.g., F. L. Morse garden, Ithaca, New York; Mueller Residences and their Allan Ravines development in Decatur, Illinois; Eastern Illinois and its counterpart, the Northern Illinois Normal Schools; see Mark L. Peisch, *The Chicago School of Architecture. Early Followers of Sullivan and Wright*, New York 1965, *passim*.
51. Clarence S. Stein, *Toward New Towns for America*, New York 1957, Ch. 2.
52. [Walter Burley Griffin], 'Trier Center Neighbourhood, Winnetka, Ill.', *Western Architect* (US), 20 (August 1913), p. 68. I have taken the liberty of making changes in grammar.
53. There is the earlier Sunnyside Gardens, New York City, 1924, which sets out the superblock principle, and the English Port Sunlight. A balanced critical view is in Henry N. Wright [Jr], 'Radburn Revisited', *Architectural Forum* (US), 135 (July-August 1971), pp. 52–7.
54. Robert E. McCoy, 'Rock Crest/Rock Glen Prairie Planning in Iowa', *The Prairie School Review* (US), 5 (3, 1968). The definitive reference on Griffin's American architecture is H. Allen Brooks, *The Prairie School. Frank Lloyd Wright and His Midwest Contemporaries*, Toronto 1972.
55. [Walter Burley Griffin], 'Rock Crest and Rock Glen, Domestic Community Development, Mason City, Iowa', *Western Architect* (US), 20 (August 1913), p. 76.
56. Roles of the various architects are complex; see Brooks, *The Prairie School*, pp. 241–4.
57. Walter Burley Griffin, 'Planning for Economy' in *First Australian Town Planning and Housing Conference and Exhibition Proceedings*, Adelaide 1917, p. 45.
58. [Walter Burley Griffin], 'Idalia, Lee County, Florida', *Western Architect* (US), 20 (August 1913), pp. 76, 79.
59. See Edmund N. Bacon, *Design of Cities*, New York 1967, pp. 217–27.
60. [Walter Burley Griffin], *The Federal Capital. Report Explanatory of the Preliminary General Plan*, Government Printer, Melbourne 1914, p. 17.
61. The industrial area, such as it is, is now located in the suburb of Fyshwick to the southeast. The market has been replaced by the armed forces buildings. The casino has been replaced by the Australian War Memorial.
62. Walter Burley Griffin, 'Canberra', *Building* (A), 8 (November 1913), p. 70.
63. *PPS*.2, 1955, pp. 10–11.
64. 'Canberra Competition', *Building* (A), 36 (January 1925), pp. 49–61.
65. *PPS*.2, 1955, p. 50.
66. Ibid., p. 13. New Delhi was opened in 1930.
67. The document is *PPS*.2, 1955.

2

1913-27: The Rise of Domestic Architecture

The economy of Australia immediately after the turn of the century was stable, if not flourishing. But it was not sufficiently vigorous to enable most clients to build more than was necessary, whether for practical reasons, or for desired pretentions. This may be construed as an apologist's view. The fact remains that except for the golden years of the late nineteenth century when much of Australia's more glorious architecture was bestowed upon her cities, the economic viability of the nation had been a delicate proposition. The effective attitude of the more prolific builders, the middle and upper-middle classes, was a conservative tendency in those areas of life concerned with the arts. The upper-class individuals or families were inconspicuous and small in number and philanthropy was not seen as a virtue. Even with their homes popular trends were, quite naturally, the norm. Quality was also degenerate by a peculiar, though not unusual twist of colonialism. The attention to design, the quality of craftsmanship and the selection of materials found in England could not or would not be matched. Those English companies with offices or manufacturing facilities in Australia were generally reluctant to indulge in the same high standards demanded, for one reason or another, in the United Kingdom. It must be noted though, that a demand for higher quality was too often not part of the architectural criteria for either architect or client. Yet, the architecture of urban and adurban Melbourne in the late nineteenth century was of a better standard than most of the British provincial cities.[1] But Melbourne was the exception.

The materials and methods of construction available to architects were typical in their universality. Native timbers were in meagre supply and quickly consumed. Most lumber was imported from the Pacific Islands, the Far East or the North American West Coast, thereby increasing costs. The 'balloon frame' was introduced in the late 1800s but brick remained the most widely used material, except in Queensland and Tasmania. Iron was imported for many years until foundries were introduced in the mid-1800s. It was seldom used structurally, but cast-iron filigree gave domestic architecture a unique Victorian character. Corrugated iron or steel roofs still were used on all types of buildings, the most auspicious, public or private, presenting a quality standard to last well into the present century. Rust was (and is) a common colour. Concrete was first used in bridges beginning in 1895 and in buildings from about 1905. One interesting application was a 114-foot diameter reinforced, shallow concrete dome, then largest in the world, over the main reading room of the Melbourne Public Library in 1912. Terracotta tile roofing came into vogue, especially the Marseilles style and red tile roofs were found everywhere corrugated iron was not, mainly in New South Wales and Victoria. The one material which was important in American high-rise architecture during the period under consideration and which was not available to architects was steel. Brick and stone of a wide variety was used for tall buildings well into the century. In 1912, architects Spain and Cosh built the Culwalla House in Sydney. It was a 170-foot high solid brick structure. Protests were raised on the prospect of dark streets, the inability to control fires, and like comments usual with the first skyscrapers. It was not long before a height limit of 150 feet was imposed and other cities followed the example. Steel was used structurally in the Equitable Life Assurance Society building built in 1895. The Sydney building, previously discussed, was nine storeys high and both the trachyte walls and interior steel frame were bearing. The first steel produced in Australia was from a small open hearth built in 1900. Slowly the process improved, until the first fully steel-framed, self-supporting building, Nelson House, by architect L. S. Robertson, was built in Sydney in 1910. In 1915 the first mass-produced steel came from a new plant in Newcastle, New South Wales. All production went to the war. By the mid-1920s steel was used rather freely in architecture.[2] There were mechanical elevators for many years prior to the introduction of electric powered ones in 1923.

Therefore, a full choice of mechanical conveniences, materials and construction methods were not readily available to the architect until the mid-'twenties. This should have caused a minimum of difficulties. Many, in fact most of the modern overseas examples were developed from basic materials and construction techniques, as witness the European Low Countries, Central Germany, Chicago's Prairie architects (including the Chicago high-rise before the 1890s) and the bungalow, whether English, Chicago or Californian. The change being sought in design was an aesthetic interpretation of not only new technologies, but of the social condition, of the philosophies of social and individual responsibility and liberation, and of scientific methodologies. The urgency which dominated the urbanized industrial nations of Central Europe or North America was beyond the physical and emotional capacity of Australia. Time and distance seemed to remove any intellectual urgency. Those aesthetic interpretations had little meaning or impact on Australia until well into the present century. Also, articulation of those philosophies was slow to mature and the built products took time to be realized. Digestion and appreciation of the analyses by Australian travellers and overseas publishers was inevitably delayed, but less than previously imagined, as we will learn about Hunt's shingle designs. In general, the circumstances and conditions were different enough from North America and Europe to inhibit initiation, let alone acceptance of other than English historicism.

Griffin arrived unburdened by local predilections. Rather brazenly he preached ideas that were received as daringly new. A few followed the evangelist while most rather resented his presence, let alone his architecture. But he was not a prophet. He was one of the practitioners: a disciple in a very real sense.

Griffin

Griffin's first commissions on arrival in Australia were not only diverse, but their number indicates the potential significance of his position as a nationally recognized figure, architect and town-planner. In view of the legends concerning Griffin a reasonable question to ask relates to Griffin's qualifications: was the disciple prepared, in a professional sense, to undertake these many commissions?

Griffin was born in the Chicago suburb of Maywood, Illinois, on 24 November 1876.[3] In the spring of 1895 he graduated from Oak Park High School and in the fall of the same year entered the University of Illinois at Urbana. The architectural curriculum at the University was rather progressive for the times and his courses were typically architectural. Also, he elected horticulture, forestry and landscape gardening. In 1899 he received his Bachelor of Science in Architecture. Before winning the Canberra competition in 1912 he was asked to be head of the Architecture School at the University. He did not accept, and the eminent Charles

Mulford Robinson accepted what was America's first chairman-ship, as it turned out, in Civil Design.

With his academic degree and his membership in the American Institute of Architects, Griffin set out for Chicago, where he began immediately to work in offices that were shared by a group of architects who were to be associated with or part of the Chicago School of Architecture.[4] During this period and independent of his employers, he executed a few landscape and architectural commissions. His first architectural commission of consequence was the W. H. Emery Residence in Elmhurst, Illinois, a pure modern design started in 1901. In about 1902 he began full-time employment in the office of Frank Lloyd Wright. It has been said that the terms of his employment were liberal enough to allow him to accept private commissions and he was considered Wright's most important assistant. In 1905 Griffin left the office. From late 1905 until leaving for Australia in 1913, Griffin maintained a private practice, accepting commissions, not only in the mid-west, but from clients as remote as Florida, New York, California and Louisiana. In 1911, the year of his marriage to a fellow colleague in Wright's office, Marion Mahony, he entered the international competition for the design of Canberra. If Canberra brought him international recognition, his architecture brought him national importance in both Australia and America. His public or commercial architecture in the United States was limited to perhaps half a dozen realized and projected buildings.

The Stinson Memorial Library of Anna, Illinois, designed in 1913,[5] was solid stone growing from the earth. The massive, random stonework was relieved at the top by a ribbon of high windows at the periphery of the reading areas. The Store and Flat Building in Chicago, of about 1910,[6] was a series of brick panels in complement to the earth and vertically composed, yet as a ribbon, and detailed almost to float on the surface between solid corners on the one elevation. With the Stinson Library there was in fact no sense of structure *per se*. Although high windows were surrounded by large concrete forms, the vertical of which were colonettes, they suggested open, unobstructed spaces within. On the other hand, the Store Building clearly expressed a series of cubicle spaces on the interior, while in fact on the upper two floors there was a continuous corridor to the exterior wall, with apartments within and a light court in the centre. Both buildings were symmetrical in plan and elevation and both were expertly developed along their single axis. For Griffin, undressed stone was not to reappear in his public architecture and brick only in the architectural projects for Canberra, in the inimitable incinera-

16 Cafe Australia, Melbourne, Victoria. Walter Burley Griffin, architect. 1915-16. (Courtesy New-York Historical Society)

tor schemes, plus some unbuilt projects. Griffin's other realized and projected public architecture in America were adaptations of the Prairie residential architecture. There was, for instance, the Niles Club planned in 1909 for Niles, Michigan,[7] and a store project for Idalia, Florida,[8] in conjunction with his plan for the community.

Again, his Australian commissions for public architecture were few, if one excludes flats or apartments and the incinerators which form distinct aspects of his career. Even fewer were realized, but two must be discussed. During and after the Canberra affair, his major architectural and landscape commissions in private practice were centred in Melbourne, where most of the Federal offices were located.

In 1915, A. J. J. Lucas asked Griffin to prepare designs to remodel his Vienna Cafe, one of Melbourne's oldest restaurants. Renamed the Cafe Australia on its opening in 1916, it continued

to be one of the prominent restaurants in Melbourne (**16**). After it opened *Australian Home Beautiful* observed:

The entrance was entirely refashioned, though the façade, from the first floor to the coping, was allowed to remain. But inside the transformation was complete, and the old-fashioned, time-stained, and rather sombre furnishings gave place to a daring scheme that ... [is] ultra modernistic, not to say bizarre, and certainly years in advance of its period.[9]

This modernistic, bizarre design was in fact a subtle translation of European Art Nouveau and the Chicago School. These inspirations of an informal nature were blended with a more formal Sullivan-inspired ornament of lace on column capitals and nonstructural vaulted ceiling (with hidden cove lighting) as well as a balcony rail. Similar ornament in similar locations was used in the chapel and rotunda of Newman College (**17**), contemporary to the Cafe. The exterior of the Cafe was a rough black granite on either side of the entry, with deep blue tiles on the recessing imposts and cement stucco in the arch, relieved by perhaps a foot from

17   Newman College, University of Melbourne. Walter Burley Griffin, architect. 1915–17. (Courtesy New-York Historical Society)

18 Capitol Theatre, Melbourne, Victoria. Walter Burley Griffin, architect. 1921–4. (Photograph Adrian Crothers)

the glazed doors and transome. Details of the interior are uncertain but other than some plaster architectural sculpture designed by Griffin, other sculpture, murals and decorations were by local artists,[10] and furniture design was by Griffin. In 1926 the Cafe was enlarged and remodelled and 'Mr. Burley Griffin's modernistic balcony and ceiling went untouched.'[11]

It was Lucas again, as partner with others, who brought Griffin into association with the Melbourne architects Peck and Kemper in 1921 to design the Capitol Theatre Building. As part of the office building complex Griffin designed one of the finest cinemas in the world, the Capitol Theatre (**18**). The office building had a stucco exterior with a rather imposing vertical parti. It had well-proportioned fenestration, not dissimilar to the typical Chicago window and nicely related to spandrel solids, and a wide, fat column expression, all capped with what was to be a restaurant on the top floor, but ended as a series of bold, deeply recessed horizontals, with an applique of rather classically inspired motifs. The office block stands flush to Swanston Street, with the theatre proper as a bustle on the rear. The structure is entirely concrete and an immense open beam carries the office block over the large volume of the cinema house.

The original entrance, lobby and grand staircases were replaced by a raucous shopping arcade, similar to perhaps one hundred in the city. The 1965 renovations preserved the auditorium ceiling and walls[12] and the lower house and balcony were brought together by raising the main floor to meet the slope of the balcony. Fortunately, the ceiling has been preserved.

There were, of course, other non-domestic buildings and projects including buildings for Duntroon (or the Royal Military College in Canberra), Leonard House office building (Melbourne), Australia House and Palais Pictures (Sydney). While a series of garbage incinerators and domestic commissions fit into a context to be developed later, Newman College should be briefly mentioned now.

Newman College at the University of Melbourne was designed in association with Augustus Fritsch during 1915.[13] The site was at the edge of a large flat area of land, a meadow in character, bordered by old residences and the University proper. The projected site plan, occupying only a portion of the meadow which was used on its periphery for other colleges and recreation, placed two large rotundas with dining and library at the two ends of the site edge. Student rooms in long wings were at ninety degrees and extended outward from the rotundas. Central to this Palladian concept was the chapel, peculiarly placed at right angles to its more recognizable axis and it closed the formal vista by the chapel's bulk. The result of this partite scheme is a double quadrangle: one for women, one for men. The northern rotunda, that is for the men's college, and its flank offices, kitchen, staff quarters and attendant dormitory wings ending in a natatorium and classrooms, were built as projected and completed by 1917.

Newman College was a successful amalgam of medieval and modern precepts; not only successful, but a unique design venture. The total effect was medieval. The internal spaces were small with low ceilings, narrow corridors and in one instance a tight flight of stairs to the balcony of the rotunda. On arriving at the balcony the space exploded. The triangular shaped ribs of the dome's structural arches were highlighted by misty light piercing the lantern and side lights. The exterior rough-faced stone bearing walls were countered by finely dressed stone about the windows. Splayed columns or mullions set against the battered lower portion of the walls, the squared proportions and heavy voussoirs over the window arches gave the building a distinctly squat effect, adding to its medieval character. This was not modern architecture in the accepted academic sense. The Palladian plan and medieval architectural elements were too conspicous. It was a traditional building, yet without revivalistic academicism.

Along with Canberra and the Cafe Australia, this building early in Griffin's Australian career became well known in Melbourne. But Griffin's position was equivocal in the community as we shall learn in a later chapter. From this brief description of his work in the United States and Australia, both architectural and city planning, it should be easily assumed that Griffin was equipped to undertake all responsibilities entrusted to him on arrival in Australia.

Between 1914 and 1918, the years of Griffin's introduction to Australia, there was quite naturally little activity in construction. After the Armistice in November 1918 a noticeable change in attitude was manifest in a resurgence of building activity in the very next year. It was then that a few tried at least to understand and explore modern architecture. This may have been due in part to the fairly large number of young men who had travelled in Europe as well as Palestine, Egypt, Turkey and Greece. Europe itself awakened from the war to begin a new era in 1919, whereas America regressed into pseudo-revivalism. In Australia a series of significant events occurred. In city planning the long, laborious yet patient efforts of a concerned few came to momentary fruition with the first Australian Town Planning Conference held in Adelaide in 1917,[14] no doubt encouraged by the Berlin and London conferences in 1909 and 1910.

In 1919 a special number of the periodical *Art in Australia* appeared with a series of essays and photos on *Domestic Architecture in Australia*. Three important people were concerned with the publication:[15] Sydney Ure Smith, artist and publisher of books and periodicals on art; William Hardy Wilson, an architect and historian who selected the illustrations (Griffin was excluded); and Harold Desbrowe Annear, Melbourne advance guard, or rather skirmisher for modern architecture. In these essays the discontent and frustration of the early twentieth-century architect, veiled in the earlier Haddon book, were now exposed, nurtured by the caprice of tasteful architecture in Europe and North America. For example, Professor Leslie Wilkinson preferred a 'tendency towards a more formal manner based on Italian and "Colonial" work'. Wilkinson was supported to some degree by Hardy Wilson who wished for 'a delightful prospect to return to the work before 1840',[16] and Adelaide architect Walter H. Bagot was more characteristic when he thought that climate 'points the way to the Mediterranean as our closest parallel'. Neither his definition of geography nor Mediterranean was offered. Harold Annear urged a more internal assessment for be believed 'The importation of ideas from other countries cannot help us'.[17] These were architects observing—if not concerned with—change. But people were fickle: as the architect wavered, the caprice of taste sustained. Situated in isolation, Australians were content with a belief that their architecture was the better part of English paradigms. Yet there was the ubiquitous bungalow.

Applications and aesthetic responses to the tall building or warehouses had little impact on the course of modernism for many years to come. It was in domestic design that architecture found sources and means for evolution. The most fertile idea was the bungalow. It was such a dominating factor of the last years of the nineteenth century and the first decades of the present century that it is appropriate to introduce a very general history of the style.

Bungalows

The bungalow fused many ideas and thoughts about the nature of housing and life styles during the period from 1913 to 1927. It reached a zenith in both style and popularity during the 1920s and carried well beyond 1930. Its significance for the architect lay with one consummating act. It brought the more humble form of architecture within the sphere of the architect, of the professional who in the seventeenth and eighteenth centuries was a man for noble patronage but who in the nineteenth century came to realize a much broader profession. The architect became part of Gothic notions and ideas of the picturesque; part of the surge of interest in healthy, humane standards for the urban dweller with studies for the 'working class'. He became part of the wealthy middle class who desired second cottages in the hinterland or by the sea (**19**); part of the search for the natural beast that Rousseau would find in all men; part of the revived interest in medieval art and social structure; part, therefore, of the nineteenth century. The bungalow was swept along with ideas of beauty in nature and acts to conserve the natural environment by establishment of national parks and preserves. It culminated architecturally with the grand hotels and magnificent lodges in the mountains of Europe or in the American parks during the 1920s and 1930s: in particular the Ahwahnee Hotel of 1927 at Yosemite Valley, California by architect Gilbert S. Underwood.[18] The bungalow was an indomitable and popular idiom that could touch the native soul of each person. Not even Walter Gropius

19 The rural ideal. From a drawing by E. W. Charlton that appeared in *The Studio*, London, in 1898.

could resist in 1921 when he and Adolph Mayer designed the Sommerfeld 'Log House' in Berlin.

European adaptation of the bungalow was a slow process which began with colonization of the Indian subcontinent in the late sixteenth century. Actual evidence of the French, Dutch and English settlers using native forms of housing began in the early seventeenth century, and in particular within the area of Bengal. The word denoting the style is Hindi and Mahratti in origin, derived from *bangla*, 'of, or belonging to Bengal'.[19] The Bengali used the world *bangala*. Also, the architectural style was quite obviously of Bengal origin although exactly which of the native dwellings found in Bengal in those early years of settlement is uncertain. There were various reports about the various kinds of housing and in the nineteenth century the number of reports increased, as did the confusion. The most probable source was taken from a description by C. Grant when writing of his travels in 1849. In plan the

centre square consists of either one or two apartments, according to the circumstances or wants of the individual, whilst the thatched roof, extending considerably over all sides, is supported at the extreme edges upon bamboo or wooden pillars, thus forming a verandah round the building.[20]

Although not a requirement, it would be difficult to imagine a bungalow without a verandah, if not surrounding the dwelling, at least of significant proportion. The basic four-celled plan described by Grant as being somewhat symmetrical, was alterable so that rooms might divide the central space, verandahs might be on any side perhaps alternating with peripheral rooms or in the extreme, as he suggested, with yet another row of posts beyond the walled periphery to form a verandah. In external appearance, two considerations were pre-eminent. First, verandah posts were exposed and second, a necessarily large and usually bulky pyramidal roof rested on the posts. At its lowest point the roof began near head height at the exterior edge of the verandah and rose rather steeply to a ridge centred over the building.

The bungalow in its native land of Bengal and in its adopted situation was a rural building. The settlers on stations or plantations used the style frequently.[21] When brought to European communities, it invariably was in semi-rural areas or well beyond normal suburban development, at least before the twentieth century.

The first bungalow to be constructed in England was apparently in 1869 in the community of Margate, which was developed as a village by the sea for recreation. 'The bungalow consisted of eight rooms, all on one floor, with a verandah at the front and back, and a basement containing wine, beer and coal cellars.'[22] It was described as being prefabricated, a 'portable' building and constructed in only two months.[23] By the 1870s the London magazine *Building News* was informing its readers of the style:

In this country the term [bungalow] is similarly applied to single dwellings on one floor. . . . The general characteristics of them being a square plan with entrance at the side or in the centre, a high-pitched pyramidal roof, with sometimes the chimney made the central feature.[24]

The late nineteenth century saw an early corruption of the basic style, probably inevitable since it was begun as a speculative, marketable item, rather than an architectural innovation. Soon the term bungalow was used synonymously with its generic term, house. And there was confusion with the popular cottage style, a much more simple form, derived also from rural settings, especially those found in the West and North of England, and brought to attention by the Arts and Crafts Movement and by architects C. R. Ashbee, C. F. A. Voysey and C. R. MacIntosh, and popularized by the Garden City movement in later years. The cottage was used extensively where new housing was required in the suburbs in and near the industrial areas. Many of the housing proposals in the later part of the nineteenth century were centred on the cottage as a semi-detached or row house vernacular. Many of the buildings called bungalow were more related to the cottage—in form and plan. In fact, the relationship suggested a classic portmanteau word. A firm in Reading advertised the 'Cottabunga'—as 'ready to erect, for £245.10 nett'.[25] A style was recognized as Bungaloid—that is, looking like a bungalow. Most people, even in the 1970s, refer to a small, single storey house as a bungalow, at least in Britain. A cottage is rural.

Therefore, through the apparent disorder there arises two aspects of the bungalow. First, there is an idea about the bungalow which we have described previously as being part of affluence, part of escape, part of recreation and cheaply built. Second, there is only one bungalow style and that has been previously described as similar, and similarity is important, to the Bengal origin. The idea of bungalow has many architectural styles. The Bengal style has only architectonic and aesthetic interpretations. The discussion to follow will almost invariably be associated with the bungalow idea, therefore with the exemplification of the implications of bungalow life-styles.

By the late nineteenth century it was considered an acceptable form for permanent housing. Dissemination of the style to Australia was inevitable. The first architectural book to illustrate the design potential of the bungalow was by R. A. Briggs, *Bungalows and Country Residences*, published in London in 1891. The spirit of the bungalow was maintained in Briggs' text, if not the architectural merit of the style. Bungalows

appeal especially to people of moderate means in a City like ours, where the grime and the smoke, the bustle and the hurry, make us long for the country and its freshness, here at a small expense we may pass a quiet weekend 'far from the madding crowd' to strengthen us for the next week's toil.[26]

He offered almost every historical style and showed only 'recently executed works' for estates near the sea or wooded country. The book does indicate the level of popularity of the bungalow.

By the turn of the century the number of books coming into Australia was considerable and they increased. C. R. Ashbee produced his exquisite *A Book of Cottages and Little Houses* (London 1906) which was in the form of a few lectures plus drawings on the plain salt-box cottage he was promulgating. Gordon Allen produced a more popular book on similar designs in *The Cheap Cottage*, which by 1919 had run to its sixth edition in London. R. A. Briggs updated his earlier work in *Country Cottages and Homes* (London 1910) but it was now a prestigious work: the freshness of his first study was gone. Belatedly he observed a parallel phenomenon: 'No Cottages or Houses, designed in the phase known as *L'Art Nouveau*, now practised by some Architects on the Continent, have been included in this volume, as the author considers it only a passing "mode"'.[27] Excluded was the bungalow and included was traditional historicism.

Country Life magazine put together a book which was diverse and rather significant in noting established trends. Author Lawrence Weaver included all aspects in *The 'Country Life' Book of Cottages Costing from £150 to £600* (London 1913) including bungalows and 'prize designs' taken from a 1912 competition. The £600 cottage of Cyril A. Farey is a peculiar blend of obvious elements of Frank Lloyd Wright's prairie houses of only a few years earlier. Also the angle and character of the perspective indicated it was taken from Frank Lloyd Wright's *Ausgeführte Bauten und Eutwurfe von Frank Lloyd Wright* (Berlin 1910) where his 'concrete' house was displayed. Of all the publications the most informative was a book by the *London Home Counties* magazine in 1905: *How to Build or Buy a Country Cottage and Fit it up*. Elevations, plans, details, materials, costs, architectural renderings, photographs, were all included. The work of English architects C. F. A. Voysey and H. Baillie Scott who were designing cottages and country houses of direct, uneffected simplicity received particular attention (**20**). All these cottage and bungalow books —and many, many more—were readily available in Australia.

In 1909 an indication of American interest was the publication of a magazine devoted to the small house called the *Bungalow Magazine*[28] which began in Los Angeles and later came out of Seattle and ran to 1918. The inimitable *Craftsman* out of New Jersey, a popular magazine devoted to crafts revival and cottage or bungalow design, was received in Australia, but in very limited numbers.

After its initial introduction in the nineteenth century a second phase of the bungalow was discernible. It was the most important, for it provided stronger theoretical bases, and therefore more independence. Three American architects took the idea of the bungalow and, blended with their own idiosyncrasies, created two distinct, yet obviously related styles in the bungalow genre. Frank Lloyd Wright blended Japanese modes, those of the wooden New England Shingle Style, the stark simplicity of midwest rural buildings, and the horizontal characteristics of the bungalow. The result was an architectural style now defined as the Prairie House. The first two completed Prairie Houses appeared in 1900: the Warren Hickox house and the Bradley house, both for Kankakee, Illinois. Also designed in 1900[29] were two projects

20 The Orchard, Chorley Wood, Hertfordshire. C. F. A. Voysey, architect. 1900. (Photograph Dr D. Gebhard)

published in the American magazine *The Ladies Home Journal*: a 'House in a Prairie Town' and 'A Small House'. The result of these designs by Wright and those to follow[30] placed him as the guiding light of a small but significant number of followers who were called the Chicago School. The houses of these architects prior to about 1910 were very similar to those of the mentor in mass, form, detail, general proportion and plan. Their work, along with Wright's, was the most advanced architectural movement in Europe or America prior to the 1914–18 war and the effect of Wright on the European architects is now well known.[31] The Prairie Houses were built almost entirely in the American mid-west—Illinois, Iowa, Indiana, Wisconsin—and by such architects as W. G. Purcell, George G. Elmslie, Dwight Perkins, William Drummon, Thomas Talmadge (who coined the term Chicago School[32]) and Walter Burley Griffin.

The Greene Brothers of Southern California, Charles S. and Henry M. Greene, present another idea of the bungalow. Directly influenced by both Wright and the details of traditional Japanese

architecture,[33] they created a singular style. The D. B. Gamble house, Pasadena, California of 1908 showed the debt to Wright more clearly than later buildings in not only detail, but formal elevational characteristics and massing (**21**). The early use of interlocking wood detailing (inherent in Japanese architecture, and seen by the Greenes in the Japanese exhibition at Chicago in 1893) along with attached pergolas, rough stone, wood shingles and a very flat gable roof, were later developed in the Pratt house of 1909. This Southern Californian style was announced to the world through books and popular and professional magazines which were eagerly sought in Australia. The work of Wright and the Prairie School (as the Chicago School is now known) was published extensively, particularly in *Western Architect* and *Architectural Record*. The former magazine was less attractive to Australian architects than the latter. The Greenes were seen not only in the two architectural journals but in magazines such as *House Beautiful* and *House and Garden*.

The information about the ascendancy of American bungalow styles was also carried by a growing number of pamphlets and books. Probably the most important was by Henry H. Saylor, published in 1911 as *Bungalows: Their design, construction and furnishing, with suggestions also for camps, summer homes and cottages of similar character*. The format of the book was emulated in many other publications to follow, the last (and perhaps the first) in Australia was Edith Walling's *Cottages and Gardens in Australia*, published in Melbourne in 1947. Saylor introduced

21 D. B. Gamble House, Pasadena, California. Greene and Greene, architects. 1908–9. (Photograph W. Current)

22 Piddington Bungalow, Mount Victoria, N.S.W. John Horbury Hunt, architect. 1876.

the bungalow and then discussed its plan, foundations, wall materials, roofing, interior, fireplace (absolutely essential), furniture, lighting, water and sewerage, and rounded out the discussion with garden considerations. The objective was to reinforce the attitude that it was wholesome and healthy to live near and with the earth's natural materials, therefore, with nature. The book contained good photographs, some plans, a few drawings and was careful about details. And, Saylor found ten types of American bungalows! The first was that derived from Greene and Greene:

This type may be recognized at once by a characteristic use of materials. Redwood shingles or redwood siding, stained dark brown, is practically always found in conjunction with piers, porch posts, under-pinning and chimneys of brick, and sometimes of filed-stone, interspersed through the brickwork surface for the sake of variety.[34]

The second type was a patio house, that is a more or less central court, similar to an atrium house. Another type was described as 'an adaptation of the Swiss chalet', while the fourth was 'the small shack' such as tent houses. Number five was the 'small unusually

picturesque' retreat or summer-house which was differentiated from the large 'Adirondack lodge or summer home in the Catskills'. The seventh was the sea coast bungalow, while eight was the Wrightian 'Chicago type' and nine 'the bungalow intended for use as a permanent home'. The tenth was more than one storey. It was a peculiar series of types without any rationale for supposed relationship (or lack thereof) but Saylor at least indicated that the bungalow idea was suitable for a complex series of uses while failing to meet his desired classifications of 'architectural types'. More importantly, he displayed some of the elements which in fact made the various styles viable: light construction, natural materials exposed, natural heat and light where reasonable, a gabled roof more often than pyramidal, exposed roof construction on the interior and exterior, verandahs (piazzas) and sometimes pergolas either attached or in the garden, a low eave line and general horizontality, casement windows and usually large areas of window for each room. If there was a second storey it was part of the roof or attic space, thereby attempting to preserve a low profile. The garden was often unkempt, rather straggly *au naturel.*

23 William Damaresq House, Rose Bay, N.S.W. John Horbury Hunt, architect. *c.* 1881. (Courtesy J. M. Freeland)

24 Phillis Spurling House, Brighton, Victoria. John Horbury Hunt, architect. 1888. (Courtesy J. M. Freeland)

After the 1918 armistice and during the 1920s the number of pamphlets or books about the bungalow was enormous, particularly in America. Most of those arriving in Australia prior to 1914 were English, while there was a fair balance between the two major publishing countries after 1918. Most were in the form of proposals using a formal perspective accompanied by a plan. Few were studies of completed works or in the vein of comparison or analysis such as Saylor's seminal work.

The verandah and the enclosure of the verandah, whether integrated initially or infilled later, was part of the Australian vernacular tradition. This is confirmed by the extant buildings or prints of the first architecture in Australia of Western tradition. As we have seen, the verandah was only part of the definition of a bungalow. Yet, within the definition previously mentioned it is quite clear that Elizabeth Farm (1793–1823) at Parramatta and the Nicholas Weston house of 1820 at Horsley, New South Wales were bungalows: so too many others of the mid-1880s. In considering contemporary ideas of a bungalow's purpose and form, the first to be built in Australia was the Piddington Bungalow at Mount

Victoria in 1876,[35] designed by John Horbury Hunt (**22**). In 1890 the new owner described it in his magazine, *The Building and Engineering Journal*, as follows:

BUNGALOO RESIDENCE, MOUNT VICTORIA

The page-sketch [by Hunt] of the bungaloo residence, Mount Victoria, represents the most substantially-built house on the Blue Mountains. It is now the residence of Mr. F. C. Jarrett, but was built for the late Hon. Mr. Piddington, at one time Colonial Treasurer of New South Wales, and was designed by Mr. Horbury Hunt, the President of the Institute of Architects of New South Wales.[36]

It was one of the most straightforward of Hunt's residential work. It was a long, low-profiled house in the best tradition of the bungalow. The plan was contained by a brick and window wall and an open verandah. The hipped roof extended out over the verandah and was supported by large square columns which were bound by plain, straight turned balusters: a sophisticated interpretation of vernacular forms. The whole was dominated by a random series of large brick chimneys reflecting a rather haphazard plan.

Hunt was born in Canada and trained as an architect in America's New England, in the Boston area, in the office of Edward C. Cabot.[37] He remained with Cabot for about six years, until he left for Australian shores in 1862 at the age of twenty-four. Cabot was fairly young, only about ten years older than Hunt. The Bostonian developed a practice based mainly on large country houses with an architecture 'marked not only by its extraordinary beauty', but by its 'delicacy, its restraint, and its schooled originality'.[38] In Australia, Hunt worked in the office of Edmund Blacket and by 1869 was engaged in an independent practice. While most of Hunt's architecture was characterized by eclecticism, it was more often than not a restrained selection and arrangement that was complex in massing and form. Amongst his work between 1876 and 1891 were a number of designs important to this discussion.

William Damaresq asked Hunt to design 'a marine villa residence'[39] at Rose Bay, New South Wales. The result, begun in 1881 and called 'Tivoli', was an imposing house, simply massed upon the rise of a hill (**23**). The Romanesque motifs in gable end, paired columns, rather flat arches as well as the general massing, round porches and dormer windows, show a strong influence of the New England Shingle Style such as Charles F. McKim's design for the Moses Taylor house in New Jersey of 1876–7. The observations of Hunt's biographer, J. M. Freeland, are worth repeating:

25 E. Du Faur House, Warrawee, N.S.W. John Horbury Hunt, architect. 1888. (Courtesy J. M. Freeland)

Apart from its size, Tivoli was a departure from all previous houses in Australia. It has none of the Classically based formality of design. . . . Tivoli is all of Hunt's earlier theories translated and expanded into an entirely new style. Its bulky broken form, its strong plain roof shapes with their prominent infilled gables, its large basically square wall openings, with low-arched heads, the tall punctuating chimneys . . . and the play of planes of veranda and house roofs, including the inevitable pyramid ventilator over the kitchen, were the break through that Hunt needed.[10]

In 1888 Hunt designed two modest sized houses which mark a distinct departure from the main current of his designs as did the Damaresq house. They stand between Queen Anne and bungalow. Form was more carefully controlled and they were surfaced with wood shingles. In some of his earlier work, Hunt used the wooden shingle as a wall surface, but only in small areas, such as at the stables at 'Booloominbah' of 1887, or 'Cranbrook Cottage'. The Phillis Spurling house at Brighton, Victoria, mixed brick on the lower floor and shingle above but the shingle does not begin at the floor line, but rather at verandah cover or above the lower

floor's window head (**24**). The subtle outward turn of the base shingle course or line (also seen as a string course at 'Tivoli') was more pronounced in later designs. The E. Du Faur house was begun the same year (**25**). It had a characteristic split or double gable; a series of very steep and relatively high roofs were all shingled, as well as the exterior walls. As with the Spurling house, fenestration was arranged in a rather picturesque fashion, seeming to suit internal need rather than formal elevational treatment.

These two houses by Hunt began the tradition of modernism in Australia. They also were designed simultaneously with the architecture they emulated: the wooden designs of New England called the Shingle Style.[41] The many Rhode Island summer homes by architects McKim, Mead and White from 1882–9 are evidence of the influence. The two Hunt houses were followed by 'Trevenna' (the P. W. Wright house at Armidale) in 1889, a much larger home, and the more famous A. Osborne 'Hamilton House' at Moss Vale, and 'Highlands' (A. J. Horden house) at Waitara, both New South Wales and both 1891 (**26**). The Du Faur and Osborne houses are stylistically comparable with the C. A. Brown house by John Calvin Stevens in Delano Park, New York, in 1886.[12]

The importance of these works by Hunt from 1881 to 1891

26 A. J. Horden House, Waitara, N.S.W. John Horbury Hunt, architect. 1891. (Courtesy J. M. Freeland)

27 'Bungalow', Pymble, N.S.W. J. F. Morrison, builder. 1892.

cannot be overemphasized. He was not an obscure figure. He was an important member of the architectural profession and in certain areas of society. His work was well known among professionals. These houses take on an added interest when one realizes their position in Hunt's career: they were executed when he was in his fifties, a time in life when most would settle for the ease of established routine.

It must be acknowledged that these houses of Hunt are more in the tradition of the inexpensive English Queen Anne than the bungalow. But it must also be stressed that that style, or perhaps sub-style, was encouraged as part of the general attitude about the nature and appeal of rural-type buildings. More formal bungalow designs closer to the rigid formula set out by the Bengal precedent were rare. The earliest we could discover—and it is a classic example—was in 1892 and built to designs of builder J. F. Morrison for a site in Pymble, New South Wales (27). Other houses titled by their authors as bungalows were more often than not a modified or simplified Queen Anne or American Shingle Style which was based on the English forerunner. The need to give the title, even if erroneous, again demonstrates the growing desirability of the type of life-style it evoked.

Probably the first to recall the Hunt Shingle Style was the Henry Gullett house, Wahroonga, New South Wales, by E. Jeafferson Jackson. The English-trained architect (who returned permanently to London in early 1908) took the Shingle, country and cottage styles and fused a marvellous, yet maturely restrained collection of roofs, bay windows and gables. The materials in this *c.*1905 house were brick below the ground floor sill line

55

28 House, Cremorne, N.S.W. Waterhouse and Lake, architects. c. 1908.

(generally), wood shingles above and in the gables, and the same material on the steep roofs. The interior (somewhat more English) was a blend of medieval spaces and a bit of Art Nouveau decoration. Jackson's architecture was characterized by an interest in overseas trends, carefully studied and refined.

Parenthetically, the work of Burcham Clamp should be noted. He worked in the shingle idiom on his own house in Cremorne, New South Wales of about 1906. Two storeys in height, with a stained shingle roof which swept down from the ridge over a sixteen-foot deep verandah, it was an imposing façade. The walls were brick, the gables stained shingle and the verandah rails and posts were stone. The verandah had a full one-half circle 'piazza' at one end with conical roof. In 1914–15 Clamp became Walter Burley Griffin's Sydney partner.

With the departure of Jackson and with Clamp showing interest in the Edwardian corruption of Queen Anne, the work of Waterhouse continued the Hunt Shingle Style. Probably the first of Waterhouse's designs to recall the Hunt Shingle Style was a house at Cremorne (Sydney) of c. 1908 (28). The antecedent is obvious in the manner of closing the gable end, the displacement of windows, the use of material (brick below and wood shingles above or on balconies) and in a long, high roof with intersecting gables. The style established in this house was carried into his later

29 Harry Martin Bungalow, Toorak, Victoria. Oakden and Ballantyne, architects. 1908.

designs such as the better known house of 1920 at Spruson Street, Neutral Bay. [43]

Two bungalows by the Melbourne architects P. Oakden and C. H. Ballantyne in 1908 provide the introduction of the twentieth-century bungalow to Australia. The first was a one-storey house with a rather jumbled plan. The exteriors, however, were very good. Two intersecting gables with wood bevelled siding and vents rested on walls of similar siding or rubble stone piers. The stone piers defined the open verandahs, which were bounded with a single post handrail. Rubble rose out of the ground to provide a rail of sorts for the steps to the verandah.

The second bungalow, for Harry Martin in Toorak, was one of the best examples of a consciously designed Australian bungalow of any period (**29** and **30**). It was two storeys and the floor plans were simple and direct. There was a modest entry to a hall which connected all rooms, an ingle-nook, a spatially open drawing and living room, and up the stairs were three bedrooms and an open upper porch or sleep-out. The two storeys were diminished visually by continuing the roof over the verandah and inserting, so to speak, the upper porch into the tiled roof. It was a wooden

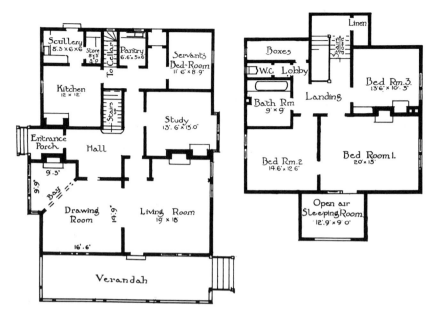

30 Harry Martin Bungalow, Toorak, Victoria. Oakden and Ballantyne, architects. 1908.

structure with wood bevelled siding and cedar shingles in the gable. Natural or rubble field stone supported the ingle-nook windows and was placed between the paired posts of the verandah. The proportions were carefully studied to produce a truly fine example of bungalow architecture.[44]

The Oakden and Ballantyne bungalows were constructed almost simultaneously with the first article devoted to the subject— 'The Building of a Bungalow: A Style That Should be Popular in Australia'. It was a very short article in *Building* magazine, only a hundred or so words, but it at least introduced the idea as reasonable for Australia in June 1908. Yet, the deed, the material fact, had already been accomplished and more were to follow.

Architect Philip B. Hudson's proposal in 1915 for the R. C. Anderson house[45] at Catham Road, Kew, Victoria (**31** and **32**) showed very clearly his knowledge, not only of Wright's concrete 'Fireproof House' of 1907—and subsequent derivations—but the heavily articulated two-storey bungalow by John C. Austin, located in Pasadena,[46] and the Prairie School architects such as Griffin. The basic massing, general proportions, method of fenestration and roof and fascia indicate a careful study of the predecessors. Early in 1913 Hudson designed the residence 'Beulah' in Gardenvale, Victoria,[47] showing a basic knowledge of Hunt's work.

The campaign to popularize the bungalow produced two results. The corrupt, commercial versions took attention away from the authentic architectural works of merit. The American magazines produced volumes on the cheap builders' imitations and Australian magazines re-used some of the corruptions. But it also placed before the reader new ideas about housing, it suggested a subtle change in life-style and it offered a new housing type that gave rise to a demand for architectural response. The corrupt versions in Australia were produced probably in the tens of thousands. The pearls, the gems of architectural interest were few and far between. As indicated above, some were worth consideration prior to 1918. Those after 1918 fitted a more precise formula.

It would be safe to assume that the initial efforts at the new types of bungalow, the post-nineteenth-century versions, would have been rare in Australia. Many architects, for many years into the century, worked tantalizingly close to many of the prevailing trends in England and America, but because of the vagueness of their designs or a lack of overall uniformity or because of additive features to more traditional and basic designs, there were few notable or even modest achievements. The Oakden and Ballantyne bungalows and the Anderson house exemplified two aspects and two styles within the early years of the rise of the bungalow. The most frequent style was the more familiar (and popular in years to follow) Pasadena form of the Greene brothers and architect James Peddle became one of its advocates.

Peddle was attracted to the bungalow in mid-career. To understand more fully the style and due in part to a slump in commissions, he set out for the comforts of Southern California in 1911.[48] He settled in the founding home of one bungalow style, Pasadena, where he set up a practice.[49] The area was also the location of some of the best of architects Greene and Greene houses and the worst of the builders' commercialized versions. Peddle's practice in Sydney was continued by his assistant, S. G. Thorpe, who had been with Peddle since 1902. When Thorpe won a competition for the design of 'single cottages' for the proposed garden suburb of Daceyville he asked Peddle to return. Peddle arrived in Sydney in January 1914[50] and renewed his career: a career which began in Australia with his arrival from London in 1889. Peddle provided a unique link between Australia and the two greatest influences on its architecture: England and America. Yet by the time of his return the bungalow was acceptable architecture. The number of houses in the new style and its various forms was increasing. He later worked on a more subtle relationship between the English cottage (and its kin, the British type of bungalow) and the Californian bungalow. There was still a use of dark stained wood,

31 Mrs R. C. Anderson House, Kew, Victoria, *project*. Philip B. Hudson, architect. 1915.

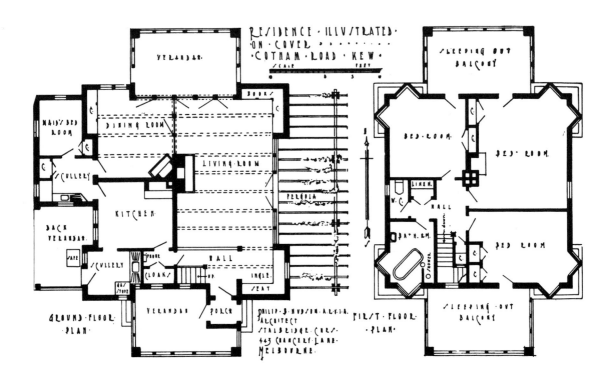

32 Mrs R. C. Anderson House, Kew, Victoria, *project*. Philip B. Hudson, architect. 1915.

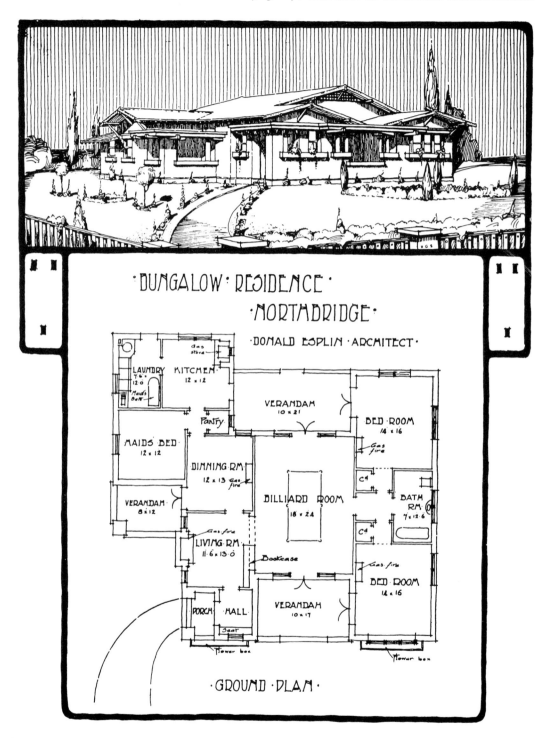

· BUNGALOW · RESIDENCE ·

· NORTHBRIDGE ·

· DONALD ESPLIN · ARCHITECT ·

LAUNDRY
7·6 ×
12·0
Maids
Bath

KITCHEN
12 × 12

gas
stove

Pantry

MAIDS BED
12 × 12

DINNING RM
12 × 13

VERANDAM
10 × 21

BED ROOM
14 × 16

Gas
fire

BILLIARD ROOM
18 × 24

Cd

BATH
RM
7 × 12·6

Cd

VERANDAM
8 × 12

Gas fire

LIVING RM
11·6 × 13·0

Bookcase

PORCH   HALL

Seat

VERANDAM
10 × 17

Gas fire

BED ROOM
14 × 16

Flower box

Flower box

· GROUND · PLAN ·

33 Bungalow, *project*, North-
bridge, N.S.W. Donald
Esplin, architect. 1915.

34 Mrs S. Toms House, Marryatville, South Australia. F. Kenneth Milne, architect. 1906. (Photograph D. L. Johnson)

low pitch of the roof, a gable usually thrust to the street, and a large verandah. There was an addition of half-timber in the gable, a use of brick and generally closed rather than open plans. These comments would, in fact, relate to most of the Australian interpretations along with an over-complication of roofs and roof forms, as well as protruding rooms in most elevations, which together indicated a lingering Queen Anne. The English cottage tended to have a steeper roof pitch than the bungalow and seldom were rafter ends exposed. Beams exposed on the interior were common, but not on the exterior until after the 1920s. The cottage was seen as masses bunched together, rather tightly, while the bungalow, at least most of its types, extended its forms and masses outward. The outward extensions were emphasized by roofs reaching beyond and over the extended plan.

Other architects seem to have specialized in the bungalow style, if not exclusively, at least to a significant extent for a definable period of time. Edwin R. Orchard built a number of bungalows

35 F. C. Stephens House, Cremorne, N.S.W. A. S. Jolly, architect. 1919. (Photograph courtesy J. Whitelock)

in the Sydney area[51] and most indicate a gentle blend as suggested above. The Claude Terry house of *c.* 1920 in Bowral, New South Wales, was a very good example, while most of his earlier designs show an uneasy quality. It may be that those of about 1914 were his first attempts at bungalow design.[52] He was more inclined to modified Tudor or half-timber schemes around this period and for his own residence he used the schemes now associated with Hunt, Jackson and Waterhouse.[53]

An interesting design of 1915 showed a knowledge of the better part of bungalow planning. Donald Esplin's design for a residence in Northbridge, New South Wales, was determined by placing a billiard room in the centre, and about the periphery of the central room a series of verandahs and rooms.[54] Restrained elevations were composed of shallow gable roofs and rather simple massing (**33**).

Another early advocate of the bungalow was Kenneth Milne. The Adelaide architect produced a large number of bungalow styles and near bungalows in the years just before and during World War I. In 1906 the S. Toms house in Marryatville was completed to a design carefully blending both Voysey and the bungalow (**34**). The Mrs J. Lee residence of a year later in Thorngate had a heavy rubble wall surrounding a linear plan, all surmounted by a large, high roof in tile. The general elevational treatment was related to both the Ashbee cottage and the Voysey country home. Yet, instead of the word verandah, he used the American term piazza.[55]

Unique among the endeavours to create homes based on the types of bungalow was the Fairbridge Home in Perth of about 1926. Following lines similar to Saylor's Swiss chalet type, the upper floor was distinct from the ground floor. Pisé walls which formed the ground floor were an oddity in themselves,[56] but done with care in this instance. The pisé was covered in stucco and painted white. Fenestration and doors were simple openings with lintels of wood. In contrast to the white stuccoed pisé, the upper floor was bevelled horizontal wood siding, dark stained, and wood casement windows, all with a dark stain finish. At the line between wood siding and pisé was a timber pergola which defined a terrace. A single and steep gable roof dominated the whole. A sophisticated interpretation in a humble manner, it perhaps epitomized variations to be found in the 1920s.

One who was inspired by the ideas of the bungalow through both Wright and Griffin was Alexander Stewart Jolly.[57] Perhaps it might be unfair to describe Jolly's architecture as being influenced only by Wright and Griffin. The house most often referred to was built in 1919 for Mr F. C. Stephens at Cremorne, New South Wales, where the low profile and heavy eave line of the entry porch, as well as the bulky pylons massed about the central portion of the main body of the house[58] indicate the more obvious elements drawn from Griffin, while the whole was of the prairie style in character (**35**). Its uncompromising presentation was most successful. It was free of half-timber gables, clinker brick and other elements which might distract from basically simple material selection—stucco and dark stained timber—and form selection—pylons in series with panels of similar kind set as infill. Only the roof's ungainly complexity disturbed an otherwise fine composition.

The original Bengal plan discussed earlier reappeared in the 1920s and 1930s. It was more often than not four rooms in each corner, with a short hall entered off a surrounding verandah. A kitchen might have been in one room or perhaps incorporated into the rear of the verandah. A single pyramidal roof reached out to the verandah posts. The toilet was separate. These were usually built from builders' plans or from books or just by word-

36 William H. Emery House, Elmhurst, Illinois. Walter Burley Griffin, architect. 1901–2. (Photograph courtesy Gerald Mansheim)

of-mouth description. They would be found in nearly all of Australia, but more usually in South Australia and in the newer suburbs and especially in the rural centres. Over the years they have been modified and the verandahs partially enclosed. Because of the simplicity of plan and form and their anonymous origin, they retain the characteristics of an indigenous architecture: a nearly spiritual revival of the bungalow not contrived by taste, tradition or follies of creative inventiveness.[59]

Such inventiveness, though, was essential to begin an open inquiry into what a new architecture might be. For Australia, the search for a new architecture was an integral part of the search for an Australian idiom. To suggest an architecture unique enough to be called Australian presumes much. Is it an architecture that uses indigenous material such as gum, jarrah or sandstone?

37 J. G. Melson House, Mason City, Iowa. Walter Burley Griffin, architect. 1912–13. (Drawing courtesy Northwestern)

This would immediately preclude buildings of iron and steel, glass and concrete. Is it an architecture with a peculiar set of aesthetic tools? That is, are the proportions, rhythms, scale, etc., uniquely Australian? Or, is it possible to speculate on the appearance of domestic architecture and the manner and mode of domestic living in Australia if the invaders had been Spanish? One could go on in a negative vein challenging a definition. We shall assume that it is a response to both natural environments and societal characteristics. At the same time there must be recognition that it is an architecture which has or will subtly change in and with time; equally important, that it will be in some respects unique in world terms.

The first Australian architect to recognize the individuality of this southern continent and its new society and in the same instant, exhibit a clarity of method and style was Walter Burley Griffin. He devised a singular style before he came to Australia and that style *evolved and changed* because his methodology was universal, and therefore it was adaptable to Australian conditions.

As mentioned earlier, Griffin's first commission of importance was the Emery house in Elmhurst, Illinois (**36**). It was a simple in-line plan with two appendages containing entry on one side and dining with den above on the other side. Four large brick piers were placed at the corners. The in-line plan flowed within the boundary implied by the piers or extended beyond that virtual boundary. Through changes of level the appendages to either side might then have been at almost any level desired. The Emery concept was clearly expressed in the exterior with the four large piers, the line of windows were tucked under the soffit of the upper floor. The appendages were carefully positioned and their levels expressed. On the long axis the upper level extended beyond the lower floor and piers and was constructed of a lighter material (stucco and frame); the implication of a floating mass was unmistakable. The importance of the Emery concept to the early work has been discussed elsewhere.[60] Suffice it to say that the idea was influential and Griffin played an important role in Wright's office.

During the years Griffin was employed by Wright he saw the design and construction, in fact helped directly some of the most significant domestic architecture to be produced in the world. He was there for the Ward Willits house, Unity Church and the Larkin Building, among many. Griffin was very conscious of Wright's genius, yet he believed that he must begin his own practice. In those first independent years his architecture was too obviously inspired by and derived from Wright. In some instances

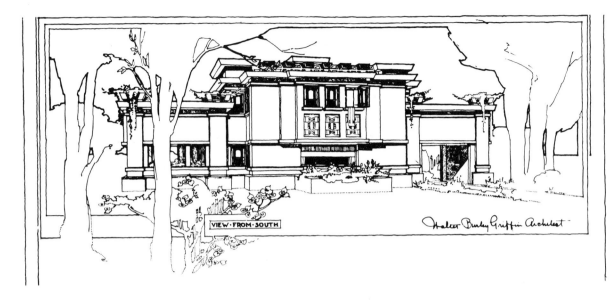

VIEW·FROM·SOUTH

Walter Burley Griffin Architect

he copied cold: Wright's Willits house of 1902 became Griffin's Sloan house in Elmhurst, Illinois, of 1909.

About 1910 Griffin began to mature. His designs were of the Prairie but less dependent on Wright and the Prairie School's idioms. If a beginning of independence were signalled by a single work, it would be the Solid Rock house. A partite plan, to be used many times, was given a solidity of expression on the exterior which was deceiving, for the ribbon of glass visually opened the spaces outward. The full maturity of this chunky, volumetric, highly personal expression was revealed in the Melson and Blythe houses of 1912–13 (**37** and **38**) and, of residential scale, the Stinson Memorial Library of 1913. Materials were stone or stone and stucco, rhythms in ribboned windows were defined with heavy mullions which, at selected points continued to the ground line almost as pilasters. The Melson and Stinson buildings suggest spaces within rock cavities and the Melson house is without doubt one of the finest domestic designs of its period. And the proportions, like Griffin's own stature, were rather squat. The low profile, the maintenance of long horizontal lines, emphasized by occasional verticals, recall the Prairie. The School's typical sweeping eave and gabled roof were gone.

In Australia the Griffins built a small house in Heidelberg, south of Melbourne. It was the first house built using Griffin's newly devised Knitlock construction system.[61] They called their diminutive home 'Pholiota' (**39**). The fully open 1919 plan was directly influenced by the theoretical pure bungalow, as was the massing. Elevations were simple and unaffected. In 1921 they moved out

38 J. E. Blythe House, Rock Glen, Mason City, Iowa. Walter Burley Griffin, architect. 1913. (Drawing courtesy Northwestern)

39 'Pholiota', Heidelberg, Victoria. Walter Burley Griffin, architect. 1919.

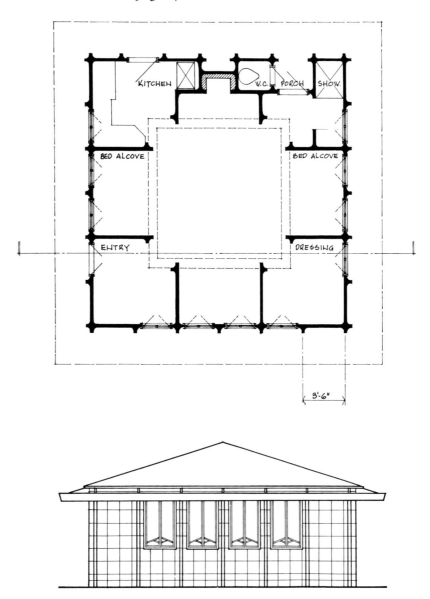

of their Pholiota, away from the melodrama of Federal political corridors and to the Sydney north shore: to Castlecrag.[62]

Castlecrag was probably purchased in 1919. The final subdivision plans were completed in 1920-1.[63] The first house was Griffin's in 1921-2 and if we discount Pholiota, it was the first statement of an architecture inspired and derived by Australia. In massing and form it had similarities to the earlier houses but was more subtle in proportion. Stone, dressed or rough, was massive for the size of the building, repetitive mullions were not

significantly developed but horizontally joined in a low profile
to the earth. It was the earth which accepted the Castlecrag house
with more grace, less forcibly contrived, perhaps, than the previous
American designs, except the Blythe and Melson examples. And
a positive indoor/outdoor relationship was designed with greater
ease.

Some motifs of the prairie years remained: diagonal muntons,
casement windows, heavy mullions and often a pronounced
continuous sill line. These were motifs, almost minor details,
yet they were so vital to the idiomatic Griffin. What was notably
new and seems to have been Griffin's repeated inquiry was a search
for form: not internal spatial flow or movement, but solid form.

They were forms, it should be noticed, which were always
derived from the T-square and triangle—geometric forms. At
Castlecrag the inventions were many. The C. W. Moon house of
1921 was probably the least successful if, in its original state, the
more interesting and very original. More successful was the
T. R. Wilson house of 1929—truly a masterpiece of the Griffin
style—internally and externally low profiled with a subtlety of
space, unrecognizable without experience. An axial plan was
distorted to receive a modest verandah or offset to incorporate
bedrooms with a court and connecting garage. The small alcoved
living room had a band of clerestory light floating an ever so small
but so important rotunda. The space was gracious, almost generous
in quality.

When Griffin again used his Knitlock it was with further
experiment. The A. E. Creswick house with a rather awkward
plan, derived from the Canberra cottage series of designs, maintained in elevation a horizontality achieved not only with the
same height for door and window head, but also the top of the
corner 'buttresses'. The Knitlock forms on the parapet gave it
a common name of The House of Seven Lanterns. The T. Felsted
house of about 1923 had a plan contemporary with and reminiscent
of the S. R. Salter house in Toorak, Victoria. Both have a central
court and are schooled bungalow plans. Both employ Knitlock
exclusively. While the Salter house tended to be with the earth,
the Felsted house rested on a podium of stone on one aspect, while
on the opposite elevation it rested on an extended flatness. The
appearance of symmetry was not fully exploited in plan but the
bold eave and soffit suspended above a band of Knitlock and glass
was a suggestion of the prairie years. Most of the Castlecrag
houses could be characterized as squarely proportioned volumes
seeming to embrace internal spaces hewn from rock.

Three houses, all in New South Wales, hint at an extension of the conceptual base of the Castlecrag beginning: the Estelle James house, Avalon, of 1935, the Winter house (to a lesser extent), Telopea, of about 1935, and the Duncan cottage of 1933 in Castlecrag. The Duncan cottage was a soft blend of stone and Knitlock. The two-roomed building, nestled on the brow of a hill and opened to patios and generous gardens, was the most direct and sensitive statement of a home in the Castlecrag community. The Winter and James houses were interesting from two points: for a design and motif uniformly related to the past, and for a nod to the rationalists' view—a view framed in the contemporary International Style. Areas of stone on the Winter house defined storage, fireplaces and pantry—services spaces. Areas of glass defined living or habitable spaces. In the James house the columned and glass habitable space was enclosed, nearly enfolded by bedrooms and penetrated by service, both expressed in stone. Situated on a steep site dropping nearly twenty feet in fifty, the garage was at the upper or street level immediately over kitchen and bath. Yet neither house was dependent on the seemingly necessary white prismatic precision required in the visual qualities of the International Style. They were houses sensitively designed for the Australian condition.

The influence of America began to wane in the mid-1920s. The peculiar ambivalence of the architect displayed in his eclectic acceptance of modes from either England or America may be a rationally stronger position than may seem at first glance. At least with more sources to draw upon the more open the selection and the less dogmatic the results. And soon the Englishness of Australian architecture was to be abandoned if ever so briefly for the central European variety of internationalism. But that variety needed some form of introduction before the architect could wholly and completely set about his task to interpret the new architecture. With the introduction of the old new (i.e. Griffin) and the prospects suggested by change to something even more violently new came an inevitable reaction.

European Strains and Local Histories

Precursor to the introduction of European strains of modern architecture was Harold Desbrow Annear. He studied engineering at Melbourne University and began his architectural practice in 1889 when he articled under William Salway, after which he concentrated on eclectic and neo-classic designs, with notable digressions. The momentary flirtation with open planning and new forms in about 1902 has been previously noted. Sixteen years later the simplicity of the house, 'Broceliande',[64] in Toorak, Victoria, anticipated in a timid manner the so-called functionalist architecture to arrive in Melbourne in 1933. Built in 1918 the house also contained influences of Griffin in the bold fascia, deep soffit, shallow pitch of the roof and the suggestion of a ribbon of similar windows with rather heavy mullions. The fenestration appeared to respond to interior necessity, rather than formal elevational composition and the severity of the plain, unadorned wall was a key to his functionalist rationalization stated later, in 1922:

it is far better to make all sleeping apartments with a maximum of window areas, so that open air sleeping can be indulged in to excess or moderation . . .

it is better to build-in all wardrobes and dressing tables and fit them elaborately and well . . .

it is not proper for anyone to have meals in the kitchen, which room being the laboratory of the house . . .[65]

In view of the date and what had passed, these words may have had a certain vitality to readers of Annear's own magazine *For Every Man His Home*.[66] In the same magazine he published plans for a 'small, semi-prefabricated modular house',[67] which indicates the inspiration of Griffin not only in plan, but in elevational treatment, suggested detail, and simple form. To call Annear the first functionalist in Australia (as some have) is obviously erroneous. But he was one of a group of people interested in the idea that satisfying function had a virtue in itself, and they came to these interests six years after Griffin's arrival. It was an idea germinated elsewhere but nurtured by Griffin in the Australian condition.

Quite independent of the movements for change coming from the United States and Europe were a series of revival groups interested in the conservation of tradition. Their position was weakened only by their insistence that tradition was seen only as a visual phenomenon. The technical and societal changes which had already occurred were constrained by a visual formula. There were, of course, some enlightened traditionalists and two, Leslie Wilkinson and Hardy Wilson, not only had widespread influence on architecture in general, but on the acceptability of the various forms of the new architecture, especially the International Style.

Leslie Wilkinson arrived in Australia in 1918 as the first professor of architecture in an Australian university.[68] Architecture had been taught for many years in the various technical institutes, mainly in Sydney and Melbourne. In spite of the acknowledged success of the architectural courses in these institutes, their general lack of credibility in academic and social circles was a burden. The profession argued for many years for the establishment of a more prestigious chair of architecture. The recipient of the first chair was a fairly young, vigorous and intelligent English architect who was steeped in traditionalism. Wilkinson was a student in the Royal Academy School of Architecture in London, where he won awards and thereafter travelled in Europe.[69] In 1908 he was appointed as an assistant to Professor F. M. Simpson at University College and he also executed some illustrations for Simpson's influential multi-volume study, *A History of Architectural Development*. In 1910 he was appointed Assistant Professor in the School of Architecture in University College. An articled and practising architect on his arrival in Australia, supported with sound academic training and experience, Wilkinson also brought a gentle but firm refinement of things architectural. Much of what he argued as correct in architecture in general, he argued as being correct for Australian architecture in a regional sense. Although his first love was Italian architecture, he saw the architecture of Spain and in particular the derivative colonial aspects found in the Americas as ideal for Australia. The plain surfaces, logias, trellised walkways and verandahs (as opposed to fully roofed), cortiles and courtyards he saw as architecturally vital, when one compared the geography of the regions where Spanish architecture had flourished and Australia. But the plainness, the simplicity of the forms and the inherent logic of his architectural sense in the 1920s provided a sound practical basis for the acceptance of new architectural forms. The bold simplicity of St John's Church of England in Penshurst, New South Wales, displayed not only a knowledge of historical precedents other than Spanish, but a sensitive response to a scheme of articulated forms. More importantly, Wilkinson's own house 'Greenway' in Vaucluse of 1923 became a hallmark (**40** and **41**).

Although arguing for different reasons and for a different architecture, the result of Hardy Wilson's crusade for a 'return to the work before 1840' was equally a resource for understanding an architecture reduced to simple geometric forms. Probably one of the most exquisite pieces of residential architecture in Australia was (and still is) 'Eryldene', the Waterhouse residence in Gordon, New South Wales, executed in 1914 (**42**). The exact compositional balance and proportions blended into an alternating series of pairs and voids, manifestly state the Vitruvian principle of eurythmy. Together with Wilson's interest in the Orient and

40 'Greenway', Vaucluse, N.S.W. Leslie Wilkinson, architect. 1923. (Courtesy *Australian Home Journal*)

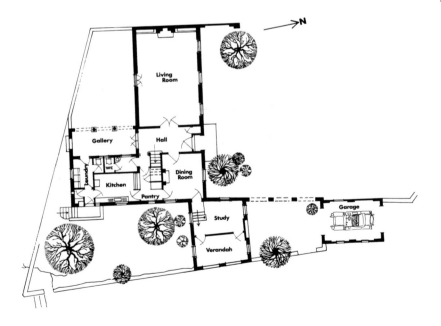

41 'Greenway', Vaucluse, N.S.W. Leslie Wilkinson, architect. 1923. (Courtesy *Australian Home Journal*)

42 E. B. Waterhouse House, 'Eryldene', Gordon, N.S.W. W. Hardy Wilson, architect. 1914. (Photograph courtesy J. Whitelock)

his client's interest in Chinese painting, a tea house with sweeping upturning roof was built to Wilson's design in the garden tennis court. Built in the 1920s, it was indicative of the interest in both Chinese and Japanese architecture during the period. Of less architectural significance but of more popularity with his architectural audience, Wilson's own house of 1916, 'Purulia' in Wahroonga, New South Wales, was a restatement of his colonial interpretations. Low in profile, with a definite horizontality and windows rather close to the soffit, the house had widespread publicity.

Wilkinson and Wilson both provided an architecture meant to straddle apparent and divergent trends. Their direct, unadorned and very cubic architecture was extremely successful not only within their own context but, as has been suggested earlier, in offering a gentle transition to more fundamental change to follow. There was another by-product: the architectural forms of what must have seemed bizarre in expressionism were more difficult to accept; in fact, expressionism in the Central European form and context was repelled from Australian shores. The influence of these two architects was a significant factor in Australian architecture, in particular Sydney, where most of the architectural awards in the 1930s and 1940s were witness to their influence. Even as late as the Sulman award of 1940, Gerard H. B. McDonell won the award with a Wilkinson-inspired hillside house in Gordon, New South Wales. In fact, the house was not dissimilar from Wilkinson's own Sulman Award for the Sweetapple house at Wiston Gardens in Double Bay in 1934.

All those attempting a new architecture were admittedly a minority, as they remained until just before World War II. That their completed buildings were important in propagandizing modern architecture was limited only by an audience, by those who consciously or not took notice of the buildings, in reality or in print, lay public or professional. That there was acceptance of these works is implied by their completion and future commissions for the architects. Only the bungalow style of the late picturesque movement received noticeable attention in local architectural journals, and these were invariably the vulgarized, popular derivations. The premier position of English Arts and Crafts or the Garden City cottages was diminished long before the 'twenties. American influence was waning, except for the tenacious if humble California bungalow. It was the Central European who was putting modern architecture in formal academic dress to evolve into the International Style.

While those formalizations of internationalism were taking place in relation to domestic design in particular, the Australian high-rise was going through a more evolutionary process. The hopeful signs offered by the simplicity of the warehouses was not noticed in subsequent years.

If one were to compress time and rather quickly scan the evolutionary process of architectural design for the high-rise during the 1920s, the view would clarify trends. The classicistic elements would slowly leave the surface, revealing simple masses and fenestration punctured in the surfaces. Large moulded forms, positive and negative, would take on almost new and certainly interesting dominance: Roman arches would stretch high into a façade of a building which might have an attic storey reminiscent of medieval English brickwork and all would be capped with a steeply sloping, terracotta tiled roof. The reminiscences held but the stripping of the elements was the trend. The first process of degradation began when stone structure was succeeded and gave way to other materials performing the structural task. The surface was then free to accept new or different or imitative materials, such as plaster or stucco, and 'cast stone' or terracotta. The great bulky façades in the early part of this century were contrived by this means. It was, therefore, possible to create some of the most ornate surfaces and the most baroque character and form that one might possibly imagine. The high Victorian, Edwardian and other eclectic forms took on a new deep undulating, if not fresh, exuberance. Unfortunately, the interiors reflected a more austere formula.

For buildings other than high-rise or domestic the evolution of slow attrition was also evident but more pronounced. The surface was relatively plain, the fenestration had modest relief above and below windows, and the mass was organized along a formal axis. By the later 1920s the design was stripped of the traditional elements about as far as possible without becoming something else. Since it was traditionally based some of the ornament took on new subjects: triangles rather than squares or circles, or corn rather than acanthus, or a bulky nude rather than a cloaked figure in contemplation. But their position on the façade, their reason for existence was part of the tradition of classicistic attitudes. Most of the buildings for the 1925 Paris Exposition (from where Art Deco received its start) fit this general description as did the later 1934 World's Columbia Exposition in Chicago.

Therefore, the arguments of the modernist had some effect on the more average client or architect in most of the Western countries during the period when modernism was being introduced and tested.

Paralleling early modern architecture was the first expression of an interest in Australia's past. In 1908, Frank Walker, a social historian, wrote a creditable series of articles on the early architecture and history of New South Wales. The emphasis was on two or three buildings and their social context. Each article was very short, a few hundred words.

John Barlow began a series of articles on 'Our Architects of Yesterday' in 1910.[70] It was a short-lived series, in fact, there was a first and last in one. But it was the beginning of an attempt to understand the progress of Australian architecture, not so much in an historical sense, but more additive toward establishing a national identity or base to work from. Studies were also made by Florence Taylor in 1921.[71] But history held no interest for the Australian, except that of his English predecessors. In fact those articles by Taylor in the early 1920s were probably directed at nurturing the growing reaction against the changes suggested as modern, against Griffin, and for the sentimental attachments and nostalgia of Colonial architecture prompted by Hardy Wilson. They were manifestly part of the post-war reaction.

Hardy Wilson was Australia's first architectural historian.

His initial study, *The Cow Pasture Road* (Sydney 1920), eulogized the soft, romantic quality associated with a Colonial innocence, as exemplified in Georgian architecture. His later book, *Old Colonial Architecture in New South Wales and Tasmania*[72] carried the same theme. Wilson stated he was writing on and designing Australian Colonial architecture, 'with a technique gathered from the masterpieces of Italy and the magnificent modern architecture in the United States of America',[73] gathered on extensive travels (including China), and nostalgically recorded in a series of superb drawings.[74] These drawings were completed during the period from 1912 to 1922. They were exhibited at London's Victoria and Albert Museum in 1923 and were published in *Old Colonial* a year later under the auspices of the Medici Society.[75] Wilson and his book had unusual, widespread influence and although the drawings are magnificent, even architecturally precise, they are not historically correct. They romanticized what the buildings and their social situation might have been or what Wilson licensed them to have been. The soft pencil technique of rendering the Lady Franklin Museum (Tasmania) resting majestically on its imagined acropolis under a baroque sky, is typical.[76] These books of Wilson's are not really histories, but at least *Old Colonial* is close enough. They portray a few buildings and the literary style, particularly in *Cow Pasture Road*, is romantically fictionalized. Wilson and the others writing about buildings of the past indicate the resolve of a few to locate in history, elements for design which might be construed as Australian. Wilson's colonial 'before 1840' was a reasonable, if limiting, idiom. Most people interested in ideas which would produce new, more viable designs and perhaps an Australian ideal, rightly or wrongly looked overseas.

Internally, four magazines set the pace of introducing the new European architecture in the 1920s: *Building*, a private publication, and *Architecture*, a professional journal, both Sydney based, and from Melbourne the *Australian Home Beautiful* and the Royal Victorian Institute of Architects *Journal*. *Building* tended to editorialize on fragmentary extracts from overseas journals, ranging its comments from modest praise of a Frank Lloyd Wright project house as 'attractive',[77] to headlines stating:

BUILDINGS THAT ARE WRONG

CRITICISM OF FREAK ARCHITECTURE[78]

These headlines were over an article on the Tokyo Imperial Hotel, by Frank Lloyd Wright, taken in part from an article in *The Architect and Engineer*, published in San Francisco. Paraphrasing by *Building* was as critical as the original—for instance:

'much carved with patterns of Yucatanese, Aztec and Navajo piffle . . . ', or later, 'The cornices are of stone . . . they have panelled perforations to the sky (possibly similar to the Griffinesque effusion on the rear of Collins House, Melbourne) . . . ', and a picture of 'A Weird fireplace', evidently designed 'to impress—or oppress—the beholder', closing with,

Sullivan deserves credit for getting away from the orthodox styles, doing something original in merely frankly clothing or covering the brute and actual structure with ornament that left the structural intent perfectly evident. He was a master and opened the way to really a new art. His disciples in most part have not proven worthy of carrying on in the way he started, for they have all striven merely for the bizarre, the grotesquely unusual, an effort to be different, and the results are generally weirdly fantastic, impracticable, dreams induced by cigarettes and absinthe, awful nightmares. And of all those disciples, Wright has sinned the most and the worst. And this last sin seems the most sinful of all past sins.[79]

Again, with the Einstein Tower (1919–21), Potsdam, by Eric Mendelsohn, *Building* found 'neither pleasure nor satisfaction of feeling that it is a scientific structure'.[80] Its view of the 'eccentric architects of Europe at the 1925 Paris Exhibition', was amply displayed with a headline,

FREAK ARCHITECTURE

Its Contempt for Sentimental Association
and Correct Principles.[81]

Commenting on Joseph Olbrich's exhibition hall in Vienna for the Secession, 1898, the magazine said it was a 'strange erection', but the 'proportions are exceedingly fine', and the trees 'exceedingly well placed'.[82] Yet *Building* magazine at the very least was presenting in its own inimitable fashion some examples of modern, overseas architecture. The exposure of the examples by local magazines gave them a certain certifiable qualification and gave the architecture greater consequence than the editorials. And exposure to contrasting tastes and ideas was and is vitally necessary.

The Sydney magazine *Architecture* continued to orient its editorials and comments towards England. It reprinted English lectures and wrote a few articles on English architecture with a frontispiece invariably of an English cathedral or eclectic Australian buildings. Exceptions were rare and concerning modern architecture only came in 1926 and 1928 when they concentrated on Germany.[83]

Australian Home Beautiful belatedly approached the subject of modernism as did the previous two magazines. It concentrated on Australiana and introduced work which appeared in slick American home and garden magazines in the 1920s. The popularity of American vogue was exemplified by the winning design in a Melbourne Exhibition of Domestic Architecture held in 1928, when Geoffrey H. Mewton and Roy Grounds won a first place with an American Colonial design.[84] Also in late 1928 there was a noticeable change in policy with a concerted effort to introduce modern European architecture to its reading audience; an audience of lay people, home owners and builders, for the magazine was a private commercial publication.

The first Australian Exhibition of International Architecture was opened in June 1927 in Sydney. Two reviewers of the photographic display, Wilkinson in *Architecture*,[85] and editorially in *Australian Home Beautiful*[86] mentioned in passing and nearly without comment that portion of the exhibit was devoted to modern architecture.

Australian architecture of the first third of this century indicates that, with the exception of rather traditional aspects of colonial architecture or a resultant hegemony of Englishness, modernism came from limited sources. The British influence was more historical and included the gentle forms of the country houses or the crisp box of the cottage with soft gardens. More diverse directions were offered by the American imports. They proved to have the most potential for independent exercise by local architects or the styles were different and new and not too radical. The early exceptions of the tall building gave way to derivations of popular themes. There was no *avant-garde* in Australia in any of the arts. But it should be noted that the delay in accepting trends was not as long as previously believed. In many instances architects responded almost immediately to the new inclinations observed overseas—Hunt, Jackson, Milne and to some extent Hudson. The impact of Griffin's arrival must be stressed again. Works which displayed the prairie style occurred after Griffin began practice in Melbourne. Suburban plans based on a response to geography and function, a more architectural approach, and simply reduced line, form and mass also followed Griffin. The presence of Griffin gave modern architecture a credibility that could not have been induced. It should also be noted that the reaction to modernism after 1918 and the acceptance of Wilson's colonial style was not only a popular action but had a devastating effect on those seeking what they believed were more rational or contemporary alternatives in architecture.[87] The fact of the reaction has been implied in these chapters by an almost negligible discussion of sources of modernism during the 1920s.

Only Griffin provided an architecture that might capture the interest of the world beyond Australian shores. His architecture in America was contemporary from the outset. It was innovative and in some instances superb. In Australia, traditional attitudes had their impact. Newman College and some houses and the exterior of the Capitol Theatre building indicate his acceptance of those attitudes. Yet, at the Cafe Australia or when he was his own client at Castlecrag, his innovative, fresh approach to design continued his own established tradition.

NOTES TO CHAPTER TWO

1. Agreement with Asa Briggs, *Victorian Cities*, Harmondsworth 1968.
2. See J. M. Freeland, *Architecture in Australia. A History*, Melbourne 1968, for a good survey of building materials and techniques up to the 1930s.
3. Cf. Mark L. Peisch, *The Chicago School of Architecture. Early Followers of Sullivan and Wright*, New York 1965.
4. Cf. H. Allen Brooks, '"Chicago School": Metamorphosis of a Term', *Journal of the Society of Architectural Historians* (US), 25 (May 1966), pp. 115–18, and H. Allen Brooks, 'Steinway Hall, Architects and Dreams', *Journal of the Society of Architectural Historians* (US), 22 (October 1963), pp. 171–5.
5. Peisch, *The Chicago School*, p. 83.
6. *Western Architect* (US), 18 (September 1912), pp. 95 ff.
7. *Western Architect* (US), 20 (August 1913), after p. 77.
8. Ibid., p. 79. The most complete discussion of Griffin's work in America is contained in H. Allen Brooks, *The Prairie School. Frank Lloyd Wright and His Midwest Contemporaries*, Toronto 1972.
9. 'The Explorer', 'A Cafe With a History', *Australian Home Beautiful* (A), 9 (October 1931), pp. 52–3.
10. 'Mural Decoration', *Architecture* (A), 8 (December 1920), p. 187, and 'Wanted—At Once', *Building* (A), 8 (December 1916), p. 61.
11. 'The Explorer', p. 56.
12. Cf. Robin Boyd, 'The Future of Our Past', in Australian National University, *Proceedings of a Seminar on Historic Preservation in Australia*, Canberra 1967, pp. 10–11, describes efforts to save the theatre. Cf. Donald Leslie Johnson, *The Architecture of Walter Burley Griffin*, Melbourne 1977.
13. Cf. Johnson, *Walter Burley Griffin*.
14. *First Australian Town Planning and Housing Conference and Exhibition . . . Proceedings*, Adelaide 1917, cf. Walter Burley Griffin, 'Planning for Economy', ibid., pp. 45–6.
15. S. Ure Smith and Bertram Stevens (eds), in collaboration with W. Hardy Wilson, *Domestic Architecture in Australia*, Sydney 1919.
16. Ibid., p. 12.
17. Ibid., p. 19.
18. Well illustrated in 'Ahwahnee Hotel . . .', *The Architect and Engineer* (US), 37 (September 1927), pp. 95–101.

I am indebted to Anton Johnson for sharing his ideas and research on the bungalow. Our thoughts often merge in the discussion and often his dominate.

19. Anthony King, 'The Bungalow', *AAQ Architectural Association Quarterly* (B), Part One in 5 (July-September 1973), pp. 6–26, and Part Two in 5 (October-December 1973), pp. 4–21, both synthesize a number of works including the important Sten Nilsson, *European Architecture in India 1750–1850*, London 1968.

20. King, 'The Bungalow', Part 1, p. 11.

21. Nilsson, *European Architecture in India*, p. 187.

22. King, 'The Bungalow', Part 2, p. 6.

23. Ibid., p. 8.

24. Ibid., Part 1, p. 25.

25. Ibid., Part 2, p. 16.

26. Briggs, *Bungalows*, p. 2.

27. Briggs, *Country Cottages*, p. 1.

28. There are no copies in Australian libraries therefore it is assumed it was not received.

29. The dates about 1900 for the various houses are uncertain, see Brooks, *The Prairie School*, Ch. 3, and Grant C. Manson, *Frank Lloyd Wright to 1900*, New York 1958, p. 103.

30. Manson, *Frank Lloyd Wright, passim*.

31. See, e.g., Vincent Scully, Jr, *Modern Architecture*, 2nd edn, New York 1974, and compare with first edition.

32. Brooks, '"Chicago School"', pp. 115–18.

33. Clay Lancaster, 'The American Bungalow', *The Art Bulletin* (US), 40 (September 1958), pp. 239–53.

34. Saylor, *Bungalows*, pp. 19–20.

35. Dated in J. M. Freeland, *Architect Extraordinary. The Life and Work of John Horbury Hunt : 1838–1904*, North Melbourne 1970, p. 92.
    Research into Queensland's nineteenth-century houses is beginning. One of the earliest careful studies is A. J. Wallwork, 'Four Early Timber Homes in Townsville', *Architecture in Australia* (A), 5 (February 1968), pp. 96–100. It predates another fine work, Ray Sumner, 'The Tropical Bungalow—The Search for an Indigenous Australian Architecture', *Australian Journal of Art* (A), 1 (1978), pp. 27–39.

36. 'Bungaloo Residence', *The Building and Engineering Journal* (A), 9 (13 December 1890), p. 438. See Preface postscript above.

37. Freeland, *Architect Extraordinary*, p. 13, and see also John Burchard and Albert Bush-Brown, *The Architecture of America*, Boston 1961, pp. 83 ff.

38. Freeland, *Architect Extraordinary*, p. 14.

39. Ibid., p. 94.

40. Ibid., p. 95.

41. See Vincent J. Scully, Jr, *The Shingle Style and the Stick Style*, rev. edn, New Haven 1971, *passim*.

42. Freeland, *Architect Extraordinary*, Figure 89.

43. For plates of Jackson's Gullett house see E. Jeafferson Jackson, 'Australian Domestic Architecture', *Building* (A), 1 (February 1908), pp. 38–9. For a plate of Clamp's house see J. Burcham Clamp, 'My House . . .', *Building* (A), 2 (March 1908), p. 50. For plates of Waterhouse's work see 'Owning a Home of Your Own', *Building* (A), 3 (January 1910), p. 55 (architects were Waterhouse and Lake), see also p. 56, and 'Australian Domestic Architecture—IV', *Building* (A), 3 (July 1909), pp. 41–4, and George Beiers, *Houses of Australia*, Sydney 1948, p. 34.

44. 'An Artistic Bungalow', *Building* (A), 3 (June 1910), pp. 52–3, and 'Cottages for Comfort', ibid., 3 (July 1910), pp. 71–3. The house should be compared with some of those in Saylor's *later* book, esp. 'The Camp Home', p. 76.

45. Philip B. Hudson, 'Modern Designing', *Home and Garden Beautiful* (A), (1 April 1915), pp. 988–95, cover, and 'Proposed Residence . . .', *Building* (A), 15 (May 1915), p. 61.

46. Saylor, *Bungalows*, p. 60. The architect is identified in Lancaster, 'The American Bungalow', p. 248. It was originally published in *Western Architect* (US) in June 1909 and republished in Australia immediately in the same year in 'Owning a Home of Your Own [vii]', *Building* (A), 3 (August 1909), p. 71 (with plan).

47. *Real Property Annual* (A), 1914, p. 54, and 'Beulah', *Building* (A), 15 (July 1915), pp. 117 ff.

48. 'James Peddle, F. R. I. B. A.', *Architecture* (A), 20 (January 1931), p. 4.

49. Howard Tanner, 'Stylistic Influences by Australian Architecture', *Architecture in Australia* (A), 63 (April 1974), p. 57.

50. James Peddle, 'Some Lessons We Can Learn From Our American Neighbours', *Building* (A), 20 (December 1912), p. 84. The issue was also titled the 'Bungalow Number' and most of it was devoted to American bungalows, especially from 'Pasadena'. Most of the illustrations were probably supplied by the Malthoid Company.

51. [Florence M. Taylor], 'Australian Domestic Architecture. How "Type" is Evolved. Some Examples of the Work of Edwin R. Orchard', *Building* (A), 16 (August 1915), pp. 108–16.

52. Cf. 'The Bungalow. Its Design and Construction. Evolving the Australian Type', *Building* (A), 16 (September 1915), pp. 85–92.

53. [Taylor], 'Australian Domestic Architecture', *passim*.

54. 'Bungalow', *Building* (A), 16 (November 1915), p. 64i.

55. F. M. Taylor, 'The Architecture of Adelaide', *Building* (A), 16 (October 1915), pp. 54–9.

56. 'Fairbridge Homes, Perth (W. A.)', *Building* (A), 35 (August 1928), p. 67. See also John R. P. Adams, *Distinctive Australian Homes*, Sydney 1925, pp. 26–7.

57. Freeland, *Architecture in Australia*, pp. 244–5. Both Freeland and this author are indebted to Richard Apperly for information on Jolly.

58. Adams, *Distinctive Australian Homes*, p. 29, also Freeland, *Architecture in Australia*, p. 244.

59. For the contrived corruptions see, e.g., *Book of Australian Bungalows*, Sydney *c*. 1925

60. Cf. Johnson, *Walter Burley Griffin*.

61. Donald Leslie Johnson, 'Notes on W. B. Griffin's "Knitlock" and His Architectural Projects for Canberra', *Journal of the Society of Architectural Historians* (US), 29 (May 1970), pp. 188–93, for a discussion of the construction system.

62. See Donald Leslie Johnson, 'Castlecrag: A Physical and Social Planning Experiment', *The Prairie School Review* (US), 8 (3, 1971), pp. 1–13.

63. Ibid., p. 7, for a site plan, and Johnson, *Walter Burley Griffin*.

64. Also referred to as 'Troon'; see W. J. Splatt, *Architecture*, Melbourne 1962, p. 22. A house of similar design for Colonel Stephenson in South Yarra, Victoria, was completed a year later, see *Australian Home Beautiful* (A), 4 (January 1926), p. 14. A heavy debt to Griffin is again evident. Mr Albert Gillissen helped with aspects of Annear's work. See also Robin Boyd, *Australia's Home*, Melbourne 1952, pp. 175–8 and *passim*.

65. As quoted in Geoffrey Woodfall, 'Harold Desbrow Annear: 1866–1933', *Architecture in Australia* (A), 56 (February 1967), pp. 104–5.

66. The magazine was launched by architects P. Meldrum, J. Barlow, R. B. Hamilton, W. A. M. Blacket, P. Everett, A. G. Stephenson, L. Irwin, J. H. Wardrop, Annear and artist A. Streeton. Apparently it ran for only two or three issues.

67. Woodfall, 'Harold Desbrow Annear', p. 106. Studs were exposed on the exterior. Annear was also interested in the bungalow; see E. W. Cole, *Australian Book of Bungalows and Villas*, Melbourne *c*. 1925, p. 17.

68. R. N. Johnson, 'Emeritus Professor Leslie Wilkinson', *Architecture in*

Australia (A), 62 (December 1973), p. 79. Wilkinson's ideas and thoughts were introduced in a series of articles titled 'The Appreciation of Architecture', *Building* (A), 27 (November 1920), pp. 80b–80d, 27 (December 1920), pp. 72–86, 27 (January 1921), pp. 74–9, and 27 (February 1921), pp. 64–70.

The first serious thoughts on architecture being taught within an Australian university were given in an address by George C. Inskip to the Victorian Institute of Architects on 7 May 1888. See 'Architectural Education', *The Australasian Builder and Contractors' News* (A), 2 (12 May 1888), pp. 315–16.

69. See also J. L. Stephen Mansfield, 'Leslie Wilkinson . . .', *Architecture* (A), 36 (October 1948), pp. 37–40.

70. The first series was in the newly founded *Building* magazine. The Frank Walker articles began with 'Early Australian Architecture', *Building* (A), 1 (January 1908), pp. 37–8. Walker also wrote on 'MacQuarie's Churches', *Art and Architecture* (A), 6 (September-October 1909), pp. 146–54. The second series was mooted in John Barlow, 'Our Architects of Yesterday', *Art and Architecture* (A), 6 (November-December 1909), p. 192. The first article was John Barlow, 'Francis Howard Greenway', 7 (January-February 1910), pp. 10–15.

71. Florence M. Taylor, 'An Australian Home: Elizabeth Bay House—The Home of the Macleys', *Building* (A), 28 (May 1921), pp. 63–5, and 'Historic Sydney Architecture . . .', *Building* (A), 29 (December 1921), pp. 75–80.

72. Published by the author, Sydney 1929, 50 plates.

73. Ure Smith and Stevens, *Domestic Architecture*, p. 9.

74. Most of the drawings are after his own photographs. See Hardy Wilson, 'Photos of Chinese Architecture', *Art in Australia* (A), (2, 1922), no pagination. The original drawings are on display in the National Library, Canberra.

75. 'Old Colonial Architecture. The Wilson Collection of Drawings', *Architecture* (A), 15 (September 1926), p. 5.

76. Ibid., p. 14.

77. 'Design for a White Pine House', *Building* (A), 35 (March 1924), p. 157.

78. Vol. 32 (April 1923), pp. 68 ff. There were similar criticisms for most of the period 1912 to 1930.

79. Written by W. F. Fitzpatrick, an American corresponding contributor to *Building*, for his name appeared frequently either for his letters or with a by-line. See also Manson, *Frank Lloyd Wright*, pp. 111–12.

80. 'Plan and Elevation of the Einstein Tower, Potsdam (Ger.)', *Building* (A), 33 (January 1924), p. 91. See a sister publication, *The Australasian Engineer* (A), for the same period.

81. Florence M. Taylor, *Building* (A), 38 (October 1925), pp. 68 ff. Inserted was a photograph titled, 'Melbourne's Contribution to the World's Freakish Architecture—The Catholic College', or Newman College by Griffin eight years after completion.

82. 'Secessional [*sic*] Art Gallery, Vienna', *Building* (A), 38 (January 1926), p. 81.

83. 'Recent German Architecture', 15 (June 1926), pp. 3–7, and Werner Hegemann, 'Modern German Architecture', 17 (September 1928), pp. 183–91, and 17 (October 1928), pp. 220–1.

84. 'A Competition in Domestic Architecture', *Australian Home Beautiful* (A), 6 (May 1928), pp. 35 and 38.

85. Leslie Wilkinson, 'International Architecture', *Architecture* (A), 6 (August 1927), pp. 144–8.

86. 'The First International Architectural Exhibition', *Australian Home Beautiful* (A), 5 (July 1927), pp. 14 ff.

87. Bernard Smith described a similar reactionary trend for the painting community that was more extreme. See his *Australian Painting 1788–1970*, Melbourne 1971, p. 168.

3

1927-34: Internalization

Hunt, Griffin and Wilkinson represent an external stimulus as well as an internal fusion of ideas and architecture transmitted not only by their own words and works, but by those who followed. Knowledge of these considerable works was spread throughout the continent not only by word-of-mouth, but by the magazine. A series of events were given credence by inclusion in magazines: there were reports of the travellers, works of other architects, personalities and activities of para or related bodies, such as landscape designers, engineers, constructors, town-planners or whatever. The magazine also may have had some persuasion in the final national unity of the various state professional bodies (without Western Australia) which took place in September 1929 and called itself the Australian Institute of Architects. The growth of the magazine as a means of transmitting ideas and (for many an architect) pertinent, practical information, was itself an event of great importance.

The allusion thus far has been clear, perhaps too obvious. The key to the development of architectural style was communication. Information has always been disseminated by some form of communication but developments were accelerated after World War I to a degree not attained before. Communication and modern architecture were often helpmates to concomitant courses which one or the other might take. Certainly the universality of modern architecture and its acceptance in Australia is linked to evolving means of communication. The progressive evolution of styles in England, the Mediterranean and Europe prior to the twentieth century often took generations to achieve their ultimate rationalization with recognizable forms and idioms, while the events which concern this discussion happened, for all practical purposes, within two generations. These events were generated not at one source, that is England, but three: England, the United States, Central Europe, and again the United States, in that order.

Immigrants were one factor in the communications link.

But before Griffin's arrival in 1913 and later, during the 1920s and '30s, it was the Australian travellers who went 'home' to England and/or took a Grand Tour of sorts. They obtained personal wherewithal that, when they returned, provided impetus and by informing others from first-hand knowledge, directed attention and ultimately productive, creative efforts toward a new architecture.

Another communication element already considered, was the magazine. Internal publications were important in disseminating the knowledge that had been gathered overseas. Internal and overseas magazines became paper platforms to educate the profession and public about new architectural idioms. Witness the many engrossing manifestoes during the first half of this century emanating from Central Europe[1] and witness the profoundly influential *de Stjil* and *l'Esprite Nouveau*. The architects were very much aware of the magazine's potential. The recognition of this relatively fresh propaganda medium was worldwide. The early part of this century saw the rise of the magazine as not only an important element in efforts to induce new apostles to new causes, but to inform on man's expanding knowledge.

Those were the three decisive factors or communicants in the development of modernism in Australian architecture—immigrants, travellers and magazines.

In any form of communication the effectiveness of the chosen form is dependent as much on content as on method. Only when the content is articulate and the method attractive, when the content is intellectually and psychologically persuasive, will there be a greater and quicker acceptance on the part of an audience. (Local magazines and journals were rather shoddy, almost cheap productions compared to those coming in from overseas, at least until 1934.) One element remains—pressure. When articulation is achieved to a degree that a recognizable programme is established then a discipline can be developed. Only then can pressure be exerted.[2] This oversimplification should be sufficient to see the fundamental problems that were inherent with conservative, insular Australia and which have been partially resolved with recent advances in communication media.[3] For architecture, two levels of articulation are necessary. Not only must the intellectual stimulus be a viable philosophy, but the deed—the physical built product—must provide a necessary substantiation of possibility *and potential extension*. For example, Italian Futurism lacked the conspicuous fact. It was full with postulates which were articulate but without the deed, let alone an immediate and real potential. Perhaps the success of Art Nouveau, as it was known to its contemporaries (and excluding architecture for the moment), was in the facts presented as accomplished followed by a descriptive outline or verbalization of its potential. Certainly this was true of Art Nouveau's contemporary movement, the Chicago School.[4] That certain elementary aspects of Futurism may now be realized is of no consequence for the fact remains that the influences directing the thoughts of Futurism's apostles, Sant'Elia and Marinetti,[5] no longer exist. The world has not only changed by almost two generations but, in a historical sense, by the compaction of time and through all the forms of physical and telecommunication there exists a much closer social proximity and pragmatic awareness.

During the first half of this century Australia was to be indelibly imprinted with the presence of immigrants, with the published notes of travels by young architects and with the editorial vicissitudes of innumerable local and overseas architectural magazines. The cumulative pressure created by the immigrants, by the travellers and by the magazines created a need on the part of their audience, to be part of and to engage in what they believed were progressive developments in the Western world. That both travellers and the press at the local or national level were staunchly conservative until just about 1930 is clear. And some remained conservative well after 1930. Still, they offered the opposite view in the tradition of a liberal press. But it was difficult to generate discourse: a vital necessity.

If there is to be meaningful discourse, there must be diversities of view. The cross-fertilization of ideas and the development of contrasting tastes are extremely important. Australia's geographical location, its insular attitude to Asia, its colonial political structure imbued with a basically one-class social system and a two-class political system, and the limitations of only two major urban centres within a 5,000-mile radius (10,000 miles to similar cultural centres) made this difficult to achieve. Also, the architectural profession was small, very small. In each capital city, which controlled the profession in the various states, their numbers were such that they formed a nice, rather large but single committee or club, which all too often was in happy, comfortable accord. Only when the fraternal camaraderie gave way to diverse views and allowed divisions to arise did various options become recognizable and, if not stable, at least provided viable programmes for discussion and later provoke action or reaction.

Before and during the period under discussion there were essentially two typical Australians. There were those of the land, the pastoralists, the people who haunted and developed the rural areas of the outback and established the internationally renowned tradition of the rugged individualist. And there were the city or suburban dwellers. The adurban and suburban people, presently 75 per cent of the population, were always a very high percentage. As so many historians have observed, he was a stubborn middle-class Britisher who transplanted the old roots in the antipodes. It was the latter, not the pastoralist, who was the architect or who commissioned by far the largest percentage of architecture.

Internal communication and cross-fertilization must be considered from another view. The distance from Adelaide to Sydney is the same as from Paris to Warsaw. The distance from Perth to Sydney is the same as Oslo to Cyprus, or Chicago to Antigua. It was talk across the back fence for Le Corbusier, Berlage, Sant 'Elia, Wagner, Hoffman, Gropius or Saarinen, as it was for architects in the mid-western United States or in California. In 1913 there were 126 architects in all of New South Wales[6] and they were 13,000 sea miles from Brussels.

Australians in the decades before 1940 subscribed exclusively to English language architectural magazines. (It was not until the 1950s that there was a beginning and gradual increase in subscriptions to foreign language journals.) Australian magazines took on a new character and format in response to the new aesthetics. For instance, *Architecture* changed in 1935 and *Building* in 1936. Occasionally architecture was the subject of an article in magazines on the periphery of the design profession, such as *Builder* in Adelaide, or *Shire and Municipal Record* or another Sydney journal, *The Australasian Engineer*. A magazine came on the scene in Sydney in 1935 that was fresh, new, without commitment to past policies and must have induced change in other magazines: *Decoration and Glass* was started by architect Watson Sharp. He was interested only in the architects and architecture of the 1930s, of his today. The *Australian Home Beautiful* befriended Griffin during its first years of publication when it was under the title of *Real Property Annual*. When in 1922 it began as a quarterly titled the *Australian Home Builder*,[7] it continued to support Griffin and his followers by periodically publishing some of his buildings, projects and writings. By the late 1920s (as a monthly) or more particularly in the early '30s, the magazine was a leader in disseminating information on buildings and ideas pertinent to the modern movement. The two other nationally subscribed architectural magazines of importance were the Sydney-based *Building* which was rather conservative, and *Architecture* (Journal of the Institute of Architects of New South Wales up to 1931, when it began to serve the national body[8]) which was conservative to the point of being reactionary, at least until 1928, and there was the *Journal of the Royal Victorian Institute of Architects*. It was not only reasonable for the young architects to approach *Australian Home Beautiful* or later *Decoration and Glass*, but editors often sought their work, real or projected, and their ideas for changes in architecture.

The changes in architectural design in both the 1920s and the early 1930s were not changes resulting from new structural materials, for as has been noted the reaction and means to such changes were transmitted to Australia. They were not changes resulting from concepts of space or changes of plan (perhaps denoting some ideas of functional determinism) or other changes induced by pragmatically philosophical bases for these were all transmitted to Australia as nearly accomplished facts. The changes were almost purely stylistic. It is difficult, if not impossible, to find any profound arguments in any journal for the changes which took place. In the 1920s reasons for this staid position were self-evident: the large proportion of architects were almost wholly concerned with style (eclectic) and saw it not only as fulfilling artistic ends, but more necessary means. And the argument that a search for an Australian architecture might provide an impetus for the changes, ever so slight, was not supportable by the evidence. The search was the concern of only a few who were more interested with a moderate attitude. They attempted to temper tradition with whatever the changes might suggest for Australia. In the *Journal of the Royal Victorian Institute of Architects*, architect Alec S. Hall summarized the general view at the end of the roaring 'twenties:

No work of art can be accepted as good unless it offers us some standard of comparison by calling to mind some previously experienced thought or accepted tradition. For this reason a new school of thought or a new style of art, cannot be invented *per saltum*, it must be born of the past and must manifest to us something of its paternity.

It is not feasible that our art should be Australian in the sense that the boomerang is: the boomerang was evolved slowly. ... So also our architecture, painting, sculpture, literature and music, if they are to mean anything at all must reflect our European origin.

Travellers and The Atelier

While the general attitude exemplified in the discussion above is what we might find not only in Australia, but elsewhere, particularly in North America, one aspect of the aculturation by Australia of the modern idiom of architecture was both typical and unique:

typical in that it had counterparts in other countries, but unique in that it *tended* to occur belatedly in Australia. We have seen that the migrant perhaps more naturally than not was to have a profound effect on the architecture of the early part of this century—Hunt and Griffin from North America and many architects from the British Isles. We have noted also that a few, a small but significant few native Australians travelled overseas for that necessary and intimate contact with the people and environment of architecture so lacking in the glossy pages of magazines and books. Some took time to engage themselves in the actual practice of architecture overseas. The group we are now concerned with travelled, but they were sponsored by their peers and mentors as travelling scholars or students. Their reports back to the professional architects in Australia were to support and profoundly influence the change to modern architecture.

Before World War I travel was gained more by the immigrant as a matter of circumstance in relation to studies and personal preparation for practice in Britain. Later, the Australian professionals who had no opportunity to travel because of distance and/or means, were given opportunities as a result of the war. Arthur G. Stephenson and Leighton Irwin were two soldiers who after the war returned to England and Europe to develop their personal expertise. The impact of these two individuals will be discussed shortly. For the most part, the architectural observers were concerned with modes of eclecticism or at the very best the geometric rationale of the stripped-down classicism of the late 1920s. The concern of this portion of the essay is with those architects who were enticed to the modern idioms for one reason or another. In the 1920s their interest in those idioms may have been more than casual, but their influence was marginal except in extreme atypical circumstances. Those who left just before 1930 were perhaps a more inquiring group as a whole because they were selected for this capacity.

Both the major cities provided financial assistance. Early in the century the profession in Sydney offered the Kemp Memorial Medal and later in the 1920s added a Travelling Scholarship to the medal. In the late 1920s the Sydney architects began the N.S.W. Board of Architects' Travelling Scholarship and the Australian Medallion and Travelling Scholarship. In the 1930s Victoria offered the Haddon Medal and Travelling Scholarship, but its resultant influence was negligible on the profession and architecture as a whole, at least during the crucial period about 1930. The significance of the Sydney scholarships lay with the editorial policy of the Institute of Architects of New South Wales to publish reports and essays of the travellers in their journal *Architecture*. The granting of the scholarships was an important act, but for the cause of architecture the reports were of inestimable value in bringing back, often after five or six years, a personal and, through their quasi-official position, an authoritative empirically gained knowledge. Two factors were important to the success of these young architects in their role with fellow Australian architects and the public: they were adequately prepared usually through the diploma courses at Sydney Technical College and they were responsible individuals.

Raymond McGrath, a Sydney University graduate, received both the Wentworth Travelling Fellow award in 1926 and the Australian Medallion in 1928[9] and his various reports indicate his evolvement as a designer, architect and historian. At the time of reporting to the Institute he had been in England, particularly Oxford and Cambridge, for three years so his activities were in full development. He collaborated with the sculptor Maurice Lambert on an unsuccessful submission for the Anzac Memorial for Hyde Park, Sydney in 1929.[10] In working on architectural projects and with the Cambridge Preservation Society, he worked with modernists such as Walter de la Mare, Clough Williams Ellis and Serge Chermayeff. His journalistic endeavours found publication in professional and popular slick (commercial) magazines throughout Britain. As a winner of an interior design competition for a Modern Art and Electric Light exhibition, he won two of the four positions with modern rather than traditional designs: 'Mr. Raymond McGrath, A. R. I. B. A., has designed two amazing rooms (a dining-room and a bedroom), which, while being keyed up to exhibition pitch, show combinations of class, colour and light that bristle with ideas.'[11] And of course his book on *Twentieth Century Houses* was in preparation. The attraction of London was too strong and McGrath became an expatriate. Many travellers sought him out during the first years of the 1930s, including Fred Anderson, Walter Greosmiths and Arthur Baldwinson.

Sydney E. Ancher received his travelling scholarship in 1930 in this twenty-sixth year.[12] He worked in London for five years, travelled intermittently on the Continent and returned to Sydney, where he formed a partnership in 1936 with R. A. Prevost.[13] By 1939 he was back in England and did not again begin practice in Sydney until 1945. Ancher was a more typical example of the architect changing his ideas. With his training at Sydney Technical College he was prepared more or less in the traditional manner about historically traditional architectural forms. While in England he was converted to 'modern in the "functionalist" manner',[14]

and sought out the architects and their buildings. He went car tour-
ing on the Continent with Frank Costello. He was impressed
by the work of the Dutch architect W. M. Dudok in Hilversum.
His introduction to Holland surprised him for he found buildings

remarkably similar to those one usually associates with the work of
the American architect, Frank Lloyd Wright; similar details which have
been made familiar to us in Australia by Walter Burley Griffin.

It transpires ... there is a disposition to regard Frank Lloyd Wright
as the Father of Modern Architecture. Volumes of his work have been
published in France and Holland; and German architects also have
used him consciously and subconsciously as a source of inspiration.[15]

Ancher's intense interest in the newly found modern developments in the 1930s induced by a 1931 visit to Berlin, led him to
a thesis on its evolution, giving particular emphasis to the impact
of technology. His own evolution or metamorphosis was apparent
on his first return to Sydney in 1936. He lamented on education:
'too much time is devoted to a study of the architecture of the
past and too little to a study of the present-day trend',[16] while
his colleagues noted the complete change in many ways including
sketches: from soft pencil or ink renderings of medieval and classic
buildings around 1930 to wholly abstract interpretations of
architectural elements at mid-decade. Ancher worked in the
London office of Joseph Emberton whose fine Royal Corinthian
Yacht Club received worldwide attention after 1932.

Frank G. Costello, as a special travelling scholar in 1928,
studied town-planning and hospital design and wrote on modern
trends of architecture and town-planning.[17] Graham A. Mac-
Donell was a 1928 travelling scholar, interested in housing and
worked with Sir Herbert Baker.[18] B. T. Stone provided excellent
sketches and photographs from Europe, concentrating on the
low countries and Scandinavia.[19] The 1930 travelling scholar was
Morton E. Herman and one of his first contacts was with one of
'the original modernists', H. S. Goodhart-Rendel.[20] Herman's
interest in the historically significant architecture of England
paralleled his interest in modern design[21] and his gift in writing
was apparent in his reports and essays. Herman, along with
Dudley Ward and Eric Garthside, were probably the most prolific
writers of the travellers and Garthside's photos of central European
modern were given considerable attention, but almost too late
in 1934.[22] Dudley Ward's studies in contemporary housing found
full expression not only in Australian journals, but American as
well.[23] A. E. Barnard won a Kemp Medal in 1923 and a travelling
scholarship in 1926. He studied in London, travelled on the Continent, and worked in the firm of Sloan and Robertson, in New

York City.[24] Brian B. Lewis travelled via Malaya and completed a Diploma at the University of Liverpool.

There were many travelling scholars, both before the critical early 1930s and after. Of course, there were some who travelled privately, without financial assistance of the profession. Norman Seabrook left for England at the conclusion of studies at the Melbourne University Architectural Atelier and in London worked for Sir John Barnet[25] where he succeeded Charles Madden, who left Sydney in 1930.[26] Jack Cheesman left the South Australian School of Mines in 1926 and Adelaide in 1929 to work and study in New York and Europe,[27] returning in 1932. And there were others.

These ever-so-brief notes on some of the travellers and the discussion to follow about these and other architects should provide enough evidence to support the contention that travel was essential, not only for the personal development of the architect, but to legitimize contemporary ideas and modes of architecture. These were individuals on sojourns meant to improve the profession through intimate knowledge of events. While these individuals might offer comparisons or opinions or bring back their expertise, they were a rather diverse group, without leadership or a mentor to provide cohesion or inspiration. What was necessary at this crucial moment was an individual or group to fuse people and events into a comprehensible unity. The University of Melbourne Architectural Atelier—or The Atelier—provided a forum for such a group.

Norman Seabrook was categorical in his praise of The Atelier:

The greatest influence on Melbourne's architecture over the last thirty years [1928–58] has been the University of Melbourne Architectural Atelier, originated by Rodney Alsop and [succeeded by] Leighton Irwin with the latter as Director.[28]

Former soldier Leighton F. Irwin studied at the Architectural Association in London after 1918. His practice had always been centred in Melbourne. Like so many young architects, he entered competitions, winning seventeen in half as many years. In 1928 he formed The Atelier. His attitude on the role of the architect was crucial to the success of The Atelier as was his experience at the AA in London. At various times he wished that architects were called 'building engineers'.[29] The term indicates what has been described as a 'passion' for verifiable facts. This, coupled with a constant surveillance of the conditions of the building industry, provided what he believed to be a sensible balance between the designer as divinely gifted and the architect as co-

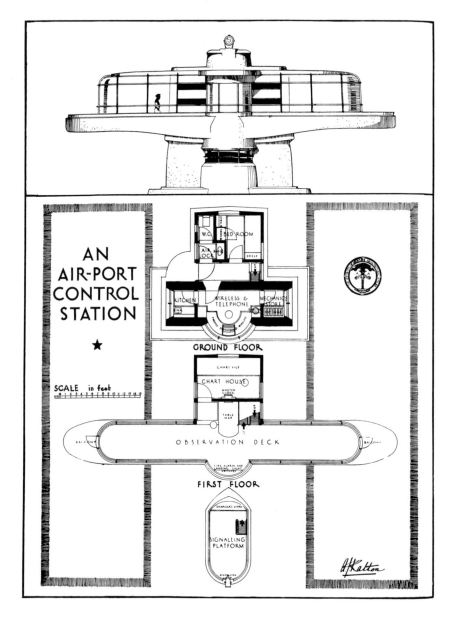

43 'An Air-port Control Station', *project*. A. J. Ralton, designer. 1930. (From Royal Victorian Institute of Architects *Journal*)

ordinator of a complex of companies and people. Therefore, his insistence on 'careful and independent basic research as a prelude to creative synthesis'[30] was seen by students as his strongest characteristic. The search for responses to more practical aspects rather than old aesthetic means was critical to understanding and accepting the changes evident overseas. So too was Irwin's own 'sense of realism, logical mind and independence of spirit', as former student Donald C. Ward recalled.[31]

From time to time (and all too seldom) the work of The Atelier students was presented to the profession. One project of note was 'An Air-port Control Station' by A. J. Ralton in 1930 (**43**): fluid forms were related to a compact and sensible design.[32] Yet, Sydney Ancher's design (as a student) for a golf club house[33] was peculiarly related to the late nineteenth-century romantic movement of residential architecture in Scotland and England, of Voysey and Lutyens, as well as local architecture of previous years.

The architectural press, therefore, began to note not only overseas works but local and student designs. Sources of design became as important as the designs themselves. A sample might be in order. Leslie M. Perrott wrote to colleagues in California on the 'tendency of Australia to adopt American methods and use American Products'.[34] In 1930 the Grace Building office block was completed in Sydney and Frank Lloyd Wright's project for the enormous high-rise National Life Insurance Company of Chicago was published in Sydney and Melbourne. Leighton Irwin gave an illustrated lecture to his Melbourne colleagues on 'The Trend of Design as Shown in Modern Architecture'.[35] Both European and American examples were shown and the works of the central Europeans were given emphasis. A debate (of sorts) was held at the end of 1930 on 'Traditional v. Modern Contemporary Architecture' with little said or resolved at the Sydney venue.[36] In 1931 the Sulman Medal, a New South Wales architecture award, was announced and in later years was to be a fairly good barometer of architectural taste. And in the same year a lecture of S. C. Ramsey in London was reprinted in *Architecture* providing some interesting arguments on the 'Fallacies' of 'Some Tendencies of Modern Architecture'.[37] *Building* magazine continued to illustrate overseas architecture and offer comment in its inimitable fashion. The longish caption for the Brinkman and Van der Glugt design of the van Nelle Factory, Rotterdam (1927) included the observation that:

Continental countries do not enjoy the beautiful hours of sunlight that we have daily and take as a matter of course, and if by these means [glass walls] the health and physique of the race is bettered, then these buildings, which at first sight appear rather strange, will have amply justified their existence.[38]

At this point in the discussion and in the evolution of events, one must not ignore a beautiful exception, the British Medical Association building at 135–7 Macquarie Street, Sydney (next to a preserved colonial townhouse, now the Royal Australian Historical Society), by Joseph Fowell and Kenneth McConnel (**44**). Design was begun in 1928, construction was under way in 1929 and it was completed in 1930. It follows on from the vertical Gothic of the Woolworth building in New York City. Also, it is the first fully composed and completely articulated design of early modern and later aberrations including Art Deco, to become so important to high-rise buildings. It represented the latest acceptable architecture, that is a design short of *avant-garde*, or, perhaps a better terminology, short of central European radicalism.

By 1930, the press, both professional and slick, was beginning to see if not the merits, the inevitable swing to the new architecture. Of all the styles available, the precise International Style ascended. The expressionistic Dutch and romantic Scandinavian ran popular seconds. The travelling scholars were reporting on their discoveries made in all parts of Europe and North America. The overseas magazines were arriving, if not in profusion, at least significantly in number and many of their articles were digested and reprinted in local magazines. The profession had grown and matured, architects had travelled and were travelling. The old retrenched with dogma, the young sought design freedom.[39]

Sydney architect J. F. Hennessy, while on a trip to London in 1932, gave a short talk to the Royal Society of Arts on 'Architectural and Engineering Problems' associated with contemporary Australia. It was a rather factual outline mixed with some personal insight: populations of sheep and people mixed with ideas of the Australian character: climate mixed with

when we consider the dominant influence of the present day, the syncopating so-called music and its impression on some painters, sculptors and architects, judging from some of their recent works, we know that this influence cannot and will not last and that it will disappear as quickly as it came.[40]

Yet, 1932 was the turning point. When the pendulum began its swing the momentum was difficult to restrain. Its effect was final, if imprecise. It centred on Melbourne.[41]

The architects P. A. Oakley and S. T. Parkes completed their Yule House at 309 Collins Street in 1932 (**45**). Many succeeding buildings in Melbourne imitated the style and its simple formula: bands of glass set in geometric patterns of fixed and opening panes, a terracotta (or stucco) surface and dominant spandrels extending well beyond the surface. Not of the earlier triangular fashion of the 1920s and not of the easy, soft lines of the more typical Depression Modern architecture of the 1930s, it was an esquisse perhaps localized in the Melbourne area. The competition for the Melbourne Herald's city office received a submission from

44 British Medical Association Building, New South Wales Branch, Sydney. Joseph C. Fowell and Kenneth H. McConnel, architects. 1928–30. (Photograph D. L. Johnson)

Stephenson and Meldrum which betrays the difficulty of transition. It was a design containing elements of the geometric modern of the 1920s, the classical, and suggestions of Regency as well as 'the new trend'[42] suggested by Yule House and its kin, The Beehive on Elizabeth Street. Yule House was an asymmetrical composition typical of the early 'thirties. Later, as architects became more proficient with the new trends, the design shifted to a more staid, more formal symmetry: not always but as a general rule. And in both the compositions the heavy forms and the concentration on solids rather than opacity or translucency or weightlessness suggested the growth out of late Victorian and Edwardian. This is also suggested by the parts, large and small, dividing the whole into vertical and horizontal aspects or stages. Peculiarly, as the 'thirties progressed, the formal symmetry was more accentuated and heaviness more pronounced, at least for those buildings derivative of the central European brick architecture.

Two other office buildings were proposed during this important year of 1932: the Shell Building, Melbourne, by architects A. and K. Henderson (**46**) and the Manchester Unity Building, Swanston Street, Melbourne, by architect Marcus R. Barlow, described in Sydney as 'An Epoch-making Achievement'.[43] The Manchester building has obvious antecedents in the influential Chicago Tribune competition and its association with the vertical Gothic. Details both interior and exterior are strongly based on Graeco-Roman elements or the Gothic. Standing next to Griffin's bulky yet prescient Capitol Theatre Building, it has a certain refinement. (On the other side of the Capitol Theatre is the extreme of simplified Gothic verticalism, the Century Building of the late 1930s.) The Shell Building (1932–5) is one of many the company built during the 1930s and is kindred with the Manchester building in its verticality but less dependent on historical precedents. The vertical was emphasized by protruding mullions which appear as columns and rise full height to extend beyond the parapet. They stopped before the ground floor which was given a more flush treatment, offering the building a husky base. The spandrels were recessed, yet the majority of the façade is seen as glass. Only one-half of the scheme was completed.[44]

In domestic design a few rather isolated events occurred which led to a more significant moment. The magazine *Australian Home Beautiful* began to offer articles often in the form of reports on modern domestic architecture overseas. One of the first was Amyas Connell's 'High and Over' at Old Amersham, England. Connell (from Canada) along with his partner Basil Ward (from New Zealand) were the first to bring the International Style of Le Corbusier to England.[45] Architect Harry Norris completed his design of the massive house 'Burnham Beeches' in 1933 in the Sherbrooke Forest of the Dandenong Mountains.[46] It is a concrete house of an architecture standing mid-point between traditional and modern, both in style and structurally, between European and English trends in domestic architecture (**47**).

Architect Geoffrey Mewton presented some sketches and offered

45 Yule House, Melbourne, Victoria. P. A. Oakley and S. T. Parkes, architects. 1932.

46 Shell Corner, Melbourne. Centre (corner) building, 1958–60, Buchan, Laird and Buchan, architects. Building immediately to the right, 1932–5, Anketell and K. Henderson, architects. (Photograph L. Richards, courtesy Shell Oil Company)

comments about architecture and modern domestic design in particular, based on his travels to America and Europe.[47] Mewton was indentured to [W. A. M.] Blacket, Forster and Craig from 1923 to 1928 with his contemporary, Roy Grounds. After a brief partnership they travelled overseas in July 1928, Grounds with a Royal Victorian Institute of Architects travelling scholarship. Mewton recalls that Dudok was the hero of every architectural student during his first years in Europe. Grounds went to New York in 1929 to work and Mewton to England in the same year. Then Grounds travelled to California where he spent two and a half years as a set designer with R. K. O. and M. G. M. Studios. Both he and Mewton returned to Melbourne in about 1933.

47 'Burnham Beeches', Dandenong Mountains, Victoria. Harry Norris, architect. 1933. (Courtesy Nicholas Institute)

They again formed a partnership which lasted until 1937 during which time they built fifteen houses. And it was in 1933 that the firm designed two houses: one was then a project for a seaside cottage[48] but later, in 1935, it became Grounds' home at Ranelagh Estate, Mount Eliza.[49] It was a simple plan with bedrooms to one side of a central entertaining space and kitchen, etc., to the other side. The ground floor was surmounted by a small sunroom and large areas of sundeck. Le Corbusier would have approved. The exterior walls were prefabricated, using steel structure and cement asbestos siding. It was an important project in the history of Australian architecture, almost as important as the Cafe Australia or the Canberra projects for Duntroon or Castlecrag

48 Critchley Parker House, *project*(?), Upper Beaconsfield, Victoria. G. Mewton and Roy Grounds, architects. 1933. (Courtesy the architects)

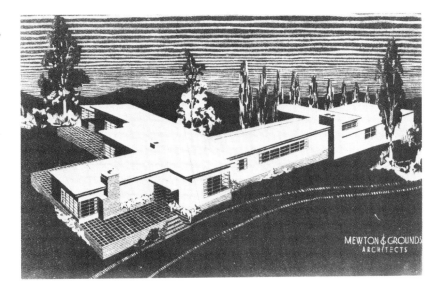

by Griffin. In 1934 the architectural observer of the *Australian Home Beautiful* could announce with more assurance than the professional journals might: 'The day of concrete, stainless steel and glass is at hand'. To reinforce the comment a project for Mr Critchley Parker by the firm of Mewton and Grounds was presented (48). It actually preceded the seaside cottage by many months and made the introduction of the International Style complete.[50] The lessons of these travellers were obvious when one compares these two projects with their 1928 competition.

These might have been isolated events, without continuity and response, if it had not been for the Melbourne Centenary. The Centenary arrived at an appropriate moment. Hurt by the depression but more by the virtual abandonment by England, Australia sensed its isolation even more strongly. For architecture there was little to offer in the vague English modes of modernism.[51] The spiritual centres of the movements were Europe and America. A tentative belief in recovery from the depression was revealed by a rise in building permits in 1934 over 1933. The average value of each permit was only £450.[52] One might speculate that the centenary was in celebration, not only for the one hundred years of Melbourne, but as symbolic of internal recovery by independent means. Part of the celebration was a Centenary Homes Exhibition, a competition with five different categories, three for the design of complete houses.[53] All three of these house awards were won by former Atelier student Donald C. Ward, then an architect with the Commonwealth Department of Interior (and not the Sydney traveller). There was one important qualification in the prospectus

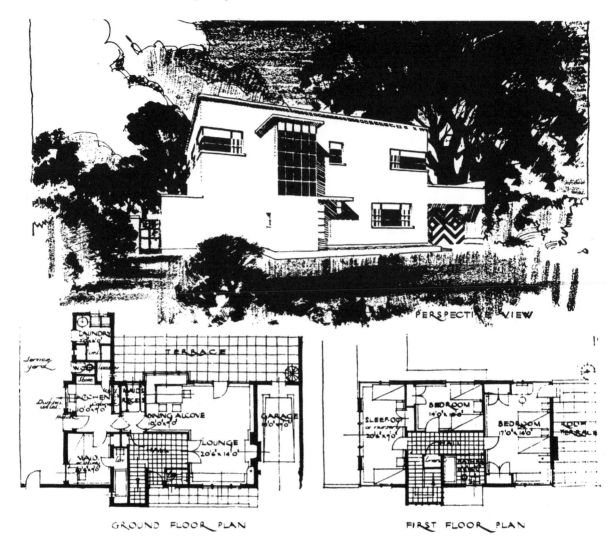

PERSPECTIVE VIEW

GROUND FLOOR PLAN

FIRST FLOOR PLAN

of the competition: modern 'tendencies' in architectural design were encouraged. Ward's houses were neat cubes with corner fenestration, vertical elements for stairs and plans that if they were somewhat congested, were at least generators of the external forms (**49**). Other winners were J. F. W. Ballantyne and Roy Wilson (second and fourth place in the 'Perfect Home Competition') with most reasonable designs, and Norman Seabrook and J. D. Fisher took third prize with a modern cream-faced brick house design. Arthur L. Peck and Hugh L. Peck presented a fairly good design for the difficult problem of a round house of two storeys. Ward's design for 'A Concrete House' was very good and similar to his previously mentioned design. But other than a competent design by L. Garrard Cahn, the medium of concrete

49 Centenary Homes Exhibition, *project*. Donald C. Ward, architect. 1934.

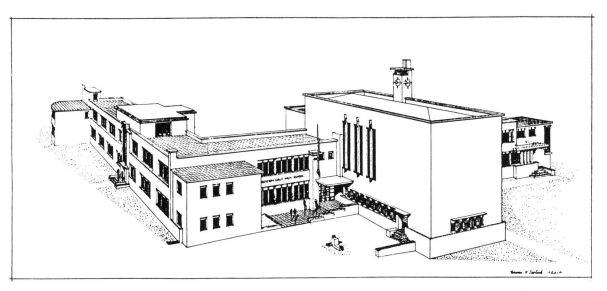

50 Melbourne (Macpherson Robertson) Girls' High School. Norman H. Seabrook, architect. 1933–4.

obviously posed problems for the architect. This was not so with those who used concrete Masonry units. Architect Leonard A. Bullen and Mewton and Grounds provided designs in the new manner. Mewton and Grounds' entry for the 'Asbestos-cement House' to cost £650 was excellent and very similar in many ways to the seaside cottage in use of material, type of fenestration and general proportions.

If one building were selected as signalling the advent of modern European architecture, it would be the Macpherson Robertson (Melbourne) Girls' High School by architect Norman Seabrook (**50**). Winner of another Centenary competition, it was designed in 1933 and completed in 1934.[54] The School was an excellent example of the kind of attention that was desperately needed in all public school architecture in almost all of the various levels of education including tertiary. The influence of the Dutchmen, especially W. M. Dudok is clear and executed with great skill. Since it became known to colleagues and the public simultaneously with the Mewton and Grounds projects, they must acknowledge the premier importance of the school.[55] In 1934 the building responded to the rationalists' view if belatedly expressed.

One would be remiss not to make a note that a similar belated phenomenon occurred in America. With the exception of key figures such as Wright, R. M. Schindler and Richard Neutra, modern architecture as finally accepted was not considered until almost the same years: the early 1930s. The differences of the early key figures are important. So too is the difference in attitude on acceptance, which tended to be more open or universal. There was a willingness to accept the theoretical and there was less content with one style. As with Australia, the changes were urged on by a significant number of immigrants such as Neutra and Schindler and then Walter Groupius and Mies van der Rohe in the late 1930s and especially the post-war period.

The early years of the depression and the resultant slack in architectural commissions seemed to allow the Australian architect a moment for contemplation about probabilities for the course of architecture. Projects, thoughts, ideas, competitions and the like urged a provocation to challenge what the future realities might be. The impact of this reflective moment was severe. Modern was to be part of the architectural *mélange*.

To emphasize the nature of the sudden change a few events are selected. In 1934 Leonard A. Bullen's long-standing series of articles on 'A Review of the Small House Problem' in the *Australian Home Beautiful* suddenly, in one issue, switched from the traditional and picturesque to European modern.[56] The magazine continued this commitment. In 1934 the Melbourne residence of Dr and Mrs Geoffrey Smith was completed with a nice façade by the architects Yuncken, Freeman and Freeman.[57] The influential and conservative *Art in Australia*, after a consistent history of discussing only painting and sculpture, appeared in May 1934 with an article on urban 'Shop Fronts and Shop Windows'.[58] It thereafter continued occasionally to publish articles on architecture with an emphasis on modern.

The seminal work of Sheldon Cheney on *The New World Architecture* published in 1930 which searched out the various ideas provoking the new twentieth-century architecture failed to include Australia. Later, Henry-Russell Hitchcock and Philip Johnson, when exploring the phenomenon of academicized European modern architecture in 1931, could not locate such a new tradition in Australia prior to or during that year,[59] nor could F. R. S. Yorke in his *Modern Homes* (London 1934). Similarly, London architect and Australian expatriate Raymond McGrath failed to single out Griffin's architecture or his influence and also missed, perhaps by months, the 'new' architecture in Australia in his worldwide survey of *Twentieth-Century Houses* finally published in London in 1934.[60]

Griffin continued to plant trees in Castlecrag, design more houses and embark on a new venture in designing buildings for garbage disposal. His students and followers were now well established professionals engaged in their own work. In the furore of discovery the profession and the public remained aloof to the revolution which faltered, the one they failed to understand nearly twenty years earlier and which so markedly changed their understanding and attitude on the nature of architecture. In 1934 Griffin was fifty-eight years old and had been practising architecture in Australia for twenty years. In 1934 he must have been encouraged by the Melbourne events, by the growth and acceptance of modern ideas for architecture—but not impressed.

Griffin

Griffin's influence was peculiarly diverse during the 1930s. Some of those who had rather presumptuously dismissed Griffin were mellowed by time, by the diminished and now softened impact of the new styles, and they saw Griffin as perhaps more important than previously suspected. Others still held firmly to the belief that Griffin was grossly misunderstood and unfairly treated, not necessarily as related to Canberra, but rather as a fellow professional. Others held fast to the belief that he was a Bohemian nut. Probably each architect and observer had a singular view. Yet all, or nearly so, would agree that Griffin had an influence on the course of events: most would make the observation with rose-tinted hindsight. Since Griffin was aprofessional in that he tended to ignore the administration and public relations necessary for private practice, the growing number of commissions during the lean years of the 1930s must be attributed to not only the presence and good works of Griffin, but his architecture. Three architectural activities evolved: Castlecrag; his work with the Reverberatory Incinerator and Engineering Company; and his residential commissions.

During the late 1920s and 1930s activities at Castlecrag became less idealized and more focused on the community. The vegetation was maturing and the roads finalized. Some of the planned houses materialized: the splendid Fyshwick house of 1929, the delightful two-room Duncan cottage designed in 1933, as well as the Nurses' Quarters for Dr Rivetts' Hospital.

While activities at Castlecrag would influence only a small number of people interested more or less directly in the community, or some fellow professionals, work with the Reverberatory Incinerator and Engineering Company—or to abbreviate, REICo —reintroduced Griffin to a larger audience for the works were built in or near four of the major capital cities. These REICo incinerators arrange themselves into three main types dictated more or less by the functional characteristics of the incineration process. A truck dropped garbage into a hopper above the furnace and the residue was taken out as clinkers from the bottom of the furnace. If one includes the movement of the trucks above and

51 Incinerator, Leichhardt, N.S.W. Walter Burley Griffin, architect. 1936. (Courtesy Cement and Concrete Association)

52 Incinerator, Pyrmont,
N.S.W. Walter Burley Griffin,
architect. 1932–5.

the carrier below, the resultant flow is a diagonal. The problem
of expressing this diagonal flow and the transition from upper to
lower levels was the design crux. The single continuously enveloping roof was the initial type used in the first buildings in 1929–30.
These were at Essendon, Victoria and Ku-ring-gai, New South
Wales.

One modification of this basic idea was the Willoughby Council
(New South Wales) incinerator which 'commenced operations

on the 7th May', 1934.[61] The enveloping roof was broken on the embankment façade into a series of shed roofs which allowed the base of the building to move out with the slope of the embankment. The relationship and use of materials, the careful variation of fenestration within a material group and the recurring rhythm of the diamond and triangle as applied form and texture, are all harmoniously integrated.[62] The continuous roof was also broken or stepped in the more dramatic Leichhardt, New South Wales, building of 1936 (**51**). The first basic type and its modifications were developed with relative ease and the results were dependent on the integral use of motifs, materials and ornamentation. In the other types this integration became a dominant factor.

When Griffin attempted to use one large volume and set it against or into the hillside, so to speak, with a small element at the base, he developed buildings of uneasy quality as the incinerators at Brunswick, Victoria, of 1936 and Randwick, New South Wales, of 1932 displayed, as well as a pyramidal roofed project of the mid-1930s.[63]

A third concept used was a stepping and interlocking of cubes down the embankment face. Thebarton and Hindmarsh, South Australia, of 1937 and 1936[64] respectively and the Glebe, New South Wales buildings fell into this type, with the Pyrmont, New South Wales building of 1935 being a slight variation.

The success of these three responses to the buildings' function were dependent on the distinctive style of Griffin's ornamental and design elements, which might at once unite his composition and still provide visual counterpoints. The triangle, whether as texture or to define panels and voids, large and small, and its related pyramidal form were used extensively. The pyramidal form appeared on both the Willoughby and the Leichhardt buildings, but first was used by Griffin on some projects in America, particularly his own house at Winnetka, Illinois of 1911-12. Later it appeared on the façade of the Melbourne Chinese Nationalist headquarters and reappeared throughout his years on exteriors and interiors—for instance, the Capitol Theatre interior. The monumental scale of the Leichhardt building did not deter the use of the pyramidal form, it was merely enlarged proportionally. At Willoughby the plastered or cement rendered forms, including the stack with pyramids growing from the surface, was a distinct counter-point to the rubble walls. Leichhardt was a superb example of an architectural design based on a triangular motif: it was continuously evolving in plan, form, plane and texture; from whatever distance or angle the building was perceived, the eye was constantly forming the intended diagonal relationships.

The Thebarton building nostalgically recalled in use of material and proportion, the school on the Chicago Prairie where it all began for Griffin. The Hindmarsh, Pyrmont, Randwick and the Thebarton buildings, as well as a project incinerator for Castlecove, all suggest that Griffin was more than subtly swayed by the contemporary European strain of architecture. The Pyrmont incinerator was an important architectural achievement, not only for Griffin, but within the Australian scene (**52**). The large horizontal mass (unfortunately softened by the hipped roof) was deftly interlocked to the lower mass. The crowning achievement was the surface ornament. On the stack or the face of the beams over the truck entrance, it was in soft layers, changing emphasis with the movement of the sun, while on the horizontal masses it appeared incised into concrete. The Mayan influence on Griffin in earlier years was recalled and unrestrained in its applique to the surface.

If the incinerators present a relatively clear, if complex picture of development from 1929 to 1936, this is not true of Griffin's residential commissions of the 1930s. As has been suggested earlier, an Australian domestic architecture began with Griffin's Castlecrag houses. The houses outside Castlecrag offer little commonality with those inside the community. They are varied in design form, style and characteristic. Some bear witness to new trends while others suggest a previous and far-away architecture, such as the Mary Williams house in Toorak, Victoria: the reminiscence of the prairie was too dominant. And therein lies a dichotomy. Griffin was inconsistent and to this degree: at Castlecrag he was, for all practical purposes, his own client. Outside Castlecrag most clients might have wished for more traditional designs and he responded. This is admittedly only a guess, but it is based on his diminished role with the designs outside Castlecrag and the relatively cumbersome quality of the designs. One exception is the D. Pratten house at Pymble, New South Wales.

Students and Followers

While the travellers, The Atelier and other Melbourne events made significant contributions to the development of twentieth-century architecture in Australia, they were not the sole instigators of the new designs nor the arbiters of taste. From the moment of their return to Australia the travellers' influence is measurable. From the moment of their activity the Melbourne architects also made a measurable contribution. And since most were still alive at mid-century, the continuity of their contribution was assured. Less obvious, but of more importance, is the definable group which continued to follow Griffin, that is, assistants, students and followers of Griffin who deserve formal consideration as a school. And here it is important not to be fooled by appearances. As the architecture of Griffin changed throughout his career, and one need only compare the Carter House of 1910 with the Lucknow University Union Building of 1936, so too would the architecture of others. But those who chose to be influenced by Griffin were more impressed with the quality of his life and his expectations of architecture, rather than with the architecture as manifest; with the integrity of the man rather than with the fashion of style; with the search for a methodology, rather than with attributes of cause. His students, as some of his assistants wish to be called, have acknowledged that working with Griffin was the most important event in their careers. They did not necessarily agree with his architectural modes at any point in his life. But they did agree about the man Griffin as an architect. With Billson beginning in Griffin's office in 1916 the argument for continuity of modernism is sustained (even if one were to ignore Griffin's own work up through 1935). The aberrations of Desbrowe Annear coincided with Griffin's early Australian work and were short lived. At the turn of the century Dods was an eclectic and Hunt was unable to generate a following, at least as related to style. Therefore, although the discussion will lapse into the previous decades, a careful, concise look at the followers' work is vital within this history.

There was not a large number of people who worked for Griffin. A speculative total of no more than twelve individuals during his twenty-one years of Australian practice would be reasonable. Before 1925, during the most productive period, the Melbourne office, for instance, was never composed of more than five or six draftsmen.

Louise (Louisa) Mary Lightfoot studied architecture at the University of Melbourne receiving a Diploma in Architecture in 1925 while articled to Griffin. Within a few months she was asked to work and live in Castlecrag and also act as a kind of companion to Marion. She performed a variety of tasks in the architectural office at Castlecrag from 1925 to 1929. But her affair with architecture was not one of love. She was encouraged into the art by her father and became one of the early women Australian professionals but another art was a stronger attraction. She studied ballet almost immediately on arrival in Sydney. Her studies with Daphne Dean at the Sydney Conservatorium led her to finally leave architecture for dance in 1929. From 1929 until the mid-

1970s she performed, produced, choreographed and promoted dance. In 1937 she travelled in France, England and India and on her return to Sydney she produced, among other works, the Indian ballet *The Blue God* in 1939. From then on she was devoted to the study and performance of Indian ballet especially the Manipur style.[65] And she took her ballet not only to Australian, but to New Zealand, American, Canadian, Japanese and European audiences.

Frederick Ballantyne worked in the office for a number of years and his brother, Keith, for a short period. Mr and Mrs Edgar Deans were both employed by Griffin. She was a typist in Melbourne and then in Sydney; he was secretary of the Greater Sydney Development Association (which administered Castlecrag) from 1927 to the early 1940s. They met at Castlecrag and after their marriage lived there for a number of years (including a residence in the Fyshwick house) before moving to Canberra.[66] George Elge,[67] a member of Griffin's Chicago office, was enticed to cross the ocean during the period of Griffin's return to Chicago in 1913 when he arranged his personal and business affairs. Elge and his wife returned to Australia with the Griffin entourage in 1914. He worked as a draftsman for about three years and then returned to the United States.

One of the most influential members within the office was Leslie Gordon Grant. He worked with Griffin from 1925 until 1936. Only Eric Nicholls and Roy Lippincott were with Griffin for a longer period. Grant was trained at the Swinburn and Melbourne Technical Colleges as well as the Design Atelier at Melbourne University. In 1925 he became an articled pupil with Griffin, completing his training in 1930. From 1930 until 1936 he worked on various projects including the Palais Pictures, the various Langi Flats, the Theatre and Shops in Malvern, some of the Castlecrag residences as well as a few Knitlock houses and the incinerators, and he became head draftsman. He was in the Melbourne office until about 1929 when he went to Castlecrag. In late 1936 he went to America and worked in the office of McKim, Mead and White and then in various offices in San Francisco. By 1939 he was back in Melbourne where he worked in the firm of Stevenson and Turner. With the engineer, W. J. Grassick, he formed a professional association and they began their Melbourne practice in 1942.[68]

Henry Pynor worked in Griffin's Melbourne office from 1921 to 1924 after receiving his Diploma in Architecture from the University of Melbourne. He then went to the United States to work and then travelled in Europe,[69] and worked in England with Yorke and Sawyer, returning in 1928. He worked in Sydney until 1930 and again travelled, this time to Canada and America. From America, in fact from a small New Hampshire town, he was invited to join a group of Americans who were to act as consultants to Russian industrial projects. Proceeding to England, and after a farewell wharfside benediction in London by George Bernard Shaw in 1932,[70] they set off and for nearly a year they travelled Russia. Pynor returned to Australia in 1935[71] and worked casually for the Griffins for a few months. In 1937 he joined the partnership of L. F. Herbert and E. D. Wilson as a full partner. In 1946 he was appointed Lecturer in Charge of the School of Architecture at Sydney Technical Institute (formerly College). Wilson was also an inveterate traveller who studied at Sydney Technical College and then in London at the Royal Academies.[72] He then travelled around England, Europe and America as a working architect from 1921 to 1927. Herbert was also a Sydney Tech student[73] and a Kemp Memorial Medalist in 1915. In 1925 he visited England, later travelling to America where he specialized in theatre design and equipment in New York City.

And there were other students and associates including Robert Haughton, Kemp McGuiness (an engineer) and Rupert Lattimer. The above career outlines indicate the diversity of background, training, travel and, importantly, influence gained and imparted in years following their Griffin interlude. This study will concentrate on four architects and investigate a few of their buildings and projects. This should be sufficient to substantiate an argument of continuity. They are: Roy A. Lippincott, Edward F. Billson, Eric M. Nicholls and J. F. W., or Frederick Ballantyne.

All who worked for Griffin pay him great homage. He was not an easy man to work for. Yet he was a humble, quiet man and a grand, generous person as can be attested. By the mid-1930s all the architects to be discussed, with the exception of Nicholls, had left the Prairie or Griffin School to work in the Australian derivations of Depression Modern and/or the International Style.

In the course of architecture there have been few formally titled schools. Yet, one of the more influential if short lived was defined early in this century. The Chicago School of Architecture was a conscious formation of young professionals who discussed the nature of mid-west, national and ideal architecture in the commercial halls and restaurants of the windy city. With the production of Frank Lloyd Wright's earliest prairie houses, the first in 1900, the as yet undefined but articulate young people found an architectural manner to encourage and then emulate. One of the first to respond in the new manner was Walter Burley Griffin. Indeed, his first house designed in 1901, the William H. Emery residence in Elmhurst, Illinois, was a fully developed concept which included a design method and geometry which structured space and form. The Emery concept had a profound influence on Wright's architecture after Griffin joined the Wright Studio.

Griffin remained with Wright for about four years and then began his own practice. In 1912 he won the international competition for a New Federal Capital in Australia, to be called Canberra. He was invited to Australia, accepted and remained until 1935. Griffin, therefore, was a direct descendant of that circle of young people who produced an architecture defined as the Chicago School. Through a peculiar twist of historicism by Carl Condit, the School's commercial buildings were defined as the only true Chicago School product. In fact any commercial building and executed by almost any architect was seen as the School as long as it was produced during the period c. 1883 to c. 1910. But not even those dates are firm for an argument was also presented for a stylistic and structural continuity up to the Mies van der Rohe buildings of the 1960s. It was H. Allen Brooks who sorted out the problem of terminology and suggested that residential works by those young people and their followers might be referred to as the Prairie School and Condit's distortion be allowed to remain for the commercial or high-rise buildings.

It was Griffin who introduced the Prairie School of Architecture to Australia when he began practice in Sydney and Melbourne in 1914. Our studies indicate that no work emulative of the School was executed prior to his arrival. Also, there was very little discussion about the School in local journals. There was the odd article about the work of Louis Sullivan and some of his essays were reprinted in digested form. Australia's interest in the architectural goings-on in Chicago was more of curiosity, that is until Griffin was announced as winner. Articles not only about him but about his school colleagues began to appear almost immediately, particularly in the Sydney based *Building* magazine, a major and important publication in the field of architecture and building from its first issue in 1908 until the late 1930s. The first illustration of Wright's architecture appeared without any form of identification on the cover of the October 1913 issue of the Melbourne slick *Home & Garden Beautiful*. It was a view over the garden of the Mary Adams house in Highland Park, Illinois, of 1905.

For a school to exist in a traditional and practical sense, it is necessary to show that assistants, students and followers used idioms of a definable group of people (as in the case of Chicago, although no attempt has been made as yet to again re-define it as the Wright School) or of the master (as in the case of Australia and Griffin). It must be definable to an obvious and measurable extent and over a reasonable period to indicate continuity in time as well as a style.

In July 1909, the year of his graduation from Cornell University, Roy A. Lippincott entered the office of Hermann V. von Holst.[74] It was von Holst who was successor to Frank Lloyd Wright's practice when Wright, with Mrs Cheney, retired in October 1909 from the rigours of professional life in Chicago to quiet pastures in Europe. Marion Lucy Mahony, who later married Griffin, was hired from Wright's office by von Holst to provide the necessary continuity to carry forward the Wright projects left to von Holst's care. In the same year von Holst moved into Steinway Hall where so many of the Prairie School architects' offices were located.[75] As was the custom, many of the draftsmen worked in the various architects' offices. As Lippincott remembers, 'there was a great good feeling and helpfulness among them, and anyone working there might be found in almost any of the offices when that office had any special pressure of work',[76] so at opportune times he was to work in Griffin's office. In retrospect he said, 'When the news arrived that the competition had been won I had already transferred entirely to his [Griffin's] office as head draftsman.'[77]

Griffin returned to Chicago after his official visit to Australia in 1913 when he made arrangements for architect Barry Byrne to become a partner and also supervise Griffin's commissions in the United States. Both had worked for Wright at the Oak Park Studio and afterwards Byrne had worked with Griffin briefly in 1908.[78] Griffin then induced Lippincott and George Elgh to return with him to Australia. Lippincott was a direct descendant and personal representative of the Prairie School (**53**), but as will become evident, he was more closely associated with Griffin's ideas and architectural manners.[79] In the mid-'twenties he introduced the Prairie School to New Zealand.

In the Sydney and later the Melbourne offices Lippincott was concerned primarily with Griffin's private practice for about seven years. In December 1920 Griffin was relieved of his position of superintending the building of Canberra—with the title Federal Capital Director of Design and Construction. Immediately before and after this calamitous event, there were few jobs coming into the private office. Lippincott and fellow draftsman Edward Billson joined together to enter architectural competitions. Their

53 Brick House, *project*. R. A. Lippincott, architect. 1912.

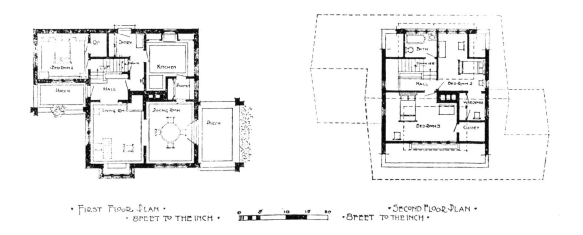

· FIRST FLOOR PLAN ·
· 8 FEET TO THE INCH ·

· SECOND FLOOR PLAN ·
· 8 FEET TO THE INCH ·

entry in 1922 for the Chicago Tribune building (**54**) received honourable mention,[80] while Griffin's was just another entry in that important competition.[81] Their design was reminiscent of Griffin's, especially at the base of the tower, but theirs must be considered the better of the two designs. In 1923 they entered a competition for the Victorian (State) War Memorial for Melbourne. They were placed fourth with a typical memorial design of the period, rather Roman, similar to the winner, and a 'beautiful drawing'.[82] With the encouragement of Griffin the team entered

54 Chicago Tribune, *project.*
R. A. Lippincott and E. F.
Billson, architects. 1922.
(Courtesy the *Chicago Tribune*)

their first competition for the Arts Building at the University of Auckland. The competition was announced as early as May 1920[83] and was to be in two stages. The first stage was due in Auckland in August 1920. Forty-four submissions were received and six were selected for the final stage that was to be submitted early in 1921.[84] The jury was composed of two New Zealanders and Professor Leslie Wilkinson from the School of Architecture at Sydney University. The announcement of the winning design of 'R. A. Liffincott [*sic*] and E. F. Billson' was published in July 1921.[85]

After considerable delay construction[86] commenced in about May 1922[87] and the building, with a slightly revised design, was completed in 1925 (**55** and **56**).[88] In 1922 the team also entered the Auckland War Memorial and Museum Competition[89] but were not placed. With the Auckland victory and ultimately the commission, both Billson and Lippincott left Griffin's office and formed a formal partnership. Billson stayed in his familiar Melbourne and Lippincott, who had already journeyed to Auckland in December 1921, remained.

From the evidence, it is safe to say that Lippincott relied heavily on Griffin's advice in architectural matters before he settled in Auckland. Where he was more or less independent (at least of Griffin) his designs were a rather unusual pastiche of Prairie School sources.[90] In Australia he built his own house in 1917–18. Griffin probably played a sizeable role in its design and attribution should include him as co-designer. Some details, such as the use and manner of brick or the vertical bands of stucco might suggest some independence,[91] but the plan, basic form and general detailing, particularly on the interior, are very much like Griffin's houses of and related to the Beverly (Chicago) group, especially the Dr Karl Stecher house of 1910.[92] With maturity Lippincott's designs improved and his association with Billson was influential on that maturation process.

In about 1923 a Lippincott house design was published in the booklet *Small Hy-Tex Homes*. While little else is known of the project it does reveal a much firmer understanding of ornament (if Wrightian), proportion and planning than in his previous independent work. His finest architecture and greatest volume, quite naturally, were executed in New Zealand over the next seventeen years.[93] In 1939 he returned to the United States. Thus, all the Americans who had emigrated with Griffin to Australia eventually returned, as did Mrs Griffin in 1938.

When Edward Fielder Billson decided to enrol for the architecture course at the University of Melbourne in 1913, the ad-

55 Arts Building, University of Auckland. R. A. Lippincott and E. F. Billson, architects. 1921–5. (Courtesy V. Terrini)

ministration had to make hasty and rather make-shift plans. At first they were reluctant to accommodate Billson. The course or programme had been in the University's Calendar for years but no one had previously applied for admission. With some persuasion[94] his course was begun under the faculty of engineering. In late 1916 he completed the course and received the University's first Diploma of Architecture, and immediately began in Griffin's office.[95] He was therefore Griffin's first Australian assistant. Billson states that his reason for starting his career with Griffin was the high esteem he had for the architect, despite the attempts of the profession—and at times the public—to hold Griffin in ridicule.[96] Upon reflection Billson offered the following comment:

I heard that he [Griffin] was commencing practice in Melbourne, but being of a reticent disposition, I could not see myself approaching him without a formal introduction. This I sought from a prominent architect of the time whom I knew. I shall always remember the appalling appraisal he gave me of Griffin. He refused to introduce me, and went so far as to say that if I went into that office, it would be the finish of me as an architect. . . . There was nothing else for it but to knuckle up courage and call upon the master myself. My shyness was soon to be dispelled, for Griffin was a very likeable and approachable man, full of warmth and kindness, but determinedly dedicated to his philosophy of architecture. In matters of design he was not prepared to compromise. He was a positive thinker, who never gave in to the negative—problems were there to be solved, he would say, and this of course is the essence of the creative mind.[97]

Griffin was aware that staff would want to carry out work for relatives, friends or admirers while in his employ. Moonlighting,

56 Arts Building, University of Auckland. R. A. Lippincott and E. F. Billson, architects. 1921–5. (Courtesy V. Terrini)

as it was called, was (and is) a general problem in the profession. It caused friction between Griffin and Wright, and for Wright a threat to friendship and a final severing of employment from Dankmar Adler and Louis Sullivan. So, to clarify the issues involved, Griffin had his senior employees sign a 'Reciprocal Co-operative Association' agreement which essentially allowed employees and Griffin to share profits.[98] No money changed

57 Alfred Arthur Billson House, Toorak, Victoria. E. F. Billson, architect. 1918. (Courtesy the architect)

hands but Lippincott (from 1915) and Billson (from 1920) could openly work on their own commissions. In fact they were often discussed in Griffin's office.

Billson's first independent commission was in 1918 for his parents. The Alfred Arthur Billson house has a rather typical plan: circulation space led to surrounding rooms and similarly so on the offset, asymmetrically disposed second level. The steep roofs are surmounted by heavily articulated stucco walls reflecting interior storage or fenestration and a series of Griffinesque windows and detail. Although heavy in appearance, accentuated by a very deep fascia and broad soffits, the interiors are handsomely lit through large areas of glass. The overall impression is of a fine piece of architecture by the young Billson (57). Another of his first jobs was probably begun in 1918 for it was under construction in March 1919.[99] The Margaret Armstrong house at Caulfield had many features of the contemporary Billson house: heaviness, materials, formality and detail, but there was a single gable roof. It too displayed precociousness.

Two more of Billson's buildings of a slightly later period should be discussed. They were begun shortly after he left Griffin's office and while he was still a partner with Lippincott. The Mr and Mrs George Silcock residence of Hawthorn, Victoria, revealed some of the more accepted characteristics of the Prairie School (58). There was a noticeable horizontality gained by an expression of the joint between the floor and foundation and, immediately above, a continuous line of the window sill broken only intermittently by large vertical elements in bold relief which expressed internal closets or the dining room sideboard. Windows set as distinct panels and a heavy fascia were reminiscent of the School.

Opposite:
58 George Silcock House, Hawthorn, Victoria. E. F. Billson, architect. c. 1926.

PERSPECTIVE

THE LIVING ROOM
FIREPLACE

PLAN

LEADED GLASS DOOR
ENTRANCE HALL

59 Woodlands (Mordialloc) Golf Club House, Victoria. E. F. Billson and R. A. Lippincott, architects. 1925–9.

60 Woodlands Golf Club House, Victoria. E. F. Billson, architect. 1925–9. (Courtesy the architect)

Also the repetition of the eave line just below the louvered attic vent, was inspired by earlier Griffin motifs such as the Niles Club of 1909. The relatively open plan of 1924 placed the little-used bedrooms near the street, while the entertaining areas, approached from the *porte-cochère*, were located in the central part of the site. The interiors included chandeliers ('semi-indirect electric light shades'), leaded stained glass doors and windows introduced with 'spots of opalescent glass of a delicate yellow-green tone',[100] and fireplace massing and style all similar in form and detail to Griffin. The presentation drawing was executed approximately two years after the house was constructed in 1924 and it was an entry in the 1928 Melbourne Exhibition of Domestic Architecture[101] under the names of Billson and Cheetham, Architects.[102]

A building committee of the Mordialloc Golf Club selected a design proposal for their club house which was submitted by Lippincott and Billson in 1925.[103] Nothing was done in putting the plans in the hands of a builder until a fire in April 1927 completely destroyed the then existing club house. After some deliberation the Billson design was again selected. By this time Lippincott was no longer a partner, for the partnership's primary purpose was to see the Auckland Arts Building to completion. By early 1929 the building, then called the Woodlands Club House, was completed to a slightly altered and enlarged plan and a more pleasing elevational treatment than the 1925 version. The plan had nothing in particular to commend it within the terms of the Prairie School or Griffin's tutelage but the elevations had a necessarily substantial

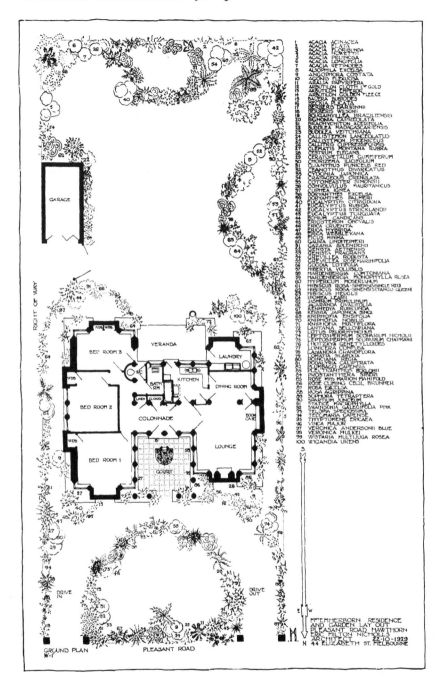

61 A. M. Herborn House, Hawthorn, Victoria. E. M. Nicholls, architect. 1928–31.

relationship to the earth, a secure horizontality and subtle undulation of the exterior wall to recall its antecedents regardless of the suggestion of the Australian Prime Minister in his speech at the official opening when he said: 'This is my ideal of what a club house should be, a true Australian bungalow'.[104] The interiors

showed a strength of design intention in a positive delineation of plaster panel and wood line similar to the School (**59** and **60**).

When free of Griffin's office Billson's next competition entry for a high-rise office building proved to be more competent in its own right. His design for the B. M. A. Building of 1927–8,[105] to have been in Sydney, was obviously of the typical American genre of the period—large, massive, suggestions of Romanesque, and the vertical Gothic begun by Cass Gilbert's Woolworth Building, New York City, in 1911–13 and associated with so many of the tall buildings in the 1920s and early 1930s.

Eric M. Nicholls' architecture was quite different from Billson's and was similar to Griffin's in one aspect—chunky, squat proportions—but very different in plan and elevation. The derivation was unmistakable but the exploitation of the Griffin influence takes on a new mode. The characteristics were amply displayed in three of the following selections.

The Joseph Lyddy Polish Manufacturing Company was designed in 1922 and construction was completed at the Fitzroy Street, Fitzroy, location in 1923.[106] A low, nearly diminutive-appearing building contained some details and a general effect similar to Griffin, all executed in brick. A delightful exposition. The plan of the Wallace Smith house in Toorak, Victoria, of 1928[107] was pinched: the small circulation spaces were riddled with protruding corners and a large selection of doors, while the rooms were for the most part a series of cubicles.[108] These plan characteristics were also true to a lesser extent in the Hawthorn, Victoria home for A. M. Herborn (**61**). The plan was derived from the modular ideas developed by Griffin about nine years before, but it lacked

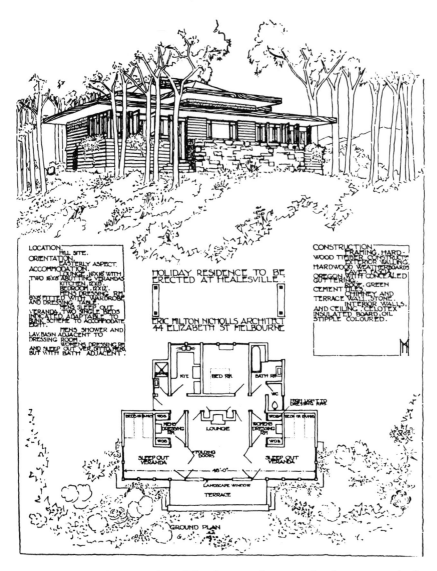

63 Holiday bungalow, *project*, Healesville, Victoria. E. M. Nicholls, architect. 1929.

a fully rational open plan. The large columns, the heavy vertical masses and the eyelids as lower fascias similar to aedicular functions over the windows provided a sense of intimacy (**62**).

The landscaping or 'garden lay-out' for both the Smith and Herborn houses was built to Nicholls' design but one assumes a free use of Griffin's wide horticultural knowledge. In their open, free-form spatial arrangement bordered by low, blooming shrubs and annuals which were backed by larger plant forms, they were not only similar to the landscape planning of Griffin, but a distinct departure from the formal, axially arranged gardens prevalent during the 'twenties and 'thirties.

Of Griffin's followers Nicholls was most dependent upon

64 Mrs G. F. Ballantyne House, Malvern, Victoria. J. F. W. Ballantyne, architect. 1924. (Courtesy the architect)

Griffin modes and mannerisms even to the drawing board tightness of Griffin in plan and elevation. Also, Nicholls' monogram on renderings was similar to Mrs Griffin's. The Herborn house was derived from a number of sources not excluding the Melbourne 'Home of Five Rooms' Griffin projected in 1920[109] with a similar entry court, or the elevational characteristics of the Mary Williams house in Toorak, Victoria, of 1923, which was designed in Griffin's Melbourne office where Nicholls was employed, beginning in about 1921.

The plan of a holiday bungalow project[110] for Healesville, a suburb northeast of Melbourne, was neat in its symmetry and the elevational treatment responded admirably well to the internal spaces (**63**). Also important, and perhaps too obvious, it was closely associated in proportion and material usage to the wood houses of Frank Lloyd Wright of preceding years (especially the C. Ross house, Delavan, Wisconsin of 1902 or the cottage for W. S. Gerts, Whitehall, Mich., of the same year[111]). This is emphasized by the rendering which duplicates Wright's rendering of 'Sommerhaus in Fresno', actually in Monticeto, near Santa Barbara, California, which appeared in the Wasmuth volume of Wright's work, a copy of which was owned by Griffin.[112]

From a family construction business, J. F. W. or Frederick Ballantyne entered the University of Melbourne in 1918, but, as he notes:

It was still necessary to be articled to a practising architect. While this was being considered, I met E. F. Billson, who was working in . . .

Griffin's office, and he suggested that it might be possible for me to be articled to Griffin. And so I became a pupil of W. B. Griffin, much to the amazement and derision of my fellow students at the University. . . .

However, this did not worry me and I have never regretted my association with such a great man. He was a man of culture and had great charm and a handsome head of light brown hair, worn long. Whatever faults he may have had, he was a stimulating teacher for a young man.[113]

Ballantyne received his diploma and completed his articles in 1921, or at twenty-one years of age. He was, therefore, Griffin's first Australian student or apprentice. In 1923 he travelled to America and journeyed by 'an air-cooled Franklin car'[114] across the barren deserts from southern California, up the Sante Fe trail to St Louis. In Chicago he met and talked with Louis Sullivan and Dwight Perkins through introductions by Griffin, and, of course, Marion, Perkins' niece. Also, he visited many Wright buildings. From 1924 to 1928 he carried on his father's building business when he again travelled, this time to Europe. In January 1929 he decided to concentrate on architecture and on residential design.

Ballantyne took the essential ideas of Griffin, and from his own education and experience and with few exceptions, applied them in his own discreet, inimitable fashion. The house for J. A. Gillespie of 1926 for a sloping site in South Yarra, Victoria,[115] was akin to the small, two-storey prairie houses of years before and to Griffin's small house designs such as the Gunn or Rule house of 1909 and 1912 in Tracy, Chicago and Mason City respectively. Many of the houses designed by Ballantyne, including this one, were built by himself as general contractor, carrying on with his brother Keith the family contracting business.[116]

A predecessor to the Gillespie house was a home in Malvern, Victoria, for his mother, Mrs G. F. Ballantyne, designed in 1924.[117] Again, there was the wide soffit and eave and gently sloping roof. As the Gillespie house set straight, vertical into the earth, this house was horizontally intimate with the ground. A visual base was below the cement rendered string course at sill line. Between this continuous course and the eave, windows were placed as a series of panels. The boldly exposed brickwork had a massive character proportionally balanced by the porch openings and the broad eave (**64**).

Shortly after leaving Griffin's office (his tenure was from 1919 to 1923) he completed the small house 'Stokesay' of Knitlock for Arthur P. Onians in Frankston, Victoria.[118] It was in many ways reminiscent of the Jefferies house, Surrey Hills, Victoria, by Griffin

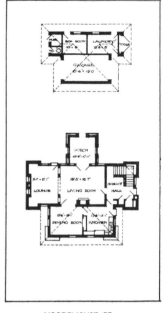

MOOREHOUSE ST

65 Mrs Craig Dixon House, Malvern, Victoria. J.F.W. Ballantyne, architect. 1924. (Courtesy the architect)

66 Mrs Craig Dixon House, Malvern, Victoria. J. F. W. Ballantyne, architect. 1924. (Photograph D. L. Johnson)

(which followed in 1924) yet a more formal and axial plan on a 3′–6″ grid. The details were as faithful and complete to the Knitlock system as the Jefferies or the contemporary Salter house also by Griffin.

Perhaps the finest house of the 1920s, and this includes Griffin's own work, was the Craig Dixon house of 1924, located at Moor-

house Street, Malvern (**65** and **66**). A masterful site plan placed entertainment to the rear and a single lane drive circumnavigated the site through the garage at the rear. The garage was free standing at the rear of the building lot but linked in form, material and detail to the house. The rather symmetrical plan was boldly revealed in elevation by formal composition to the street. In proportion and employment of material, as well as planning, it was a truly excellent piece of residential design.

The house for Dr Carl Stephens of Healesville, Victoria (**67**), was derivative of or perhaps inspired by Wright, the teachings of Griffin and more obviously traditional Japanese architecture which was of growing interest during the 1920s. The massing form and proportion of the roof were intrinsic to the 1927 design. The horizontally lapped wood siding (unusual outside Queensland after 1910) in a continuous band below the sill, formed a strong visual liaison with the ground and the extended soffit. The stark simplicity and manner of panelling between these broad horizontal lines was honest to its design sources. Unfortunately, nowhere was this expressed on the interior, in fact the interior had a continuous plastered wall surface with stained wood trim and a wood valance at door head height—typical of builders' houses in the 1920s. Here was its weakness in an historical and design context.[119]

The attraction of European architectural strains was magnetic, as well as professionally fashionable. Eventually these architects

67 Dr Carl Stephens House, Healesville, Victoria. J. F. W. Ballantyne, architect. 1926.

switched allegiance. For instance, change for Ballantyne was complete in 1934 when he, in partnership with his cousin Roy Wilson, placed second in the 'Perfect Home' competition of the Melbourne Centenary Homes Exhibition in 1934.[120]

We have looked at the work of some of those architects who began their professional life with Griffin as assistants or students. The work of followers (in a more traditional sense of the word) in Australia is not clearly defined as yet. A great deal more research needs to be completed. Some suggestions can be offered, however, where the influence is evident from association or by visual inspection. There is, for instance, the Hayward house in Knitlock at 6 Third Street, Blackrock, Victoria; the Kew Croquet Club, Victoria of 1934, a truly fine emulation in proportion and form; the Workshops, Moonee Ponds, Essendon, Victoria, near the incinerator; the Jenkins house, 139 Manning Road, East Malvern, Victoria, in Knitlock, probably speculatively built by the builder who helped Griffin develop the patented structural system; the E. Healing house at 34 Fellows Street, Kew, Victoria; the remodelling in 1927–9 of the N. E. Laurance row houses, 15–21 Rose Street, Toorak, Victoria (perhaps by Nicholls); the community plan for Station Estates, East Keilor, Victoria, in the late 1920s, perhaps stage three to Griffin's Milleara plan; and the White house at 5 Ophir Street, Moonee Ponds, Victoria (perhaps by Pynor or Lippincott).

The works just suggested are by anonymous followers, at least as of this writing, but architect G. J. Sutherland completed his house at 54 New Street, Brighton, Victoria, and other houses with School details. Ray C. Smith displayed his role in the School in some of his designs, particularly the F. J. Smith house at Thornleigh, Sydney. E. J. A. Weller suggests that his old Sydney employers, architects G. C. Thomas and F. G. Briggs, were strongly influenced by Griffin since Thomas, Briggs and Griffin were associated in a manner of assistance during the late teens and early 1920s.

A study of the work of only four of Griffin's followers has provided partial evidence that the lineage from Wright to Griffin to Australian architects in general can at least be argued with conviction. It should no longer be assumed that architecture's modern movement in Australia began, as so often suggested, in the early 1930s. It began when Walter Burley Griffin started his architectural practice at Melbourne in 1914.

NOTES TO CHAPTER THREE

1. Cf. Ulrich Conrads, *Programmes and Manifestoes. Twentieth-Century Architecture*, London 1970.
2. Cf. Raymond Williams, *Communications*, rev. edn, Middlesex 1968.
3. John Moore, 'The Recent Past and the Contemporary Scene', *The Architectural Review* (B), 104 (July 1948), pp. 14–18, touches on the problems of communication—and attitudes—in Australia.
4. As a unified process of architectural thought, the Chicago School was well established before its intentions and philosophy were verbalized, initially by Thomas E. Tallmadge in 'The "Chicago School"', *The Architectural Review* (US-Boston), 15 (April 1908) pp. 69 ff., reprinted in *Architectural Essays from the Chicago School*, Chicago 1967. Cf. H. Allen Brooks, '"Chicago School": Metamorphosis of a Term', *Journal of the Society of Architectural Historians* (US), 25 (May 1966), pp. 115–16.
5. Cf. Reyner Banham, *Theory and Design: the First Machine Age*, London 1960, pp. 127–37.
6. *Salon* (A), 2 (December 1913), p. 183.
7. *Real Property Annual*, 1910 to 1921, succeeded as *Australian Home Builder*, 1922 to 1925, succeeded as *Australian Home Beautiful*.
8. Now titled *Architecture Australia* (Journal of the Royal Australian Institute of Architects). Predecessors were *Art and Architecture* (1904 to June 1912), *Salon* (July 1912 to December 1916), *Architecture* (1917 to June 1955), and *Architecture in Australia* (July 1955 to December 1975), all published in Sydney.
9. 'The Design of Broadcasting Studios', *Architecture* (A), 20 (June 1932), p. 139.
10. 'ANZAC War Memorial, Sydney', *Architecture* (A), 18 (October 1930), p. 536.
11. 'Reports of Travelling Scholars', *Architecture* (A), 18 (October 1930), p. 529, see also Raymond McGrath, 'Quantity and Quality of Architectural Illumination', *Architecture* (A), 18 (April 1930), pp. 93–4.
12. 'Reports of Travelling Scholars', *Architecture* (A), 20 (July 1932), p. 154.
13. 'Sydney Ancher', *Decoration and Glass* (A), 15 (July-August 1949), p. 41.
14. 'Reports of Travelling Scholars', *Architecture* (A), 20 (July 1932), p. 154. Cf. Donald Leslie Johnson, 'Sources of Modernism in Australian Architecture', Art Association of Australia *Architectural Papers 1976* (Sydney 1978), pp. 103ff.
15. 'Reports', *Architecture* (A), 20 (July 1932), p. 155. See also his final report, Sydney Ancher, 'The Evolution of Modern Architecture' (extracts), *Architecture* (A), 28 (December 1939), pp. 244–9.
16. 'Travelling Scholar Returns. Sydney Ancher's Views on Architectural Education', *Architecture* (A), 24 (March 1936), p. 76, and see also Sydney Ancher, 'Whither Architecture', *Architecture* (A), 24 (June 1936), pp. 148–9.
17. 'Board of Architects' Travelling Scholarships', *Architecture* (A), 18 (January 1930), p. 314.
18. Ibid., and 'Reports of Travelling Scholars', *Architecture* (A), 18 (October 1930), pp. 529–30.
19. 'Board of Architects' Travelling Scholarships', *Architecture* (A), 18 (January 1930), p. 314.
20. 'Reports of Travelling Scholars', *Architecture* (A), 19 (October 1931), p. 218.
21. 'Reports', *Architecture* (A), 20 (July 1932), p. 161. See also David Saunders, 'So I Decided to go Overseas', *Architecture Australia* (A), 66 (February 1977), pp. 22–8.
22. Eric Garthside, 'The Lessons from Modern German Architecture', *Architecture* (A), 22 (July 1934), pp. 145–66. He remained an expatriate.

23. Cf. Dudley Ward, 'European Policies and Practices', *The Architectural Forum* (US), 70 (February 1934), pp. 141–51.

24. 'Australian Medallion and Scholarship in Architecture', *Architecture* (A), 18 (July 1930), p. 455. The impact of travellers on Australia in a general sense is more difficult to evaluate. Charles Higham and Michael Wilding have gathered together reflections and impressions by the literary fraternity in *Australians Abroad. An Anthology* (Melbourne 1967), but it is a peculiar mixture of non-fiction and journalism. A more definitive and properly edited study is yet to come.

25. 'Who's Who', *Decoration and Glass* (A), 3 (July 1937), p. 60.

26. 'Personalities', *Decoration and Glass* (A), 15 (March-April 1949), p. 36.

27. 'Who's Who', *Decoration and Glass* (A), 6 (June 1940), p. 51.

28. Norman H. Seabrook, 'Some Notes on a Life in Architecture', *Architect* (A), 66 (March-April 1968), p. 23. Alsop began The Atelier after 1918. The Diploma was begun in 1916 probably as a result of E. F. Billson.

29. Donald C. Ward, 'Portrait of Leighton F. Irwin', *Architecture* (A), 40 (October-December 1952), p. 123.

30. Ibid.

31. Ibid., p. 124.

32. 'An Air-port Control Station', *Journal of the Royal Victorian Institute of Architects* (A), 28 (September 1930), p. 64. The design has some features of streamlining that would have pleased Norman Bel Geddes. The extent of Bel Geddes' influence in Australia—or indeed North America—during these early years of the century's fourth decade is not at all clear. So much of what we associate with him is of the mid and late years of the decade, in particular his theatrical designs and the General Motors building and exhibit for the New York World's Fair of 1939–40. Perhaps a study of his influence might be encouraged by the republication by Dover in 1977 of Bel Geddes' book *Horizons*, first published in 1932.

33. 'A Golf Club-House', *Building* (A), 41 (August 1930), p. 89.

34. Leslie M. Perrott, 'American Influence on Australian Architecture', *The Architect and Engineer* (US), 103 (October 1930), pp. 133–4.

35. L. F. Irwin, 'The Trend of Design as Shown in Modern Architecture', *Journal of the Royal Victorian Institute of Architects* (A), 18 (July 1930), pp. 65–74, and *Building* (A), 41 (June 1930), pp. 83–6.

36. 'Traditional v. Modern Contemporary Architecture. A Discussion', *Architecture* (A), 19 (December 1930), pp. 565–9.

37. *Architecture* (A), 20 (May 1931), pp. 119–22.

38. 'A Tobacco Factory at Rotterdam', *Building* (A), 42 (March 1931), p. 85.

39. Leslie Wilkinson stated the prevalent view, 'The evidence of the past is a surer guide than the promise of the future', 'Traditional v. Modern', p. 568.

40. J. F. Hennessy, 'Australia: Some Modern Aspects with Special Reference to Architectural and Engineering Problems', *Journal of the Royal Society of Arts* (B), 80 (June 1932), p. 726.

41. Robin Boyd, *Australia's Home*, Melbourne 1952, pp. 297–8.

42. 'Yule House . . .', *Journal of the Royal Victorian Institute of Architects* (A), 30 (September 1932), p. 83.

43. 'The Manchester Unity Building, Melbourne', *Building* (A), 43 (September 1932), pp. 55ff., a very complete article including construction, furniture, and other aspects.

44. The project was presented in 1932, see 'Shell Building, Melbourne', *Building* (A), 43 (July 1932), p. 65. Comparison with English and German Shell offices was made in 'Office Architecture Abroad', *Journal of the Royal Victorian Institute of Architects* (A), 31 (July 1933), pp. 52–3.

45. Basil Ward, 'Houses of the "Thirties"', *Concrete Quarterly* (B), 85 (April-June 1970), pp. 11–15. Ward attributes Connell as designer and the date as 1929 (p. 13), and interview 1974.

46. W. E. J. Harrison, 'Burnham Beeches . . . ', *Australian Home Beautiful* (A), 12 (March 1934), pp. 6–14, 60, and 'Xanadu in Jazz', *Architect* (A), 3 (July-August 1969) p. 15.

47. [Geoffrey H. Mewton], ['Impressions of Modern Building Abroad'], *Australian Home Beautiful* (A), 10 (December 1932), pp. 46–7, and Geoffrey H. Mewton, 'Modern and Medieval', ibid., 11 (January 1933), p. 14. I am indebted to Ms Julie Ewington for some of the information about Mewton and Grounds.

48. At the suggestion of the editors—interview, Geoffrey Mewton, February 1969: see 'A Seaside Cottage Built of Prefabricated Units', *Australian Home Beautiful* (A), 12 (June 1934), pp. 32–3.

49. Elizabeth Auld, 'Ship Aground at Ranelagh', *Australian Home Beautiful* (A), 14 (May 1936), pp. 8–11, and 'Modernism in Victorian Home', *Constructional Review* (A), 11 (September 1938), pp. 22–3.

50. 'La Mabelleion: Modern by Circumstance', *Australian Home Beautiful* (A), 12 (January 1934), pp. 24–5.

51. European modernism was introduced, so to speak, to Britain about five years earlier. The book, *Recent English Domestic Architecture* edited by H. de C. Hastings in 1929, was a reprint of the December 1928 issue of *The Architectural Review* which contained a review of current architecture. Among those illustrated was 'A bungalow at Hong Kong' by M. H. Baillie Scott, Jr, a Southwest American Spanish pueblo design, and a very large number of designs of the European white box school by architects Behrens and Bassett-Lowke, as well as Tait and Burnet & Partners. Their debt to Le Corbusier is evident.

52. 'Master Builders Offer Services to Government', *Constructional Review* (A), 7 (December 1934), p. 3.

53. The Homes Exhibition was fully covered in the December 1934 *Australian Home Beautiful*. The jurors for this important competition were John F. Freeman, Marcus W. Martin and John F. D. Scarborough.

54. 'A Contract . . .', *Journal of the Royal Victorian Institute of Architects* (A), 32 (March 1934) p. 23. This building is selected only because it fits into established academic traditions as they evolved in Europe. Cf. 'The Mac-Robertson Girls' High School', *Art in Australia*, 61 (November 1935), pp. 91–4. Burnham Beeches has many modern attributes, but is also full with sentimental traditional elements. Perhaps this author is hasty in placing this house in an aberrant category.

55. Norman H. Seabrook, '1935', *Australian Home Beautiful* (A), 13 (June 1935), p. 23.

56. Vol. 12 (March 1934), p. 26.

57. Nora Cooper, 'A Very Much Discussed House', *Australian Home Beautiful* (A), 13 (May 1935), pp. 5–11. The plan is a typical compartmentalized arrangement. It is the façade or elevational treatment which attracts our attention.

58. H. O. Woodhouse, 55 (May 1934), pp. 64–74. A sister publication, the society slick, *The Home*, showed a few modern interiors in 1929–30 and as early as October 1928 ('Are Our Architects Obsolete', 9, pp. 40–3) extracted snippets of Le Corbusier's *Towards a New Architecture*.

59. *The International Style*, New York 1966 edn.

60. See also, J. J. P. Oud, 'Towards a New Architecture', *The Studio* (B), 105 (April 1933), pp. 249–56.

61. Donald Leslie Johnson, 'The Griffin REICo Incinerators', *AAQ Architectural Association Quarterly* (B), 3 (October-December 1971), p. 48. This is the basic reference for discussion of the incinerators, as does Johnson, *The Architecture of Walter Burley Griffin*, Melbourne 1977.

62. James Birrell, *Walter Burley Griffin*, Brisbane 1964, p. 174.

63. Johnson, 'The Griffin REICo Incinerators', *passim*.

64. Donald Leslie Johnson, 'Adelaide's Incinerators', *Architecture in Australia* (A), 58 (August 1969), pp. 665–71.
65. Correspondence, 1977. She published *Dance Ritual of Manipur, India . . . an Introduction to 'Meitei Jagoi'*, Hong Kong 1960.
66. Interview, February 1969.
67. Research has shown another spelling, George Elgh, but it has failed (in both America and Australia) to identify the architect or draftsman.
68. The partnership lasted about one year. Interview, February 1969, correspondence, 1977.
69. 'Who's Who', *Decoration and Glass* (A), 5 (February 1938), pp. 53–4.
70. H. Pynor, 'An Australian Foreign Specialist in Russia', *Architecture* (A), 25 (May 1937), p. 96.
71. [Marion Mahony Griffin], 'Magic of America', typescript, New York Historical Society, *c.* 1949, sec. I, p. 35, recalls the date as 1936.
72. 'E. D. Wilson', *Decoration and Glass* (A), 5 (February 1938), p. 39.
73. 'L. F. Herbert', ibid., p. 52.
74. David T. van Zanten, 'The Early Work of Marion Mahony Griffin', *Prairie School Review* (US), 3 (2nd q., 1966) p. 13.
75. Cf. H. Allen Brooks, 'Steinway Hall, Architects and Dreams', *Journal of the Society of Architectural Historians* (US), 12 (October 1963), pp. 171–5.
76. Letter from Lippincott to Mr V. L. Terreni dated August 1956; a copy was kindly given to this author.
77. As quoted in Birrell, *Walter Burley Griffin*, p. 19. See also Mark L. Peisch, *The Chicago School of Architecture*, New York 1965, p. 37.
78. Sally Anderson Chappell, 'Barry Byrne, Architect: His Formative Years', *Prairie School Review* (US), 3 (Fall 1966), p. 8.
79. As early as 1913 Lippincott reviewed the 26th Annual Exhibition of 'The Chicago Architectural Club', (*Architectural Record* (US), 33 (June 1913), pp. 567–73) and presented the array of the exhibition and gratuitiously inserted a Griffin design not discussed in the text.
80. *The International Competition for a New Administration Building for the Chicago Tribune MCMXXII*, Chicago 1922, Plate 257.
81. Ibid., Plate 171.
82. Blamire Young, 'The Designs for the Victorian War Memorial', *Art in Australia* (A), 7 (March 1924), no pagination. Mrs Griffin assisted with presentations (interview 1969).
83. 'Architectural Competition', *N.Z. Building Progress*, 15 (May 1920), p. 787.
84. 'The Auckland Competition', *N.Z. Building Progress*, 16 (October 1920), p. 38.
85. 'New Arts Building for the Auckland University College', *N.Z. Building Progress*, 16 (July 1921), p. 250.
86. 'Auckland Arts Building Competition', *N. Z. Building Progress*, 17 (October 1921), p. 55.
87. 'Auckland's University', *N. Z. Building Progress*, 17 (March 1922), p. 156.
88. 'The New Arts Building, Auckland University (N.Z.)', *Building* (A), 38 (February 1926), pp. 46, 48.
89. 'Auckland War Memorial and Museum Competition', *N.Z. Building Progress*, 18 (October 1922), p. 39. There were over sixty entries from the Commonwealth.
90. See, e. g., Northrup house, 420 Miramonte Drive, Santa Barbara, now altered, or his design in Brick Building Association, *One Hundred Bungalows*, Boston *c.* 1912, p. 34.
91. Cf. Johnson, *Walter Burley Griffin*, p. 63.
92. Ibid., p. 48.
93. Information supplied by Mr V. L. Terreni and first-year students (1968), School of Architecture, Auckland.

94. Interview, February 1969. See Robin Boyd, *Victorian Modern*, [Melbourne] 1947, p. 12.

95. Interview, February 1969, and Boyd, *Victorian Modern*, p. 30; also Robin Boyd, 'Griffin in Melbourne', *Architectural Review* (B), 137 (February 1965), pp. 133−6.

96. A great deal of the initial biographical and historical essays concerning Griffin have been based on interviews with Billson.

97. Edward F. Billson, 'A Life in Architecture', *Architect* (A), 2 (September 1968), p. 22.

98. Correspondence, 1977.

99. Information with assistance of John Kenny, Melbourne.

100. Edward Fielder Billson, 'Seeking the New-Note in Architecture', *Australian Home Beautiful* (A), 4 (October 1926), p. 32.

101. W. A. M. Blacket, 'The 1928 Exhibition of Domestic Architecture, Its Organization and Aims: a Forward', *Australian Home Beautiful* (A), 6 (May 1928), p. 13.

102. Ibid., p. 25.

103. 'Picturesque Golf House', *Australian Home Builder* (A), 15 (May 1925), pp. 64−5.

104. As quoted in K. McEwan, 'The Golf Clubs of Victoria. III—Woodlands and Croydon Club Houses: A Study in Contrasts', *Australian Home Beautiful* (A), 7 (March 1929), p. 25.

105. 'Design by E. F. Billson . . .', *Building* (A), 40 (May 1928), pp. 56f and 56g. Two other houses might be mentioned. The M. B. Cragg house at 18 Findon Street (Crescent), Kew, of 1922 was a fine example of wood and stucco design while the Cox house at 236 Gotham Road, Kew, of 1925−6, was a tall squarish house in deep textured stucco similar to the Billson house and by Lippincott and Billson.

106. Other Nicholls houses of interest of which little is as yet known but which should be mentioned are the Baumant house at 33 Uvedale Road, Kew, which is a rectilinear composition, with flat roofs and a plan similar to Billson's 1918 house, including the offset second floor. There was Nicholls' own house of 1924 and a remodelling for Mrs Mary Williams, who used three designs by Griffin (her own house, and the two Langi Flats), a house called 'Stanton' on Kooyong Road of 1923.

The author would like to thank John Kenny for his interest and continuing and valuable assistance.

107. Frank L. Walker, 'Planting a House and Garden', *Australian Home Beautiful* (A), 6 (December 1928), pp. 12−18.

108. 'A Suggestion for a Harbor Front Residence', *Australian Home Beautiful* (A), 8 (February 1930), p. 19.

109. W. B. Griffin, 'The Problem of the Basic House. Home of Five Rooms', *Real Property Annual* (A), 10 (July 1920), pp. 30−1.

110. *Australian Home Beautiful* (A), 7 (December 1929), p. 27. Nicholls' business address was the same as Griffin's, i.e. Leonard House, Melbourne. He moved to Castlecrag (the Moon house) in the early 1930s. After Griffin's death in 1937 he continued to design houses for the Castlecrag community and other buildings in the Willoughby area. Cf. 'The Albert Chowne Memorial Hall', *Building and Engineering* (A), 57 (October 1947), p. 32. His Castlecrag houses are often confused with Griffin designs.

111. Grant Manson, *Frank Lloyd Wright to 1910*, New York 1958, p. 129, and Reyner Banham, *The Architecture of the Well-Tempered Environment*, London 1969, pp. 110−11.

112. See Plate XLIII. The house was called 'Stewart House' by Wright but is now owned by the Blickenstaff family.

113. Frederick W. Ballantyne, 'Carrying on a Family Tradition', *Architect* (A), 2 (July 1968), p. 27.

114. Ibid.
115. 'M.R.', 'A Small House Set on a Hillside', *Australian Home Beautiful* (A), 5 (September 1927), p. 16. See also Freeland, *Architecture in Australia*, pp. 225–33.
116. Interview, February 1969. Ballantyne graduated from the University of Melbourne in 1918.
117. R. Chandler, 'An Architect and His Hobbies', *Australian Home Beautiful* (A), 6 (March 1926), p. 28.
118. 'A Pretty Australian Home', *Australian Home Beautiful* (A), 12 (December 1925), p. 18. The architect should be listed as J. F. W. Ballantyne (not C. F. Ballantyne) and completed in 1922. Griffin's name is erroneously associated with the building.
119. M. Ramsey, 'A Country Home with the City's Comforts', *Australian Home Beautiful* (A), 6 (March 1928), pp. 15–18. Lapped siding was introduced into other Australian states in the nineteenth century. The house replaced a building built by Ballantyne's father for Dr Stephen's father, which burned to the ground.
120. 'The Centenary Homes Exhibition', *Australian Home Beautiful* (A), 12 (December 1934), pp. 11 ff. See also [J. F. W. Ballantyne and Roy Wilson], 'An Attractive Layout', *Australian Home Beautiful* (A), 13 (January 1935), pp. 17, 58.

4

1934-47: Reaction and Resolve

It should not be assumed that there was a sudden burst of creative activity solely in modern idioms. The period was also notable for its uncertainty. Many of the houses of 1932 to 1934 which were flat-roofed were altered to receive a gable or hipped roofs. The box form was too harsh, apparently, and many people needed a more traditional referent for home. Few professionals practised the new architecture and the variety of architectural forms, ideas, styles was enormous—from neo-Classicism through Edwardian, from Dutch brick through the bungalow. In many ways the frustration of the architect was exemplified by the work of Arthur G. Stephenson. Completing his articles in both Melbourne and Sydney, he finished off his training with studies at the Architectural Association in London after the War. He returned to Melbourne in 1921 to form a partnership with P. H. Meldrum.[1] The firm of Stephenson and Meldrum and later, in the 1930s as Stephenson and Turner, was a profoundly influential office.[2] Stephenson made extensive trips overseas. He encouraged and financed members of his firm to do likewise and he promoted an excellent training for young aspiring architects. His hospitals gained him a national and international reputation and it was after his trip to Russia and America in 1932 that his designs changed from traditional to something close to modern in style. A very rational plan and attention to function were the key to the hospitals' success, as well as the clarity of their expression. The first in modern dress was Mercy Hospital in East Melbourne, notable more for the open balcony's long, deeply shadowed line and a full expression of verticals (**68**). Others followed such as the Freemasons' Hospital, also in Melbourne, a more neatly arranged plan and maturely resolved façade.

Two buildings by Stephenson and Turner exemplify the frustration of pre-war trends. The first, designed in 1938 and

'The average Australian'—that composite picture of seven and a quarter million people living here in this part of the globe and far removed from all its most experienced and dynamic centres, has been, and still is, shut off from events. . . . He has fought through two major World Wars, has won his spurs, and now stands on the threshold of maturity ready to find his full soul. How soon he will find it will depend on the depth and quality of his experience. Until he does do so he cannot go forward to express himself fully in art and architecture.

JOHN MOORE, 'The Recent Past and the Contemporary Scene', *The Architectural Review*, July 1948

68 Mercy Hospital, Melbourne, Victoria. Stephenson and Turner, architects. 1936. (Courtesy the architects)

completed in 1941, was the Australian Consolidated Industries[3] Building on William Street, Sydney (**69**). The other building was the new Collins Street branch of the English, Scottish and Australian (E.S. & A.) Bank, completed in 1942 for the Melbourne site.[4] It contained the resolutions in a more traditional manner. The façade was a tripartite scheme with base, shaft and termination (or capital) identified as a deeply recessed attic floor and over-hanging roof, rather than parapet. The two façades (the other being Elizabeth Street) were nearly identical. The A. C. I. was clean of line, with a rather jumbled ground floor façade, and a more modest interior than the E.S. & A. The structure was given clear exposure on the recessed attic and strikingly circular holes in the roof of the attic overhang. The E.S. & A. building's compositional treatment was found at the Bank of New South Wales in Adelaide by architects Claridge *et al.*[5] and also a more refined contemporary, the offices for the Orient Steam Navigation Company at Spring Street, Sydney, by the English architect Brian O'Rorke.[6]

If there was a kind of schizophrenia revealed in some of the firm's architecture, either in detail or in composition, this was not the case of the Darwin Hotel of 1939–41 (**70**). It was an excellent blend of traditional south seas openness, of nineteenth-century English Colonial Asian hotel, and of 1930s modern. The hotel commanded an excellent site near a peninsula. The clarity of structure in concrete, the consistency of motifs and general

69 Australian Consolidated Industries Ltd, Sydney. Stephenson and Turner, architects. 1939-41. (Courtesy the architects)

horizontality, surmounted by a bold hipped roof, presented a building unequalled in the northern town. It was certainly of far greater dignity and architectural merit than the city's post-war governmental buildings to follow.[7]

Dudley Ward in Sydney followed rather closely the forms of central European modern. Having studied housing and made extensive trips to Europe and America, it was only natural that a significant portion of his work would be housing. The block of flats called Ruskin of 1935 exemplified his work and one of his interests, a blending of Dutch brick work and what might be termed a very modified expressionism.[8] Most of the Melbourne architects had taken what must be termed a regressive step by

70 Darwin Hotel, Northern Territory. Stephenson and Turner, architects. 1939–41. (Photograph D. L. Johnson)

capping their designs with bulky hipped and gabled roofs. There were exceptions. The excellent George Stooke house in Brighton, Victoria by Mewton and Grounds (**71** and **72**) was particularly refreshing.[9] There were other indications of the continued acceptance of modernism. Seabrook and Fildes' Royal Exchange Building at Pitt Street in Sydney was the first of the high-rise buildings to present a face of simple glass and spandrel without resorting to ornamentation (**73**). The ground floor rose nearly three storeys, and was faced with glass set in a bold screen.[10] Architects Reid and Pearson completed McPherson's Ltd at the Collins Street site in Melbourne (**74**). Designed in 1934[11] the building was a very good example of modern at mid-decade with a bold terracotta pattern and characteristically different sets of glazing (and in 1974 the building was in mint condition). Emil Sodersteen's City Mutual Life Assurance Society building[12] was completed in 1936 and was one of the best examples of the architect's ability to blend traditional and modern in stripped classicism mode popular in 1930s American architecture.

More indicative of the persuasion of the central European forms was the terracing or stepping scheme of the Wyldefel Gardens home units at Potts Point, Sydney by the architect John Brogan in 1935–6.[13] The scheme was apparently based on the owner's familiarity with similar housing on a similar site in Oberammergau, Germany. The interpretation of Brogan was very good indeed. The white units terraced down the hillside as a series of two-

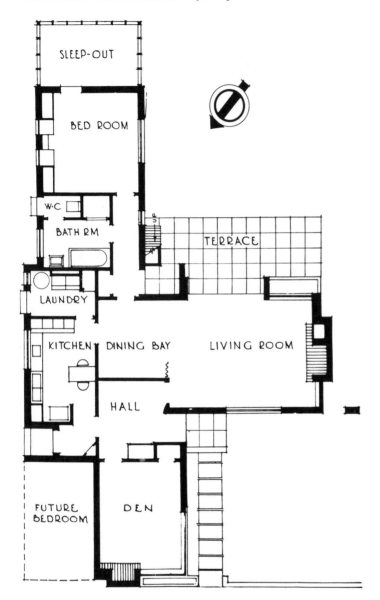

storey platforms. Each floor protruded out, not only for definition but for deep shadow. The roof of one unit formed the garden of the next higher unit and each garden was surrounded by a simple pipe rail. The white, round-corner cubes were complemented by rugged outcroppings of rock. A view to the water dominated the concept (**75**).

72 George Stooke House, Brighton, Victoria. G. Mewton and R. Grounds, architects. 1934. (Courtesy the architects)

With the work of Sodersteen, Brogan, Samuel Lipson and others to follow, the lead given by Melbourne in the first years of the decade gave way to the Sydneysiders. The growth of Sydney, with a flurry of building activity, as well as the influence of the travellers previously mentioned, helped to make Sydney a centre of modern architecture before the war. Two buildings which were completed almost simultaneously are worth comparison. The Hastings Deering building for Riley and Crown Streets, East Sydney, was by architect Samuel Lipson (**76**). It merely wrapped alternating bands of glass and concrete spandrels for seven storeys.[14] Columns were set back from the face of the building similar to its antecedent by Wells Coates, the Embassy Court building at Brighton, England of the previous year or 1935. Unfortunately the Sydney building was covered with steel trusses and a corrugated metal roof. The Melford Motors extension on Queensberry Street, Melbourne by architect Harry A. Norris in 1937, although occupying a corner site, was somewhat similar.

The columns were on the surface of the building and the facing was terracotta but only every third column was continuous to the ground.[15] The overall scheme and effect was not too different from his G. J. Cole's store in Adelaide of 1941.

In the 1930s Hardy Wilson commanded attention as an architect, author and artist. In a talk to a Melbourne audience on 'A New Era in Architecture' one might expect thoughts on the architecture of the 'thirties, but the man who did so much to instil a sense of pride in Australia's colonial architecture, and in many ways, to begin a revival in the 1920s, was more interested in Chinese architecture and the relationship of Australia and China. In the following year, 1937, he published his *Grecian and Chinese Architecture* of minimal text and fifty drawings in reproduction.

One event is necessary material for this discussion. In 1937 returned traveller Morton Herman became interested in the Sydney publication *Architecture* and in June he instituted a series of photo-essays comparing Australian architectural and urban conditions with those overseas.

The purpose of these comparisons is to show, side by side, various buildings in Sydney, and the solutions that have been found abroad for identical problems in design.[16]

Comparisons between the sophisticated results overseas and the local efforts must have been a shock to those who had not travelled. The visual comparison was 'so obvious it needs but little comment'.[17] For reasons unknown, the series ended rather abruptly in December.

Other literary efforts were rather typical with one exception. R. M. Edmunds produced a book on architecture that contained a general history of Western architecture as well as mention of some Australian buildings in the past (but not as a historical text). Also, there were fifteen pages about modern: something about functionalism (but of course, she argued, all great 'periods of the past' were 'extremely functional') and something naive about 'One thing is sure: that some fundamental change is occurring in architecture, since it is occurring in life itself'.[18]

Some of the buildings which were dependent on the precedent of the Yule House scheme began to dominate the later part of the 1930s. Notable among those buildings was the Mitchel House, Lonsdale Street, Melbourne by architect Harry A. Norris and completed in 1937. More obvious was the Askew House, Melbourne, by architects Twentyman and Askew, completed in 1938;[19] the Oddfellow Building (now Jensen House), dominating its neighbour Christ Church, was by the architect Marcus R. Barlow

73 Royal Exchange Assurance, Sydney. Norman H. Seabrook and Alan L. Fildes, architects. 1936–8.

74 McPherson's, Melbourne, Victoria. Reid and Pearson, and S. P. Calder, joint architects. 1934-5. (Courtesy McPherson's)

in about 1939; and one is tempted to include the stylized 44 Bridge Street building in Sydney by architects Brewster and Manderson, completed in 1938.

There were two other tall building styles which also dominated the designs of the 1930s. The second in order of appearance was the mixture of European low countries brick and German horizontality, which most contemporary observers credit Dudley Ward with introducing. It was taken up by such architects as A. M. Bolot in his Ashdown home units at Elizabeth Bay, Sydney of 1938.[20] Although the exterior walls have been cement rendered, the design source is quite clear. A number of houses would also follow this scheme. The third design style was related more to industrial, school and some commercial buildings. Brick was the principle material, divided by bands of glass which were set in bulky cubic forms. The compositions were to vary from a strict symmetrical organization to more informal. The more isolated buildings tended to follow symmetry, such as the Administrative Offices for Lysaght's at Port Kembla, New South Wales, by architect R. J. Magoffin of 1938-9, or NESCA House, Newcastle by Emil Sodersteen and Pitt and Merewether, completed in 1939 (**77**). The NESCA building exemplified the heavy massing and symmetrical frontal composition so typical of many of Sodersteen's buildings. The first unit of the Royal Melbourne Institute of Technology Electrical and Radio School of about 1938 was also a very good example of the brick and glass style. Edward F. Billson's Sanitarium Health Food building[21] in Warburton,

75 Wyldefel Gardens, Potts Point, Sydney. John Brogan, architect. 1934-5.

Victoria, of 1937 was an excellent interpretation and much the better design than his Signs Publishing Company of one year earlier. The refined compositional treatment of the Sanitarium building, careful proportions and the sensitive use of materials epitomized its design style (**78**).

It would not be difficult to argue that most of the buildings and ideas discussed in relation to the 1930s, or more particularly after 1933–4, have been ephemeral or tasteful attempts to rationalize the changes that had taken place in Europe in preceding years. With a hope that repeating will not diminish the basic premise of the discussion, there was no reason for Australia to promote an architecture to meet whatever new pragmatic or philosophic ideals which might have existed. Therefore, stylistic changes were to a

76 Hastings Deering, East Sydney, N.S.W. Samuel Lipson, architect. 1936–8. (Courtesy the architect)

very large degree matters of taste. On the other hand, much of what did occur happened because of a more pragmatic attitude about the role of architecture, not only in relation to attitudes about the machine or in the use of scientific reasoning and process, but in solving social problems through methodology, or, perhaps, simply to instil an Australian vigour. Emulation was a necessary factor of architectural design.

In what was described as a House at Bayview, New South Wales, architect W. Watson Sharp produced a *tour de force* of 1930s architecture which culminated the stylistic period.[22] Eleven-inch cavity brick walls were finished with a smooth cement rendering in an off-white. The L-shaped plan stretched out from a connecting hub to partially embrace an open courtyard. One of the stretching wings ended in a raised swimming pool. Corner windows, round windows, deep columns at the entry, were employed as well as pipe handrails on the roof decks, all blended with the utmost care (**79** and **80**). One is reminded of the much earlier Wyldefel Gardens and most certainly of those early houses of Amyas D. Connell and Basil Ward in England—white in the deep, damp green of the English countryside. (Of interest: in 1941 Connell was to win a second premium with a modest Gothic design in a competition not too distant, the Auckland Cathedral, assessed by Sir Giles Gilbert Scott. First premium went to Charles Towle of Sydney who blended English cathedral plans with Scandinavian forms in a tower and spire, and tall slit windows about the nave.) And in Melbourne an urban architecture, similar to Sharp's country domestic style, was the delightful E. W. Tilley building on Latrobe Street.

Oddly enough, two sets of flats come closer to achieving architectural designs more in keeping with their intended paradigms, yet they are quite different in appearance and justification. One is very European and the other very much of California. The Newburn Flats in South Melbourne by Romberg and Shaw, of 1939–40, responded to a plan of angled flats to a straight line access-way (or balcony on upper floors) to gain privacy.[23] The flats were a simple one-bedroom scheme with the living room opened to a balcony. The dramatic off-form concrete and bright colours in the fenestration panels and a mural were contrasted by the deep shadows of the private and public balconies (**81**). In contrast, the flats by Roy Grounds on Glendon Road, Toorak, Victoria, were brick with white trim and wood fencing. While the Newburn Flats were designed with vigour and flair, the Glendon Road Flats were restrained in their direct cubic massing.[24] Newburn was solid design for the period while Grounds' flats were rather more prophetic. Both were a promise for the future.

The future, though, was many years away. There was an architectural limbo created by World War II. The war years were difficult, in fact the period 1942–8 was one of the most frustrating for Australian architects. Productivity of the profession was for the most part depressingly myopic and unstable. Yet it was also a time for new resolution. Architects who remained in a civilian capacity did not engage in private practice, or if they did, it was limited by the government. The larger firms managed to continue professional services, but the smaller offices, the large majority, simply closed. Many architects worked for governmental agencies or for the American armed or support services in their architectural or engineering capacity. Some architects,

77 NESCA House, Newcastle, N.S.W. E. L. Sodersteen, and Pitt and Merewether, associated architects. 1937–8. (Photograph Universal Photography)

78 Sanitarium Health Food Company, Warburton, Victoria. E. F. Billson, architect. 1936–7. (Courtesy the architect)

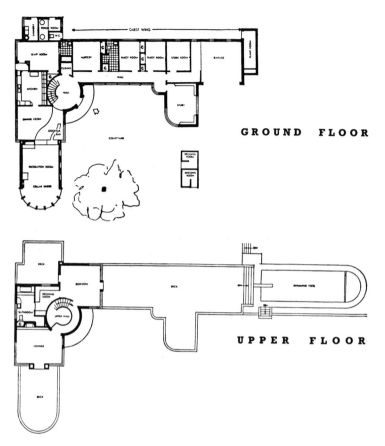

79 House, Bayview, N.S.W.
W. Watson Sharp, architect.
1940.

GROUND FLOOR

UPPER FLOOR

the young, went overseas. Two groups of Australians, therefore, were confronted with the realities of what the change in architecture was about. The first group came in contact with those peculiar American traits of initiative and of management. Although a small group, their attitude on initiating and maintaining an offensive position, so to speak, was critical. Rather than reassuming the traditional (and passive) role of arbiter over a series of post-mortems on the efforts of others, particularly overseas, their persuasion was to establish the architect in an important position in the community, especially through ideas which they believed were nationally based. Conversation about what was happening in North America or Europe was to be no longer of worth unless it could be related to what could be done in Australia. It was a search for a potential of real value.

The second group confronted modern idioms of architecture in their forced journeys overseas. A much larger group than the select few of the immediate past generation, they were to demand an avoidance of the gentle architecture of the depression years. There was to be no return. Nostalgia, that human element which

80 House, Bayview, N.S.W.
W. Watson Sharp, architect.
1940. (Courtesy the architect)

so damned the first attempts of modern architecture after World War I, was to be vigorously and scrupulously dismissed from consideration. Australia was to be built anew. The bracing, sustaining attitude of isolation—in this instance with a concomitant demeaning attitude of insulation—was fractured by the global war. It had touched native shores. Distance might be overcome. A national integrity might be sustained through internal will and international response. For the architects, the desire was for a new *and* indigenous architecture.

A third group must be considered again—the immigrant. Not the English or American, many of whom stayed after the war, but the Europeans, a significant group who could not or would not return to their homeland just before or after the war. We will look carefully at the architecture of one such immigrant, but only after a general survey.

How did these groups wage themselves against the depressing norms of egalitarianism?

One problem which engaged the architect after the war was housing, in fact it was the only problem to engage the nearly destitute professional architect after hospitals and factories were no longer in desperate need. Housing spawned a series of inducements to invigorate the economy and labour market—returned servicemen's housing, housing estates, suburban factories, suburbs, electrical power projects, apartments and flats, etc. Yet, when the economy, labour market and the architect were in desperate need, the national and various state governments turned to prefabricated housing from England, rather than fully developing a domestic industry. The English model was competent, but its parts and/or components were not designed for Australia. Yet the English wood sheds were used for houses, semi-detached living units and schools. Combined with poor site orientation by local agencies, the results must be viewed as depressing. In general, architects were bystanders.

The suggestion has been made that the first prefabricated buildings in Australia were constructed in 1804. William Paterson, of the New South Wales Corps and also Lieutenant-Governor, sailed from Sydney carrying soldiers and convicts, settlers, livestock and stores, 'and two wooden houses'.[25] They were temporarily unloaded at George Town and five weeks later, in December, they were reloaded on another ship, the *Lady Nelson*, and moved across the harbour to the site of the selected permanent settlement and seat of government for Northern Van Diemen's Land, York Town, where they were erected. One hundred and forty-four years later people were again moving into Australia for settlement. They were encouraged by national and state government schemes of assisted migration to help build Australia anew — mines, dams, power plants, roads. In spite of some existing industries concentrating on prefabricated housing, noticeably the Victorian Housing Commission who took over the Fowler prefabrication company,[26] the governments went overseas to help satisfy the demand created almost wholly by the influx from abroad. The neat and completely sound product called the 'Sectionit' house produced by Vandyke Brothers of Sydney,[27] begun in 1946, was bypassed. What was secured for Australia were more traditional plans with tedious entries and wasteful corridors and jumbled elevations: less than satisfying in their wholesome character of English precedent and purpose. A local observer commented: 'Naturally, the design of State-sponsored homes is guided more by economy than aesthetic demands'.[28] It was a normal egalitarian suggestion that aesthetics are added and not an integral design factor; a suggestion which has dominated most opinion. Even the Victorian Minister for Development, R. G. Casey, had to defend the imports:

I know that there are people who do not favour the importation of pre-fabricated houses. To them I say, 'Neither do I, but we have no immediate alternative, except a disastrous curtailment of the migration programme'.[29]

81   Newburn Flats, South Melbourne, Victoria. Romberg and Shaw, architects. 1939.

Minister Casey's peculiar logic was in response to criticism of 'Operation Snail'. The operation was a search for prefabricated housing not wholly justified in the view of many for it excluded Australian based firms. It eventually became the first 'mass importation' of such houses, in this instance from England, in spite of the fact that the Victorian government owned its own plant.

There is no question that there was a need for housing. Rather, the question was 'Why not an Australian product?'

Vandyke Brothers also produced a more traditional-appearing house with a large hipped roof pressing down on low walls. John Paine Company was producing homes in Hobart and the Beaufort Division of the Department of Aircraft Production produced a nicely designed house by Sydney architect Arthur Baldwinson.[30] And there were other Australian products.

The attraction of the market in Australia also encouraged other firms in other countries to test their products and hopefully wedge open the market. The Stex organization from Sweden, comprising two firms from Finland and one from Sweden,[31] set up prototypes in 1948. Probably the largest order for English prefabs came from the Australian government when it purchased a batch of factory-made timber dwellings called the Riley-Newsum house as late as 1951: cost £1,250,000.[32] It was made in Lincoln and shipped to Australia as a series of panels. The states followed the national precedent, especially South Australia.

While such acts were demoralizing, the architect persevered

and struggled for professional independence through initiative and chance.

Publishing firms sought to assist the independent home buyer and builder in a post-war market by producing pamphlets on houses and designs. They invariably contained houses of all sizes and description unless the pamphlet was directed to one house type, such as a vacation cottage. The architectural designs varied in type and quality, as did the pamphlet itself. One of the better products from Sydney was edited by Florence M. Taylor: *The Book of 150 Low-Cost Houses*.

One other factor of the post-war depression must be recounted. The period saw the rise and entrenchment of state and national architectural offices. The word entrenchment is carefully presented. At first agencies would assist in determining needs and standards and allow, even encourage, architects to provide professional services, not only to the agency, but privately. Then, the various governments assumed more control until full architectural services were conducted by the state. They employed the architect, the engineer, designer, and other professionals. The result was bureaucratic control of most of the profession and all services related to state and federal (or public) works. Some argued that standards might rise to the lowest level of bureaucratic trivia or that the governments were being fooled by pennywise policies which had nothing to do with economics or design excellence. But the old Colonial architect system sustained itself again in a non-Whig world. One, and only one consoling factor can be counted: after the war there was direct employment in these agencies. For other architects, the road to professional security was unpredictable and apparently circuituous.

Many architects promoted their professional wares by producing their own pamphlets and brochures. Most did not display their past accomplishments but their potential. They presented possible architectural achievements, particularly and invariably houses. These brochures were similar to those of the 1930s but the incidence of non-traditional design was much greater. Most were a catalogue of sorts. Some were more concerned with relating their designs to Australian conditions which were as yet ill-defined in an architectural sense.

John Moore's 1944 book *Home Again!* anticipated a return to normal after the war.[33] He discussed the geographical conditions, looked briefly at the city and he analysed the home, both its plan and location. He then urged his reader not to be afraid of change in architectural appearance and pointed to modern architecture (in words only) in other countries as offering something of value but he failed to identify the visual and architectural character of his proposals for change. Kenneth McConnel concentrated on rural conditions in *Planning the Australian Homestead*, published as late as 1947.[34] The book approached the subject of function but with some naivete. So-called open plans were not open, and functionalism was not fairly represented. By comparison with information available from overseas on the subject, the book was somewhat misleading. It also perpetuated the soft, nostalgic, oft-repeated reality—corrugated iron roofs and similar sheds; nobby, wobbly fences; randomly enlarged and ungainly cottages— a reality in the past that should not have been in the mid-century, a spartan almost tasteless reality that Edith Walling was trying to avoid within the same conceptual framework in her contemporary book previously mentioned: *Cottages and Gardens in Australia*. There were no dreams of what might be in McConnel's book. Neither the Moore nor McConnel book clarified the visual result of what they argued as rational architectural planning. Their designs (most of McConnel's were of completed buildings) were sensitive to tradition.

A more comprehensive work which anticipated domestic construction and urban rehabilitation after the war was Walter Bunning's *Homes in the Sun* of 1945 vintage. The first forty pages were a history of architecture (other than Australian) and of the development of Australia's cities. The remainder of the book was a critical appraisal of Australian urban planning or lack thereof. It also dealt with ideas for the dwelling that would take advantage of the sun and enhance privacy. Merits of some of the ideas were obviously gained through the growing knowledge of the rational or functional approach to planning but the architectonic response to the approach was unresolved. Perhaps this was due to concentrating on the presentation of how a new home might be ordered under the Australian sun and ignoring intrinsic aesthetic values.

Home Plans was a small pamphlet put out in late 1945.[35] It presented the ideas of architects (and a few students) from Melbourne and Sydney. It included a few houses by American architects (they were not identified) 'whose distinguished presentation of the new and unfamiliar forms in housing has won them fame'. This was true to some extent and the statement does emphasize the importance of the American import. Of equal, or perhaps of more interest was the presentation of some excellent designs by the Australian architect. Those of John Mockridge and Edgar M. Gurney with L. E. Rowell were notable for their clarity, direct plans and elevational treatment. They also showed, as did others, the American influence, with the exception of Mockridge.

82 Two-storey maisonette, *project*. Leslie T. Brock, architect. 1946.

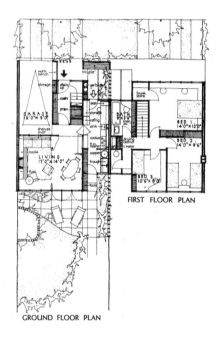

FIRST FLOOR PLAN

GROUND FLOOR PLAN

His plans were simple yet unorthodox, elevations unaffected but showing a distinct bi-partite scheme of a box hovering above open space or at least the suggestion of an open space. In his 'Holiday House' the ground floor was for car and play with rooms above. The open-plan extended living schemes through indoor/outdoor relationships so typical of Southern California were used with care in architect Trevor Bain's 'Expandable House'. Designed for a narrow city lot, the functional positioning of the parts of the house on the site was more than suitable, as was the treatment of the elevations in relation to house orientation. Some architects presented two proposals: one contemporary and one traditional. In fact most of the pamphlet was devoted to the more historical designs, as was a later compendium that was concerned with completed homes.

In 1948, under the banner of modern architecture, architect George Beiers included American Colonial, English and American Georgian, Venetian, Chinese, Spanish Californian, Queen Anne and a few others in his book *Houses of Australia*.[36] He provided a few selected photographs of nineteenth- and early twentieth-century houses and some of the latter were not historically based. Obviously the word modern was not a definition of style but of time. The discussion was nil and there were no plans or sections to compare. As a picture book it missed the mark: the photographs were too dark for study, especially the reproductions of the Colonial prints and paintings. It was a pictorial survey of domestic architecture with a theme 'anything goes', yet in a very modest, superficial manner it was the first 'history' of Australian domestic design in book form.

Competitions were held by a variety of sponsors and literally hundreds of out-of-work architects entered their ideas and drawings. The results varied from pre-war to post-war styles. One of the more productive in previewing a post-1945 potential was the Sun Post-War Homes of 1946. Leslie Brock's rather fine two-storey maisonnette design precisely fit the rationalism predicted by the pre-1939 North American precedents for both urban living and design (**82**).

Of course city or urban planning and replanning was a serious focus of government agencies and many architects were involved. The replanning of Darwin was a major undertaking. The original master plan was finally published in 1948[37] but it was not acted upon in following years except in a piecemeal fashion. Some of the proposed residences showed a logical extension of the tropical house—bulk raised on posts or stumps, cross ventilation, sloping roof, substantial construction[38]—but they too were quickly forgotten. Treatises of a more theoretical nature were forthcoming. Some were by government or quasi-government agencies. One was directed to urging a logical survey (more on social aspects) before preliminary planning. Architect Ernest Fooks displayed these methods with utmost clarity in a series of essays published just after the war. His training in Vienna was both in architecture and urban planning. His years in Victorian planning agencies, mixed with theoretical study provided a basis for the work.[39]

The number of planning books (or pamphlets) which might have been of practical value by setting out contemporary methodologies and resources were too few and this was an exception.

The local journals and magazines concentrated on overseas countries. In fact, *Building and Engineering* showed more foreign architectural work than Australian during the period from 1943 to 1949. A fair indication of the dearth of commissions: recovery was painfully slow. The published designs were often the only outlet for creative activity. The local journals either had favourite countries and architects, or more probably, there were only a select few countries willing to engage in the game of public relations. Sweden, Brazil and America were popular countries. Seldom was England's architecture displayed or discussed. It was Oscar Niemeyer from Brazil, the American Frank Lloyd Wright, W. Dudok in Holland, along with Le Corbusier, who were catching the editors' eye. The architects and libraries were also showing increasing interest in other English-speaking countries, indicated by subscription of architectural journals. Except for Le Corbusier, France produced little of interest. The Australian journals and magazines did show local work by both the young and old professional architect, but it was in the form of ideas, projects, thoughts and the like. Concepts of function, especially the plan form, were topical subjects—resolving wind, sun, privacy or other problem related to domestic design—particularly around the year 1948.

It was a year earlier, in 1947, that Australian architectural histories began. All prior attempts were imprecise historical outlines or ill-conceived blandishments on an English heritage or short articles of fact without necessary interpretation such as those of the 1920s. Only Wilson's brief comments in his two books written in the early 'twenties engender praise or interest from either the historian or architect. In 1947 Robin Boyd's seminal work, *Victorian Modern*[10] focused most of its attention on twentieth-century Melbourne architects and their buildings. Boyd was concise, losing nothing in brevity. His research has proven to be more than adequate. Boyd's book made Australians aware of a small portion of their architectural heritage and of the people who had reputations that extended beyond local, state and even national boundaries. He also suggested that although it may not be the best architecture in the world, it was at least not the worst, and it was a sufficient foundation for a future architecture. If the suggestions offered above may sound somewhat trite now, they were absolutely necessary in 1947. A responsible, carefully constructed history was also necessary in 1947. Boyd tried to emphasize that the architects he discussed (A. G. Stephenson, Griffin, Roy Grounds, Leighton Irwin, etc.) were unique in that they were Australian or designing for Australian conditions. This first history and first architectural criticism (at least enough to warrant that distinction) had the seeds of what was to be a life-long crusade: a plea for integrity. If the prosperous influences from everywhere abroad were an irresistible magnet, let Australia's selection (importation) be more refined, more sensible and sensitive to Australia's needs. Often Boyd was too didactic, too negative. Often he did not encourage, did not guide his audience to rational observations. Strength was gained by consistency, by repetition of his concern in his many essays and books to follow *Victorian Modern*. He became Australia's first architectural critic. Therefore, his collective works were to be an added inducement in recognizing merits in the past and damning lethargic concern for the visual and architectural environment, past and present.

The frustration which faced Robert Haddon when he tried to discover an Australian architectural idiom after Federation, dogged the architect forty-five years later at mid-century. The desire, in fact the acknowledged need, not in a political sense but of a spiritual nature, for an image conveying a national architecture was real. The means—theoretical or material—eluded the architect. There was a hesitancy to copy directly the overseas idioms. There was a great and obvious gap between the paper design of projects and ideas and the material thing; between artefact and architecture. In spite of the noble attempt of Boyd to isolate and analyse architects and architecture, there was not enough evidence to convince architects and clients of the reasonableness of the new ideas. Nor was there enough evidence to indicate that change was in fact necessary, a view held by many. The moody independence of Roy Grounds or Sydney Ancher, the rallying cry of Robin Boyd, the hefty, granulated concrete of Frederick Romberg, the eclectic delicacy of Robert Hanson with his ranch houses, the renewed Edward Billson, the quixotic large architectural firms— nothing was persuasive enough to solidify opinion or engender a following. All were, after all, part of the problem.

While a panel composed of important figures from Europe and the Americas (including William Holford, Henry-Russell Hitchcock and Lucia Costa) sat in London and discussed the idea of a 'new monumentality' for mid-century,[41] it was obvious that symposia and discussions of this nature were too much of a rhetorical exercise when viewed through the lens of those lean post-war years. The more pragmatic Australian architect (as he was to say of himself) wished to see results, and results were slow in coming to fruition. The United States' recovery after the war was the quicker. The result of post-war American architecture was strikingly modern, and in physical appearance a free and open design. It was a cause of interest throughout the world. Australian architects were keen observers of its architecture especially that in California. The magazine *Architectural and Engineering News* from San Francisco was not only watched by Australians, but it watched Australia with occasional articles (nearly the only American magazine to do so). The popular slick magazines were received not only by libraries but by private offices. *Art and Architecture* from Los Angeles was put in a new format under the capable and progressive editorship of John Etenza. It was watched with some hesitancy, for it was seen as too biased to the trends of internationalism. As in the 1920s Australia had a spiritual affinity with California in many ways including architecture. The architectural yield of the matriarch England was practically nil. Europe was in the throes of redefinition. The import was generally Californian.

While the focus was to be on California after the war one house suggested the Californian source much earlier. In 1941 Norman Seabrook and Alan Fildes completed a truly fine example of modern architecture in their Country House at Croydon, Victoria (**83** and **84**). The plan was superbly balanced and read like a textbook example. The open plan suggested the California influence but more particularly this was noticed in the materials employed and manner of the façades. Wood post and beam structure was exposed and infilled with glass. Where a partial wall was required, they used brick to sill height. The chimney was brought away from the fascia and the roof was an ever-so-gentle gable. The consistency of the design into the interiors and the quality of space and light made this one of the outstanding houses of the decade from 1935 to 1945.

Arthur Stephenson continued almost single-handedly to provide an architectural export that England was willing to accept and acknowledge. Of course, much of the export knowledge was provided by Stephenson himself, not only through his tours and speeches overseas, but through articles by him or the firm he directed. The ability to promulgate his own architecture was praised by his contemporaries and colleagues. Just a few years later Harry Seidler was damned for the same ability. Yet, Stephenson's hospital designs continued to intrigue international audiences. In 1942 the large Royal Melbourne Hospital was complete.[42] Also in 1942, after slightly less than two years' design and construction, the Repatriation General Hospital in Concord, N.S.W.

83 A Country House,
Croydon, Victoria,
N. Seabrook and A. Fildes,
architects. 1941.

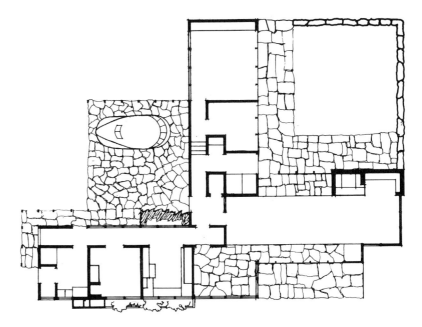

84 A Country House,
Croydon, Victoria,
N. Seabrook and A. Fildes,
architects. 1941.

was complete.[43] If the Nurses' Home of the Concord complex was confused in massing and lacked a sense of deliberate intention, the Main Block of rooms and wards was a splendidly mature balcony scheme so typical of Stephenson, as was the 'Y' plan. The elevations were very similar to a contemporary, the King George V Memorial Hospital, Camperdown, N.S.W. of 1940.[44] Both won Sulman awards: the first in 1946, the second in 1941. In recognition of his designs, principally of the 1930s and 1940s, his contribution to hospital design and his professional activities, he was awarded the Royal Gold Medal of the Royal Institute of British Architects in 1954, an honour which was reserved for few, such as Frank Lloyd Wright and Walter Gropius, and the first by an Australian.

During the war most hospitals were one storey and spread out in an endless series of blocks and covered walks. Just before these emergency 'temporary or semi-permanent'[45] facilities were begun the hospitals of Stephenson and others were to be completed. One of the finest ward and operating block schemes was by Leighton Irwin: the Heidelberg Military Hospital, Victoria, also completed in 1942.[46] The plan was a blunt 'T' with operating wing crossing the base of the stem. The balconies off the beds and wards on the upper floors were straight and of the Stephenson mould. In this instance the balcony rails were in highlight against their own shadow and contained by solid mass blocks at either end, thereby neatly enclosing the façade composition.

Although architects were faced with little work and a shortage of materials and money after the war, at least there were competitions. Home magazines, quasi-professional journals, newspapers and the various institutes conducted competitions which were almost exclusively related to domestic architecture. The Melbourne newspaper *The Sun* received 1,000 entries for a competition in 1945.[47] The results were disappointing compared to the 1934 competition in Melbourne.

One non-domestic competition which aroused national attention was for Anzac House. Promoted by the Returned Sailors, Soldiers and Airmen's Imperial League of Australia (New South Wales Branch), it had sentimental importance, as well as occupying a major site in Sydney and a healthy first place premium of £1,000. First prize for the 1948 competition went to a design submitted by architects W. R. Bunning and C. A. Madden of Sydney.[48] It was a design overburdened with too many different forms of fenestration on the façades. Two other designs are worth mentioning. The submission of Best Overend of Melbourne was an undulating glass box of many storeys resting on a solid stone base. It was

85 Anzac House, Sydney.
W. R. Bunning and C. A.
Madden, architects. 1948–52.
(Courtesy the architects)

described as difficult to follow 'because of its "clever boy" very sketchy kind of presentation'.[49] The other submission was that of Yuncken, Freeman Brothers, Griffiths and Simpson, also of Melbourne, who employed a flush surface material from ground to parapet with individual windows carefully proportioned in the surface. When the Bunning and Madden design was finally executed on College Street in the 1950s (85), it was to a far superior design to the original, a much shorter building and very reminiscent of the well-known Casa del Fascio, Como (Italy) by Guiseppe Terragni, done 1932–6. The suggestion arises not only from the square proportioned voids of the exposed post and beam frame (in this instance not exposed concrete) but the direct openness of the top floor or attic as it recedes from the front surface.[50]

What characterized so much of the architecture of the 1940s was a lack of clearly defining the design intention in visual terms. Form and detail were befuddled by a compounding of elements. There was a lack of restraint in that buildings had too many ideas, too many varieties of form, too much of the plan was given expression, too many parts described in mass or material as different rather than similar. Much of this described characterization was brought about through immaturity, by simply not working with design idioms but rather in imitation. With few exceptions, and they were important, the architects were responding rather than proposing; reacting rather than acting. More precisely, architecture lacked a concise definition of what in fact the Australian conditions were in architectural terms for the proponents of regionalism, or, of what was international about internationalism.

In 1951 and therefore seen in retrospect, an American, Dr John E. Burchard was a visitor to Australia. He was Dean of Humanities and Social Sciences at the famed Massachusetts Institute of Technology when he made his tour. He gave speeches, viewed works in all states of the continent and talked to architects, who also looked at the post-war period retrospectively (and squarely at 1951). The architects spoke of their lack of sophisticated materials, of shipping delays or other lamentations. Burchard was sympathetic, but his comments were critical:

At first you think this shows lack of imagination and energy. . . . Then you begin to come across the skeletons of people who have tried to be expeditors in Australia. There is no doubt that a heavy hand is laid by what is acceptable, by what can be permitted in the 'crises', by legislation, and by custom. Then Australian brickmakers and bricklayers [for instance] are simply unwilling to make something different. All this limits the materials which an Australian architect can use.

But the basic ones are still there. There is handsome stone. There is plaster. There is steel. There are brick and tile (and paint to cover them with). . . . There are more materials now in Australia than Australia's best architect, Francis Greenway, had to use in 1810.[51]

There were exceptions as both this book and Burchard suggest. While much of the commercial work was the brick architecture of the late 1930s, two dissimilarly styled buildings stood out from the red heaviness. The offices and factories for Wormald Brothers at Waterloo, New South Wales by architects Stafford, Moor and Farington,[52] displayed a consistent attitude about the nature of the building type, as did its contemporary, the Automatic Totalisators Limited building at Meadow Bank,[53] New South Wales by architects Herbert, Dennis and Odling. The first group of buildings was light in appearance with an extended roof beyond the offices, a window pattern and a modular constructional characteristic which strongly related to the California vernacular of the building type. The second building was a sophisticated re-interpretation of the smooth flowing lines of the 1930s. And there were other exceptions.

The architecture of Griffin in form and material was carried into the post-war years by Eric Nicholls. While the remodelling of Palings on Ash Street, Sydney, was in the vein of European modern, the houses at Castlecrag suggested Griffin. This was noticed in some of the details, the squat proportions and the granular stone masonry. After Marion's return to America,

86 W. R. Hamill House, Killara, N.S.W. Sydney Ancher, architect. 1948–9. (Courtesy the architect)

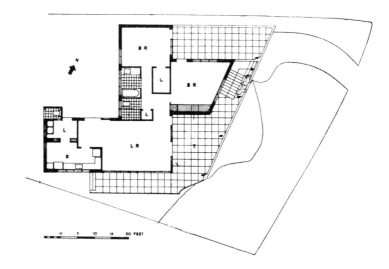

87 W. R. Hamill House, Killara, N.S.W. Sydney Ancher, architect. 1948–9.

88 Studio, Curl Curl, N.S.W. Sydney Ancher, architect. Perspective. 1948.

Nicholls was more-or-less left in charge at Castlecrag and a few houses were built to his designs in the 1940s, designs reflecting not only Griffin but contemporary ideas of form. The J. S. Thompson house on Edinburgh Road of 1946 clearly displayed the new and lingering influences.[54]

Two houses by Sydney Ancher revealed the clarity of his planning and the direct, unaffected simplicity of his residential work which was unique in Australia around the decades of the war. The W. R. Hamill house in Killara, New South Wales, had a simple 'L' shaped plan with one bedroom jutting to an angle.[55] A garage was located under a large deck or verandah. Glass was full height to the view in the living space. A simple post and beam structure extended beyond the walls on two sides (**86** and **87**). The other house was more a cottage for a site at Curl Curl, New South Wales (**88**). It contained only one bedroom but the pattern established in the late 1930s and again at Killara, was used in this earlier house[56] including a flat plan or verandah extending the internal space. At Curl Curl an exterior wall defined the private deck off the bedroom from the more public entertaining area of the 'L' shaped plan. But the cottage had a rugged history. Although the design was finally approved, the local council initially made a condition to approval. It wished to have a surrounding parapet two feet high 'to hide as far as possible what is in this Council's opinion the ugly view of a flat-roofed building'.[57] Date: 1948.

The Wormald building and the Ancher houses exemplify the growing enthusiasm for the idioms of European Internationalism,

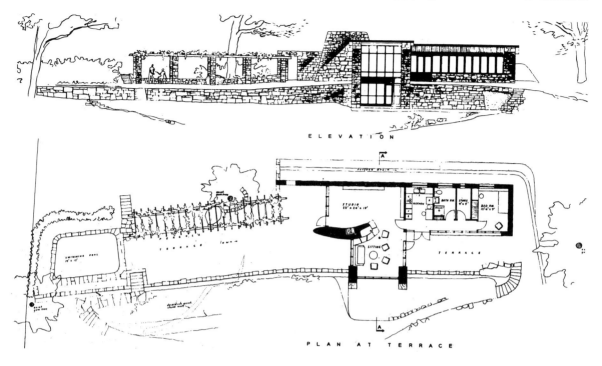

ELEVATION

PLAN AT TERRACE

89 William Dobell Studio, *project*, Church Point, N.S.W. Gibson and Baldwinson, architects. 1947.

as did some of the proposals published just after the war in pamphlets, brochures or in the competitions. The reaction or non-acceptance of the idioms must not be disregarded. Quite often architects (and designers) would engage in a wide variety of styles. Some designs were ambivalent. Some were superb. In 1947 architects Gibson and Baldwinson designed a blend of internationalism and regionalism, two attitudes on conceptualizing architecture at a very basic level. Their's was a schooled, textbook design of a very high calibre. Their words are worth repeating:

Aesthetics.

It was felt that the beauty of the wild, rocky, timbered environment should be preserved, or rather, played up to. The building, terracing and planting should harmonise with the natural terrain, both in colour and texture. To this end the abundant stone on the site was chosen (random jointed) as the principal building material.

Design emphasis, if any, is towards easy romanticism rather than formalism, the composition being based on an asymmetrical grouping, pivoted about a massive chimney wall. Long parallel lines of terrace, pergola and main form of building are contrasted in direction and mass by the boldly jutting living room wing, with its further emphasis of vertical raking stone piers.[58]

Not to detract from the Gibson and Baldwinson house for the painter William Dobell (**89**), but in just three years architect

Philip Johnson and then Mies van der Rohe proved beyond doubt that a fully glassed prismatic cube resting within a wooded site does more to enhance the natural site and to bring it within the internal spaces than a fully harmonious use of materials and form. Or did they?

In 1940 artist Danila Vassilieff, a European immigrant, began to build his own house at Warrandyte near Melbourne. Journalist Wynn Scott visited the Vassilieff house in 1949 and reported the following:

Materials for building were handy, and he had a creek bed which could be dammed to provide the water for mixing cement and for household purposes.

... [The site] held all the sandstone anyone could want. When the supply of trees ran out, there were tall gums for the cutting on adjoining land. Cement could be had in any quantity for the buying in those days and windows were to be picked up at city wreckers' yards. ...

Stone was blasted and quarried, and the blocks of sandstone—blue grey and tawny—were piled up for building. The silica was carted down to bed the dam wall and to form the filling for the terrace. ...

Trees, set in the stone floor, support the roof, and trees (one could hardly call them logs) form the tremendous beams, which are covered with split logs. This is, of course, where fence splitting experience played its part. Over the split logs bark was placed, then stone chips and a coat of cement. ...

An island fireplace in this [living] room is a new architectural feature. Round the fireplace the floor is paved with stone and a step behind it leads to a hardwood floor. Much of the furniture was made by the builder.

A large studio is now being built.[59]

It is difficult to evaluate such a highly personal expression of home and life style. Yet, in the last analysis there is no need to impose an evaluation. It is quite simply an extension of aesthetic selection and experience. Where one might select a paint colour for a room and paint the room, or select a floor material and lay the material or select a painting and hang it, this marvellous house was similarly built. It is just a more complex and complete experience. That does not imply the experience or house have greater virtue. Nor does it suggest more value, except, perhaps, to Mr Vassilieff. But the experience of others is increased and viably enhanced by not only a vicarious knowledge of the activity of building, but by a full impact on an otherwise repetitively similar aesthetic environment. For such small, tasteful gifts we must all be grateful.

Although not an architect, Vassilieff characterizes the resolve developed during the period for a fundamental indigenous architecture.

NOTES TO CHAPTER FOUR

1. See 'The Royal Gold Medal For Architecture', *R.I.B.A. Journal* (B), 61 (January 1954), p. 94, and 'The Work of the Royal Gold Medallist 1954', *R. I. B. A. Journal* (B), 61 (February 1954), pp. 144–8.

2. Ellison Harvie, 'The Changing Profession of Architecture', *Architect* (A), 3 (May-June 1968), pp. 26–8, provides interesting background.

3. ['Australian Consolidated Industries'], *Decoration and Glass* (A), 7 (September 1941), pp. 9ff.

4. 'Bank', *The Architectural Review* (B), 93 (March 1943), pp. 65–8.

5. 'The Bank . . . ', *Architecture* (A), 37 (January 1948) pp. 37–8, completed in 1942, by Claridge, Hassel, McConnell and Laybourne-Smith, architects.

6. 'Offices . . . ', *The Architectural Review* (B), 90 (August 1941), pp. 49–52.

7. The preliminary plans of 1939 were very disappointing in their complication; see 'Perspective Drawings of New Darwin Hotel', *Decoration and Glass* (A), 5 (March 1939), p. 36. As finally built (first stage) see 'New Hotel at Darwin . . . ', *Decoration and Glass* (A), 7 (May 1941), p. 30. Visited December 1974.

8. 'Model of Flats', *Building* (A), 45 (February 1935), p. 105, and 'Ruskin, Dudley Ward adds Another Continental Contribution', *Decoration and Glass*, 2 (December 1936), pp. 10ff.

9. 'First Prize . . . ', *Journal of the Royal Victorian Institute of Architects* (A), 34 (March 1936), p. 19.

10. 'Proposed Royal Exchange . . . ', *Building* (A), 46 (June 1936), p. 13, shows original façade.

11. Correspondence. See also 'Australia Shows Way to Modernism', *The Architect and Engineer* (US), 46 (May 1936), pp. 31–2, 52.

12. 'City Mutual . . . ', *Decoration and Glass* (A), 2 (November 1936), pp. 11ff., for very complete coverage. Sodersteen (1900–61) is the object of great interest among 1930 design aficionados. Many of his buildings still exist: the War Memorial in Canberra, of course, and of controversial character. Two that appeal to this author are located in Sydney: Bryant House, 80 Pitt Street (now Queensland Insurance building) and the charming if inelegant No. 7 Elizabeth Street.

13. 'Wyldefel Gardens', *Decoration and Glass* (A), 2 (July 1936), pp. 7–11, for excellent photographs.

14. 'Glass Predominates in Modern Factory Construction', *Decoration and Glass* (A), 2 (November 1936), p. 56. The building was designed in 1936 and completed in 1938.

15. 'Modern Functional Architecture', *Decoration and Glass* (A), 3 (November 1937), pp. 26–8.

16. M. E. Herman, 'Comparison of Architectural Solutions', *Architecture* (A), 25 (June 1937), p. 121.

17. Ibid.

18. R. M. Edmunds, *Architecture. An Introductory Survey*, Sydney 1938. Sadly the book was praised in the introduction by Leslie Wilkinson.

19. 'Horizontal Motif in Askew House', *Decoration and Glass* (A), 4 (July 1938), pp. 18–19.

20. 'Ashdown', *Building* (A), 46 (October 1938), pp. 34–5.

21. 'Victorian Factories in Peaceful Rural Setting', *Decoration and Glass* (A), 4 (June 1938), pp. 18–23. This fine building won the Street Architecture Award in 1940. Billson was in and out of many partnerships or semi-partnerships including one or two with Geoffrey Mewton. Billson had a chance to remodel his old mentor's Palais de Danse at St Kilda, executed by Griffin in the 'teens. He and Mewton completed the remodelling in 1940. See 'Nautical Notions', *Building* (A), 49 (August 1940), pp. 32–3.

22. Extensively covered in 'Little Mountain', *Decoration and Glass* (A), 7 (June 1941), pp. 7ff. See also 'House at Bayview . . . ', *The Architects' Journal* (B), 112 (May 1942), pp. 373–5.

23. 'Newburn Flats in South Melbourne', *Art in Australia* (A), 1 (March-May 1941), pp. 73–4.

24. 'Modern Flats in Toorak', *Art in Australia* (A), 1 (March 1941), pp. 78–9. Cf. [Conrad Harmann], 'Early Romberg', *Architecture Australia* (A), 66 (April 1977), pp. 68–75.

25. As recounted in 'Tasmanian Prefabrication Project', *Architecture* (A), 38 (October-December 1950), p. 130.

26. Cf. 'Housing in Victoria', *Architecture* (A), 33 (April-June 1945), pp. 180–5.

27. 'Australian Prefab', *The Architectural Forum* (US), 83 (March 1947), pp. 122, 124, but more particularly 'Prefabrication Down Under', *The Architectural Forum* (US), 79 (November 1943), pp. 75–8.

28. 'Housing in Australia', *The Builder* (B), 176 (February 1949), p. 254.

29. '"Operation Snail" The Victorian Precut Housing Project', *Architecture* (A), 38 (October-December 1950), p. 124.

30. Ibid., pp. 122, 132.

31. Ibid., p. 129. Samples of various British units had been on display as soon as early 1946; see 'British Prefabricated Homes', *Building and Engineering* (A), 55 (July 1946), pp. 24–5.

32. 'The Riley-Newsum Factory-Made House', *The Builder* (B), 181 (August 1951), p. 294. Cf. 'Prefabricated Buildings for Australia', *The Architects' Journal* (B), 115 (10 April 1952), p. 448.

33. John [D. M.] Moore, *Home Again! Domestic Architecture for the Normal Australian*, Sydney 1944.

34. Sydney 1947, with notes on 'Garden Design' by Rex Hazlewood.

35. E. Gye, *Home Plans*, Sydney *c*. 1945.

36. George Beiers, *Houses of Australia*, Sydney 1948.

37. 'Re-planning of a New Darwin . . . ', *Architecture* (A), 36 (April 1948), pp. 32–7. It is interesting to compare these plans with those in 'Cable Station . . . in tropical, sea-girt Guam', *Architectural Forum* (US), (July 1947), pp. 93–7, by architects Antonin Raymond (who worked with Wright on the Imperial Hotel and then stayed in Japan) and L. L. Rado.

38. See also 'Tropical Planning and House Design', Housing Division, Ministry of National Development, *Australian Housing*, 21 (September 1950), pp. 401–6.

39. Ernest Fooks, *Xray the City! The Density Diagram: Basis for Urban Planning*, Melbourne 1946.

40. Robin Boyd, *Victorian Modern*, [Melbourne] 1947. Cf. 'W.B.', *Architecture* (A), 35 (October 1947), p. 29. 'W.B.' writes in the style of Walter Bunning. See also Robin Boyd, *The Australian Ugliness*, Melbourne 1960, and cf. Donald Leslie Johnson, 'Australian Architectural Histories 1848–1968', *Journal of the Society of Architectural Historians* (US), 31 (December 1972), pp. 323–32.

41. 'In Search of a New Monumentality, a Symposium', *The Architectural Review* (B), 104 (September 1948), pp. 117–28.

42. A. G. Stephenson, 'Medical Center at Melbourne', *The Modern Hospital* (US), 57 (August 1941), pp. 65–7; 'Hospitals in Australia', *The Architectural Forum* (US), 85 (August 1946), pp. 109–13; A. G. Stephenson, 'Contemporary Planning Down Under', *The Modern Hospital* (US), 66 (June 1946), pp. 43–51.

43. A. G. Stephenson, 'Repatriation General Hospital', *The Modern Hospital* (US), 70 (March 1948), pp. 66–9; 'Sulman Award, 1946', *Architecture* (A), 36 (July 1948), pp. 35–8.

44. 'King George V Memorial Hospital for Mothers and Babies', *Art in Australia* (A), 31 (September 1941) pp. 82–3.

45. 'General Military Hospitals', *The Architectural Record* (US), 90 (August 1941), pp. 82–3.

46. 'Heidelberg Military Hospital', *The Architectural Record* (US), 100 (August 1946), pp. 76–80.

47. 'Australian Prize-winner for Post-War Homes', *The Architects' Journal* (B), 103 (February 1946), p. 158, and *The Sun Post-War Homes*, Melbourne [1946], paper.

48. 'ANZAC House, Sydney, Architectural Competition', *Architecture* (A), 37 (January 1949), pp. 14–20. Second prize was given to E. W. Andrew (Melbourne) and third to G. W. Finn (Perth).

49. Ibid., p. 40.

50. See 'Australia', *The Architectural Review* (B), 126 (October 1959), p. 198. For the architects' own analysis cf. Walter Bunning, 'Anzac House, Sydney', *Architecture and Arts* (A), 44 (April 1957), pp. 24–9. The Terragni building also appeared adulterated in the Melbourne C.E.G.S. in the 1950s. A competition for Melbourne's Western Market Site (consisting of parking and a large office block) was held just one year later, in July 1949. There were only thirty-nine entries. The very complex planning problems probably deterred many architects. 'Melbourne Western Market Site Competition', *Architecture* (A), 39 (October 1949), pp. 104–10.

51. John Ely Burchard, 'The State of Architecture in Australia', *The Architectural Record* (US), 112 (August 1952), pp. 108, 110. See also the comments to Burchard in Florence M. Taylor, 'An American Looks at Australian Architecture and Thinks We Can Do Much Better', *Building and Engineering* (A), 61 (January 1952), pp. 29–35.

52. 'Sulman Award, 1947', *Architecture* (A), 37 (January 1949), pp. 6–8.

53. 'Automatic Totalisators Limited', *Decoration and Glass* (A), 13 (November-December 1947), pp. 16–21.

54. 'A New Castlecrag Residence', *Building and Engineering* (A), 57 (April 1948), p. 27, and Helen Wentworth, 'His Home was His Hobby', *Australian Home Beautiful* (A), 27 (April 1948), pp. 40 ff. See Nicholls' fine design, 'Factory at Croydon, N.S.W. for W. E. Smith, Printers', *Architecture and Arts* (A), 24 (August 1955), p. 12.

55. Sydney Ancher, 'House at Killara', *Architecture* (A), 38 (January 1950), p. 32.

56. 'Home at Curl Curl', *Decoration and Glass*, 14 (July-August 1948), pp. 24–5, and 'At Curl Curl, NSW', *Architecture in Australia* (A), 44 (October 1955), p. 114.

57. As quoted in 'Australian Architecture', *Current Affairs Bulletin*, 6 (April 1950), p. 51.

58. 'Proposed Studio for Mr. William Dobell at Church Point, N.S.W.', *Architecture* (A), 35 (June 1947), p. 20.

59. Wynn Scott, '"Stonygrad"—Home in a Quarry', *Australian Home Beautiful* (A), 28 (October 1949), pp. 27, 76–7.

People familiar with Australian architecture might wish to compare the Vassilieff house with one of similar appearance: Morrice Shaw's 'bush' house outside Melbourne (cf. 'Cottlesbridge House, Bachelor House in the Outback', *Progressive Architecture* (US), May 1971, pp. 96–7, and published in England—*Design*—and Australia during the same year). But the comparison should be done with care. Shaw, an architect, produced a thoroughly pre-designed house, fully contrived, so to speak, whereas Vassilieff's grew rather organically. Conceptually they are quite different architecture.

5

Harry Seidler: Maturity at Mid-Century

In 1952 the designer George Nelson, a student, practitioner and careful observer of so much of the struggle for a contemporary design and its transition into mid-century, was nearly in a state of lamentation when he announced: 'Now the battle, for all practical purposes, is over'. By the time of the announcement,[1] an observation with which most agreed—even in Australia—the traditional seats of tradition, the architectural schools—even Australian—had accepted surrender. The four, perhaps five years previous to Nelson's observation were critical years for Australian architecture. We have noticed a rather mild but firm reaction to modernism in the mid- and late 1930s and we have noticed that the architects and clients responded by accepting a gentle, softened outward appearance. After World War II a similar response was only in the market place or in government housing. While it is true that a feeling of purpose rested in many architects, they were a significant minority. It could be argued that both the societal conditions and aesthetic attitudes were at an optimum which needed only a forceful lever to swing, if not the majority at least enough architects and clients to a position where compromise was unthinkable, to an acceptance of the international aesthetic. It is an argument with much in its favour. It might also be argued, perhaps with less vigour, that one individual was the lever to swing society's attitudes on approvable architectural tastes. This is the history-makes-man or man-makes-history argument. Either way it is necessary to emphasize that Harry Seidler was a catalyst and that he became the focus of a great deal of attention. After the introduction of a few rather modest houses, the architectural profession in Australia was reluctant to return to a previous aesthetic rationalization.

If Griffin proved to be an enigmatic figure and much of the arch-

Architecture belongs to the university, the profession to the market place.

LOUIS KAHN, quoted in Romaldo Giurgola, 'Louis I. Kahn, 1901–1974', *Progressive Architecture*, May 1974

itecture in the first fifty years of this century was tempered by moods of indecision, the converse was true of Harry Seidler, the second immigrant to cause change. His career appears to be a conscious, straight line development: his architecture consistent, always correct, and if appearing sparse it was always more than less true to the spirit of its time. And there, in his clear statements emphasizing and rationalizing the contemporaneous, is the clue to understanding, to positioning his nearly synonymous designs in Australia. To fully appreciate his synthetic position we must again look back to the early years of this century and eventually at what will become obvious influences on both his method and resultant architectural formulations. It will become clear that Seidler was a product of his experience, at least up to the moment where we terminate this study, about 1951.

The people of the Bauhaus proved to be the dominant influence on Seidler. True, he spent a summer with Oscar Niemeyer but the Brazilian's ideas did not fit the already fixed methods of the young Seidler—only form aberrations lingered for a few short years. Walter Gropius and his pupil (and later his partner) Marcel Breuer were at Harvard where Seidler engaged in graduate studies. To Gropius and Harvard, Seidler's debt was to an unfettered method or approach to architectural design: design in a more exact sense. To Breuer, Seidler's debt was to architectural form. To Joseph Albers, part-time teacher at Harvard, the debt was to an inner yet sustaining inquiry into virtual form, the illusions of line and plane which Seidler manifested three-dimensionally in architecture. If this debt is less noticeable in Seidler's architecture today, it was most assuredly evident in his architecture of the 1940s and 1950s. Although method is the most useful generating tool to the architect, it is form which manifests the result caused by those generative investigations. Thus, Breuer haunts the spaces and forms in most of Seidler's architecture like a spectral image.

Marcel Breuer was born into a comfortable social position as the son of a doctor in Pēcs, Hungary.[2] In 1920 he won a scholarship to the Art Academy of Vienna and, to paraphrase, he walked in one door of the Academy and out the other—it was not for him. Later in 1920 he entered the Bauhaus. Through a friend he read of the Bauhaus and began studies at Weimar almost immediately.

First as a student then a master of the carpentry shop Breuer was an intimate part of the Bauhaus (both at Weimar and Dessau) until 1928, when he opened his architectural office in Berlin. The Bauhaus and its own programme of self-education during this formative period were to have a lasting effect on Breuer.

The self-education programme was not conceived as such, but rather it was a programme of investigating all movements and ideas current in Europe. By providing a place for display and exhibition at the Bauhaus, *de Stijl*, suprematists or constructivists would not only have a venue but the Bauhaus had a continuing programme of studying contemporary art. Two such movements have lineage delineated through the Bauhaus or Breuer directly to Seidler and therefore to Australia.

With its commitment to abstracting forms through line and plane extensions and colour inferences the *de Stijl* claimed an aesthetic which would unite the arts, define a common language of communication between the artist and the community, or as historian Gilbert Herbert has summarized, 'the Bauhaus was seeking a common denomination in Design'.[3] The articulate and persuasive Theo van Doesburg went to Weimar in 1921. His influence on a means for an aesthetic demonstration of the rational processes encouraged by the Bauhaus and Gropius is obvious and well known. Breuer accepted these persuasions and extended them into furniture design and, reacting as did Gropius and Ludwig Hilberseimer, extended them into city planning. The results were a series of coldly ascetic images of what were believed to be conceptually coherent, orderly and socially responsible housing estates. In architecture, not a subject at the Bauhaus (until *c.* 1927) but the inferred sum of the total experience of technical and aesthetic studies, Breuer followed too closely the style of Gropius and the then popular Le Corbusier. That is, until the full impact of the Constructivists' theories and particularly the results in sculpture and architecture (especially in Russia) were familiar to the still young Breuer. The first Constructivists exhibition was held at Weimar in 1922. In the late 1920s he began fully realized explorations. For architectural theory, the following summary is explicit:

The separation of functions in any design-object, and the expression of the separation by visual and structural means ... *is a fundamental precept of Constructivism.*[4]

The first chrome-plate structured chair of 1925 was designed by Breuer and made the separate articulation between compression and tension or legs and seat, so to speak. In the 1920s he was primarily a furniture and interior designer and the projects and completed designs were in those areas. Few projects were architectural and of those, almost all were concerned with the construct proposition in its meanest sense by exposing structure or in many ways blatantly contriving to express the structure. The difference between Breuer and Le Corbusier was the difference between the end result for an object (Breuer) and the conceptual result desired for architecture (Le Corbusier).

The Bamboo houses of 1927 were box forms alternately sitting on stilts or on the ground. The stilts freed the upper box from the ground but this was the conceptual limit. With Le Corbusier the stilts ('pilotis') freed the ground, the plan, the skin and the roof to free the designer, enabling him to explore a full range of aesthetic potentialities: form consequences were not important in themselves. With Breuer the form consequences were inherent in the idea. This, of course, was a parcel of the Bauhaus. These fundamental explorations of form continued through Breuer's career when in the 1930s more of his practice became architectural. The difference between Breuer and Le Corbusier and Bauhaus white box concepts was a search for forms which would complement the box—stairs, a diagonal, for instance, or for large buildings a partial free form plan, or segment of an arch—forms clearly generated from an esoteric aesthetic impulse.

Like Gropius, Breuer left Germany in 1934. An invitation of F. R. S. Yorke provided the impetus. An important innovation was immediately employed during their partnership: stone. Stone for walls and not as a skin but full stone walls exposed on the exterior and interior—an attempt to humanize, to soften the International Style as it was proclaimed by Henry-Russel Hitchcock and Philip Johnson. The same conclusion was reached at the same moment by Alvar Aalto using his native Finnish wood and stone. Two differences between Aalto and most of those exploring the International Style were important. Breuer extended roof and ground planes beyond the interior. He defined and emphasized that implied extension with a vertical plane. The small Pavilion for the 1936 Royal Show at Bristol (by Yorke and Breuer) was the first fully mature statement recognizing this visual extension of space. It was a more obvious statement than those employed by Frank Lloyd Wright and the Chicago school thirty years earlier. The other difference was a search for extended inner space, especially in houses, yet maintenance of privacy. This search ended with a series of houses executed in the United States.

In 1936, Mies van der Rohe was invited to be Chairman of the Architecture Department at Harvard University. Sensing an old established university might impose limitations Mies refused. Some months later he accepted a similar position at the Amour Institute (now with the Illinois Institute of Technology).[5] Gropius was then approached and after deliberate consideration, accepted. He then initiated the Harvard Graduate School of Design (or

GSD). The Bauhaus system of education had to be surgically altered to fit the concept of the American university and the needs of a profession. At the old Bauhaus the student was introduced to crafts through new methodologies born in the essentials of the arts and crafts or Werkbund. Those who wished to become professionals had to continue at one of the technische Hochschule. Harvard and the American professional required a total educational experience and commitment to produce young, eager architects. The burden on Gropius was eased somewhat. The School of Design was placed in the graduate section of the University. Therefore Gropius did not have to concern himself with the idea of a general, liberal education as sought at Harvard College. He concentrated only on architecture and the architect. Many new teachers had to be encouraged or trained. Of course some of the old stalwarts accepted invitations to help begin anew. Among these was Breuer. He and Gropius immediately entered into a partnership while at the same time encouraging, stimulating and coercing the GSD into existence.

The houses of Gropius and Breuer during this pre-war period introduced to North America not only some of the initiators of the International Style[6] (admittedly under controversy before their arrival), but the idea of the Bauhaus, a system of art education that was well known in Central Europe, whereas the vast majority of American architects could proclaim absolute ignorance of the system. It was not just a matter of a lingering attitude of isolation for that majority, as much as a lack of providing an intellectual stimulus where attitudes would encourage notions such as the *avant-garde*. Yet, for Gropius and Breuer and others, those houses (and projects) must have appeared rather gross compromises to their work of only a few years before. Two are worth mentioning in the context of this essay. The first was the Gropius House, Lincoln, Massachusetts, of 1937-8 (Gropius and Breuer): a box with space flowing through and elements thrust out. The other was the precisely articulated Chamberlain Cottage, Weyland, Massachusetts, following by two years in 1940,[7] also by the two architects. The division of spaces related to structure and its expression, together with the sculptural effect of the fireplace dividing and anchoring the small spaces (dining, living and screened porch), had a profound effect on the profession when it was published. Its principals, as well as the Breuer house interiors and the collective judgements discussed above, were carried to full expression by Breuer after the war when a young Harry Seidler studied under and worked for the Hungarian immigrant.

If their paths failed to cross before Harvard, their cultures were similar and their journeys were nearly the same, if not for comparative reasons. Their careers as architects are inextricably woven one with the other.

Seidler attended a rigid, authoritarian 'humanist-classic gymnasium',[8] or high school, in the city of his birth, Vienna, Austria. In 1923 it was a city of Baroque and Rococo, of late nineteenth-century pastiche and, by the 1930s, the odd modern structure. It was also a city of style for Seidler's upper-middle-class family. The apartment in which the family lived was completely remodelled 'by an "avant garde" Viennese architect, Fritz Reichl', but such influences are of speculative value. When Seidler was fifteen, in 1938, the family moved to England. Seidler attended a building crafts course at Cambridgeshire Technical College from 1938 to 1940. Professor Duncan McAlister, of the Dublin University architecture school, often visited his sister, Lady McAlister, in whose home Seidler was living while attending school in Cambridge. It was through Professor McAlister's encouragement that Seidler seriously considered architecture. But before his studies could begin he was interned in May 1940 and after being shunted off to various camps in England and the Isle of Man he was sent to Canada. During internment a number of architects and students formed an informal architectural design group stimulated by lectures, imaginary design projects and the building of the camp's canteen. In October 1941 he was released to begin his studies.

Seidler entered the University of Manitoba in the city of Winnipeg in 1941 and received his Bachelor of Architecture with honours in 1944. For about a year he worked in Toronto and then, in 1945, he received a scholarship to attend the Harvard GSD.[9] Ideas, ideals, practical and visionary whirled before those students who first experienced the GSD—methodology, each problem a new problem, each problem a unique cultural/social context, the modulation of space by line and plane, abstraction as neutral, methods of detailing and construction, housing and prefabrication, structural integrity and expression—for those young, budding architects the atmosphere was electrifying. The year Seidler obtained his masters degree he was asked by Breuer, who left Harvard, to work in his office. Before going to New York he studied with Josef Albers at the experimental (and unfortunately short-lived) Black Mountain College. The college was a school in the southern state of North Carolina devoted to assimilating and reviving the arts, not dissimilar to the Bauhaus and with some of its former staff. But the emphasis was more on an aesthetic response primarily on visual aspects and not necessarily based on social need or study.

Gropius had suggested this to me and I feel now that I learnt more about basic design there than I ever did at an architectural school. Albers was, and still is, a great pedagogue. He really opened my eyes to perception—he made us understand just how our eyes react in predictable ways to visual phenomena. . . . He really made us break sterile habits and trained us in active visualisation—just as he did in the preliminary course he taught at the Bauhaus.[10]

It was a summer devoted a *re*study of the basic principles of design, a series of problems relieved of achitectonic impedimenta. For Seidler, it was a discovery of stimuli that he had not received in his early years of architectural training in Canada and had known only by the faintest suggestion while at GSD. Much of the preliminary study and experience usual at undergraduate level had to be assumed by the Gropius team at graduate level. Again, Gropius was right. The intellectual stimulation and the live-in situation at Black Mountain, fused with the methodology learned at Harvard, provided an essential basis for the reason of architecture. It only remained for Seidler to discover the means.

The first few years of Breuer's practice in New York were less than spectacular as far as obtaining jobs. But the few which came to the office provided the maturing Seidler with a knowledge of how to detail the most concise architectural statement in the simplest yet most effective manner.

The so-called 'H-house' of 1943[11] and the 'Bi-nuclear house' projects to follow were the object of continued study at Harvard. When Seidler went to Breuer's office he worked on the Robinson house, Williamstown, Massachusetts, completed in 1947.[12] The plan followed the bi-nuclear scheme: to the east were the public or entertaining spaces, to the west the private or sleeping spaces. The umbilical link contained the entry. Spaces were extended by plane and surface beyond the interior while forms were softened by natural materials of stone and wood. The Tompkins House, Newlett Harbor, Long Island of 1946[13] was tightly organized about a direct circulation from entry to stair leading to private areas on a second floor. The ground floor (almost entirely paved with stone) was modulated by a free-standing fireplace and book-shelves. The areas of study, living, dining and entry were thus defined only in a virtual and implied sense. A vigorous plan form surmounting an inelegant asymmetrically placed box characteriz-ed the Ariston Restaurant, Mar del Plata, Argentina of 1947 (with Coire and Catalano) and shows again that Breuer, no doubt encouraged in this instance by Catalano, was still willing to explore form within a reasonable context. While these buildings were of some persuasion it was Breuer's own house in New Canaan,

Connecticut of 1947 that displayed all the axioms and influences from his past connected to the traditions of New England—the flow of space internally (within) and to the exterior, bold cantilevers, and inferred structure, independently formed sun shades, a precisely articulated plan and a small box surmounted by a wooden box roofed by the most gentle (and obvious) of slopes. Seidler did the working drawings.

The experience of studying under Breuer and then seeing how his buildings came to fruition was the final encounter necessary to encourage Seidler to seek his own fortune. He had been with Breuer since 1945, both at GSD and since September 1946 in his office. The entreaties of his parents to join them in Australia where commissions were assured by their friends was an added impetus.[14] In March 1948 he left Breuer and as a kind of working holiday went to Rio de Janeiro and the office of Oscar Niemeyer. He stayed with Niemeyer, working on some housing for the aeronautical centre at Jose dos Campos, until August. He found that 'the flare and exuberance of Brazilian architecture appealed to me a lot' in those days but 'much less so the social conditions in the country'.[15]

He arrived at Sydney in September 1948. Between 1948 and 1952 Seidler completed ten buildings and designed a number of projects, some of which were eventually constructed. Without exception the completed buildings and some of the projects had a direct and immediate influence on Australian architecture without parallel. Some were recognized as superlative architecture without equivocation by the wider international audience. All owe their debt to Harvard and Breuer. Seidler did not see his role as prophet but in a more direct, causative way as a disciple. The twenty-five-year-old architect was not concerned with creating new ideals from which to offer new prophecies. He was totally and completely convinced in the appropriateness, in the correctness in a very moral sense, of what he had learned from his mentors. He distilled an essence from his learning and practical experience which was displayed in a series of buildings of simple plan and form—he applied the lesson of working with a 'limited palette'. Yet, there is a distinctive variety presented to the aficionado in the first series of 1949 to convince one that many ideas were released from paper architecture into a joyous revelation in reality.

The first house I built (for my parents) [**90** and **91**] caused quite a stir. It was very much part of the form vocabulary of the Eastern United States which centred in Cambridge, Massachusetts.[16]

This is a statement in retrospect by some twenty-five years, yet

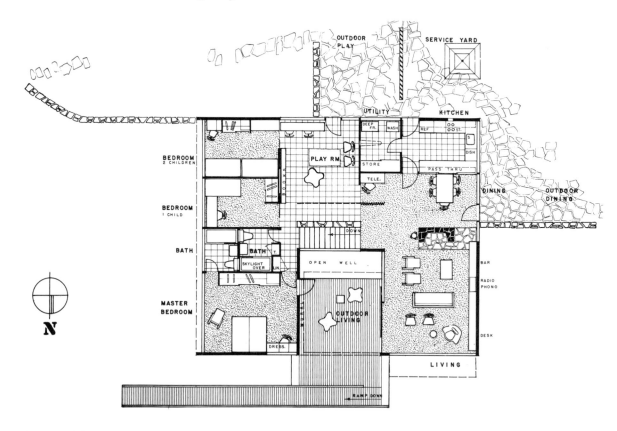

it was said without hesitation and with full awareness of the position he presented then as a disciple. But he was an evangelizing disciple. Others had experience with the Europeans. Ludwig Hirschfeld-Mack studied at the Bauhaus under Albers and Lyonel Feininger. During the 1930s he emigrated to Australia and taught for many years at the Geelong Grammar School.[17] He was primarily concerned with the two-dimensional visual arts. Sydney architect Arthur Baldwinson had worked with Maxwell Fry and Gropius in England. But only Seidler was educated in the system and worked for the architects.

His first completed design was a remodelling of an old waterfront basement apartment into an office: a small space simply divided by a bookcase into reception and work areas with basic white contrasted by bright primary colours, an all-glass front and direct geometric lines and forms. Although this small office portrayed with the utmost clarity the principles of progressive architecture at mid-century, his next two buildings establish the precedents for personal development and emulation.

Seidler has set out in his own words some of the basic principles which he found important to the development of his architecture

90 R. Seidler House, Turramurra, N.S.W. Harry Seidler, architect. 1947–50. (Courtesy the architect)

91 R. Seidler House, Turramurra, N.S.W. Harry Seidler,
architect. 1947–50. (Courtesy
the architect)

during this period in his book *Houses, Interiors and Projects*[18]
and there is no need to repeat them here. But there is a need to
analyse his buildings in a proper historical context.

During the mid- and late 1950s there was a significant reaction
to 'the box'. The simple prisms of the school engendered by Mies
van der Rohe were found wanting, sterile, and of uncompromising
severity. The idea that the whole should dominate the subordinat-
ing parts, that purpose and place should evoke an aesthetic
response, was attracting a reaction in and by the name of regionalism. American architect Paul Rudolph, writing in 1957 on 'Regionalism in Architecture', made two observations worth noting:
'Regionalism is one way toward that richness in architecture
which other movements have enjoyed and which is so lacking
today'.[19] That is, regionalism was one way; architecture lacked
something, and blandness may be one insufficiency. Exactly

92 L. Waks House, North-bridge, N.S.W. Harry Seidler, architect. 1949–50.

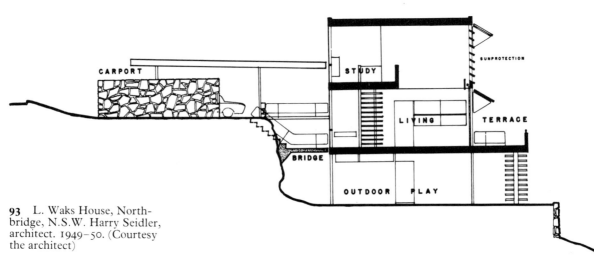

93 L. Waks House, North-bridge, N.S.W. Harry Seidler, architect. 1949–50. (Courtesy the architect)

94 L. Waks House, North-bridge, N.S.W. Harry Seidler, architect. 1949–50. (Courtesy the architect)

what the other movements enjoyed was not clear but one of the supporting arguments was in reference to Australia. The R. Seidler

house of Harry Seidler's jumped from Cambridge, Mass. (It might be described as the Harvard house incarnate ... pre-Sert) to Sydney, Australia, without any modifications whatsoever. It is difficult to believe that it would not have taken on a new significance if the principles which formed its prototypes were better understood.[20]

Rudolph's vantage point was of one who believed that his work in Florida did reflect its location. One can discover some indications of this belief manifest in his work of mid-century. What provoked the comment was the design of Seidler and R. D. Thompson

95 T. Meller House, Castlecrag, N.S.W. Harry Seidler, architect. 1949–53. (Courtesy the architect)

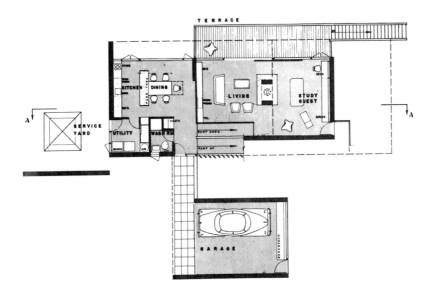

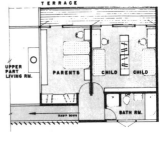

96 T. Meller House, Castlecrag, N.S.W. Harry Seidler, architect. 1949–53. (Courtesy the architect)

(who also worked for Breuer) of a house for a Foxborough, Massachusetts location designed in 1947.[21] The plan of the Foxborough house and the R. Seidler house were for all practical purposes identical. The elevational treatment was not identical but the change was of such a subtle difference as to be important only in this respect: there is a maturity gained in the Seidler house in proportion and plane inference as well as a nod to sun shade. What Rudolph's article ignored was the subtle difference in purpose for not only Seidler's design in 1947, but most assuredly Rudolph's own designs of the same period. The dominant overriding consideration of the designs in the era of the late 1940s was plane inference and space modulation of the cubic form. All the more delightful if one's empathy can be challenged by floating the cube above the earth and also introduce opposition of tactile surfaces and contrast by an incline of the ramp. While the reaction in North America was exemplified by Rudolph's comments there was, oddly enough, a reaction in Australia to Seidler's architecture. Australia too was employing the term regionalism as well as nationalism. It was not only a reaction but a search which ended in two brief years. But to fully understand that search it is necessary to complete our study of Seidler's limited but important series of architectural achievements.

The R. Seidler house of Turramurra, north of Sydney, was finally completed in 1950.[22] A plan revolving about a service or 'wet' core had two relatively blank walls to the sun and two opened to the view. The glass area had a very strong geometry and contrasted to solid planes. The basic compositional bulk described above sat easily on a gentle slope. The L. Waks house of Northbridge, also north of Sydney[23] was placed directly on a high rock ledge overlooking a harbour (**92, 93** and **94**). From a free carport one entered the house down a set of stairs leading to the entertaining level with bedrooms on the second level while the lowest floor was nearly fully open. The living room space rose the full two storeys. The flow of space was accentuated in wood panels, in the diagonal of an open stair and horizontally through the glass to the cantilevered deck. Again two solid walls were placed against not only the sun, but neighbours. A neat, tidy, fully comprehensible plan exploited the space within vertically as well as to the outlook. The architectural elevation to the view was a generalized restatement of Le Corbusier in the 1920s and more particularly of Breuer in the late 1920s and 1930s. The module of space implying structure in three equal bays was subtly offset at each level. Line, plane and texture were exploited with professional sophistication as if by formula.

Two other houses were designed in 1949. Both were the object of a great deal of controversy and both seemed to be as different from one another as the R. Seidler and Waks houses. The T. Meller house[24] was planned for a magnificent site in Castlecrag. The design was objected to, not only by the administration of the Greater Sydney Development Association, but also by the Willoughby Council. Seidler approached E. M. Nicholls, acting for the Association, to intervene. Nicholls suggested Seidler discuss in a letter the problem with Mrs Marion Griffin, but she referred it back to Nicholls.[25] The matter rested in a state of limbo until it was taken to court by Seidler, where it was resolved in his client's—in the design's—favour. Like Griffin and Sydney Ancher, Seidler had to resort to court decisions 'to have my house designs declared innocent',[26] as he very succinctly and correctly summarized.

The Meller house (**95** and **96**) was a composite of Gropius and Breuer, a manifestation of prevalent attitudes and in particular the growing interest in forms generated out of the inherent need of the internal configurations of space: forms other than rectilinear. The section displays (as does the interior experience) the fact that only one bedroom was enclosed. The kitchen, dining, living, entry, study, ramps, guest and parents' bedroom were all within a single, diagonally contrived space. It was an expression that received full attention on both the interior and exterior, both in form and detail. The building section read as if from a Breuer text of just a few years before. The plan/section were reverently referred to as the 'open plan' concept. The elevational treatment appeared as if in direct response to the needs of site and plan: view, sun, privacy; entry, terrace, service. The bedroom terrace floor line became part of the exterior wall and then the roof to create a flowing line highlighted against shadow and sky and glass for the view. The three other elevations were nearly enclosed with only minor fenestration carefully composed not to interfere with the full expanse of the wall. The roof sloped back to a point tensionally tight with the lower terrace/balcony handrail which was a line counter to the roof, which suddenly flaired away from the building. In all, it was a textbook example of earlier lessons, only marred by the bulk of the carport. With the interior a mirror image of the exterior in softer more natural materials, the house was a total conceptual realization.

The Rose house design in 1949 for a site in Turramurra and finally completed (unchanged) in 1954, predicted the constructional emphasis of the 1950s and established Seidler as one of the more important architectural designers at mid-century (**97** and **98**). Like most of Seidler's work during his first few years of practice, the Rose house[27] was small, only one bedroom with a small study/office. It may stretch the argument to suggest that the scheme was based on Breuer's own house with a double cantilever, but couple that house with Seidler's proposal for an apartment complex in Boston of 1946 and with the general investigations conducted at Harvard, and the precedents were established. Yet, the fresh design and exacting finish seems without paradigm, a *tour de force*. It is appropriate to examine the house by two observers. Seidler's own comments:

The structural system restricts all support to four columns only from which a cratework of steel beams is suspended by diagonal steel hangers. The infill is of timber for the upper levels and of brick below.

All structural elements are freely exposed and become a decorative feature in the general theme of complete suspension and visually negligible support. To offset the clearly suspended rectilinear building form, the diagonal lines of the suspension members find their counterpoint in both stair shapes. Plastic interest is added by these to the simple silhouette by the solid stair end on the 'void' Northern terrace glass side and the projecting stair form on the more solid South side.

The interior reflects the lightness of structure by merging completely with the outdoors, through two long sides entirely glazed in the living area.[28]

If one were to approach a criticism of the building from the standard view then prevalent of structural purity and expression, then the house has some disappointments: the diagonal suspension rods are lost, buried in the wooden handrail of the stair on the north side, as was the balcony handrail; the east and west elevations did not reflect the structural system except in the most subtle manner of turning the wood siding (which is not an infill) horizontally above the window head and below the sill (of course, the wood siding is on the second floor, which thrusts over and beyond its support); and the diagonal suspended supports are lost completely behind a screen of wood on part of the south elevation, yet they were revealed in the transparency of the glass; if the south elevation was the least successful, it also shows the lower spare room and utility room to be too large and intrusive into the space created by four columns raising the bulk of the house to supposedly free the space under (lateral support easily found elsewhere). These are criticisms which should not detract from the historical importance of the building, but should only emphasize prevalent attitudes of architectural design at the moment of its creation. And at that moment it wrote a new book. Others were to emulate the disciple who engaged in exacting statements. The consolidation of that position was accomplished by the completion of only

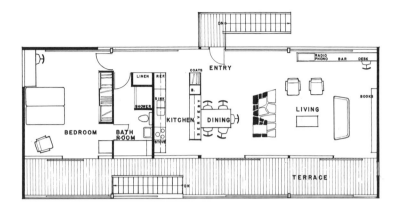

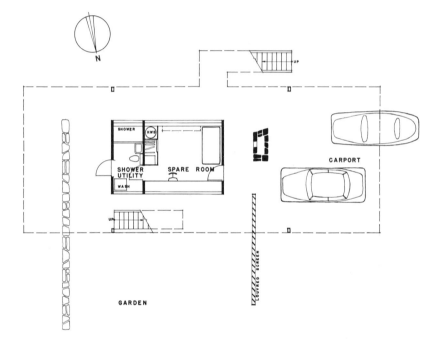

a few buildings in 1950–4, and their publication throughout the world.[29] We will discuss only those of 1950–1. These will be sufficient to make the case for the introduction to Australia of the new Post War architecture—and its acceptance.

The Dr S. Fink house of 1949–51 built in Newport, New South Wales,[30] was similar in plan and elevation to the R. Seidler house with the exception of a broken or 'butterfly' roof form. The same roof form was employed in 1950 on the Bowden house in Deakin, Canberra,[31] where the bedrooms and kitchen enclosed two sides of the entertaining area. The Lowe house also of 1950 for a wooded site in Mosman, N.S.W., was on a theme of a box on stilts.[32]

98 The Rose House, Turramurra, N.S.W. Harry Seidler, architect. 1949–54. (Courtesy the architect)

Two elements were of interest. First, the garage was part of the box and thrust its form into the interior of the house or box form, where it was close to servicing the kitchen. This garage form (and interlocking stair) was accentuated on the interior. The other element was the deep penetration of exterior space, diagonal stair and attendant terrace. This penetration almost touched the entry vestibule and at the same instant separated the entertaining and sleeping areas. The rationale of a functional plan can take subtle or explicitly overt architectonic form. This was sustained in a number of projects executed in 1951.

The Spears house at Beecroft was projected in 1951[33] with a plan of the R. Seidler theme but realized in a larger format in the Marcus Seidler house at Turramurra[34] in 1952. A more obvious debt to Breuer can be found in the bi-nuclear schemes for the Barnes house,[35] proposed for Lane Cove, New South Wales, where a carport was placed between the two nuclei, and the larger Rubensohn house proposed for Quirindi, N.S.W. in

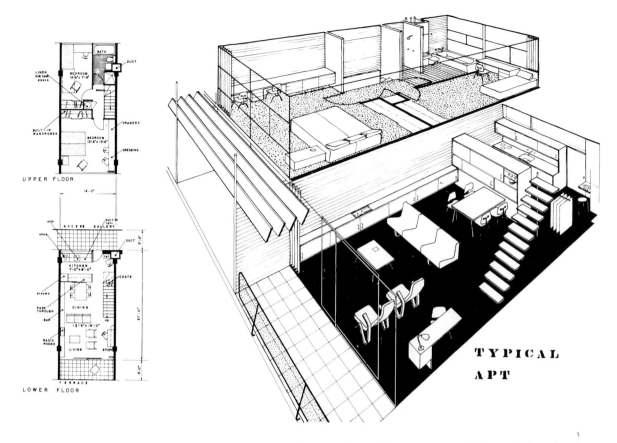

TYPICAL
APT

UPPER FLOOR

LOWER FLOOR

1951. This latter house had the roof form of Breuer's Robinson house of 1947.[36]

Apartment living was a long and strenuous study of both the Bauhaus and Harvard GSD. Gropius' investigations of the 1920s should be well known.[37] Seidler made his own apartment block proposal for a site in Boston in 1946 and worked with Niemeyer on housing (if ever so briefly). In 1950 and 1951 Seidler received commissions for apartments but none were fully realized. Two exploited the idea of skip-level entries, that is, entering an apartment on every other floor from a single-loaded exposed corridor and within the apartment a second level was gained by internal stairs to bath and bedrooms. The Ithaca Gardens Apartments of 1951 (**99**) were by far the superior in elevational treatment[38] with the whole raised on *pilotis à la* Le Corbusier in his initial Unite Habitation at Marseilles.[39] This raising of the bulk was also employed in the Glenvue Apartments for Bondi[40] but the *pilotis* were stubby and the forms on the roof contrived and without the free juxtaposition found on the Marseilles roof. The other apartment proposal was a Student Hostel for Sydney University.

99 Ithaca Gardens Apartments, *project*, Sydney. Harry Seidler, architect. 1951. (Courtesy the architect)

Of Seidler's projects in these early years, this would be the least successful: a hodge-podge collection of exposed structural elements, of materials, of oddly related forms—for the architect and historian, features in plan and basic form bearing a kinship to the Swiss Students' Hostel of Le Corbusier at University City, Paris of 1930. Yet what was the influence of the Sydney project on Le Corbusier and Lucia Costa for the Brazilian Students' Hostel at University City of 1959?[41] Were both Seidler and Le Corbusier persuaded by Breuer's garden house for the Museum of Modern Art in 1949?[42] The sloping roof form was distressingly similar in the later emulative works. The Sydney Hostel was not built. The proposal was very quickly absorbed into the tired politics of a middle-aged university and it withered in committee in camera.

The Royal Australian Institute of Architects has maintained a Small Homes Bureau in most of the major cities since the 1940s, an idea initiated by Robin Boyd in Melbourne. In 1951 Seidler's proposal for a basic three-bedroom house of under 1,000 square feet was essentially a square box made of two side-by-side rectangular boxes, one for sleeping and the other for, of course, entertaining. The square box was then able to accept a variety of orientations and positions for garages or carports and also courtyards. The project was eventually realized in nine Staff Houses for the Australian Oil Refinery at Kurnell, N. S. W., completed in 1955.[43] The plan was further extended in the Model House for the Architectural and Building Exhibition at the Town Hall in Sydney, 1954.[44] The inline plan could be altered by additions to a two, three or four bedroom house with or without garage. The entire house was built in a week of prefabricated components. The interior was composed of simple planes, exposed structure of steel bar joists and steel deck, wood component panels and a prefabricated fireplace and bathroom (**100** and **101**). Although somewhat outside the period under discussion, this small house was part-and-parcel of the earlier Rose house and exemplifies contemporary attitudes toward what was described as 'structural integrity', which more often than not meant exposing the structure. Charles Eames' own house in California, with components selected from catalogues in 1949 and this Exhibition House exemplify Western architecture at mid-century with the utmost clarity.

There remain only two houses to consider. Seidler's fleeting romance with forms introduced by Niemeyer and so haphazardly employed by Seidler in the Glenvue apartments and at the Sydney Hostel, met with a great deal more success in the Williamson house (**102** and **103**) in Mosman of 1950.[45] The reason was very

100 Exhibition Model House, Sydney. Harry Seidler, architect. 1954. (Courtesy the architect)

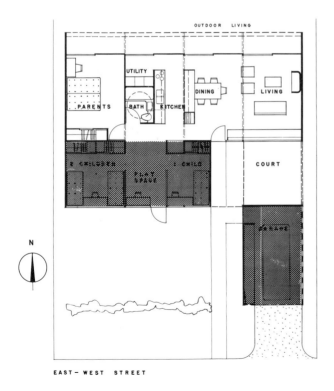

101 Exhibition Model House, Sydney. Harry Seidler, architect. 1954. (Courtesy the architect)

simple. The box form of the house resting on free columns was symbolic, if not real in a man-made sense, of the rocks on which the whole rested. The roof, therefore, was no less than another rock ledge on which the forms enclosing the garage and private sun terrace resided. The scheme was adopted with powerful simplicity, directly and uneffected. Seidler's own rationale of providing 'opposing shapes to the angularity of the rest of the building'[46] is not convincing: it is an arbitrary statement, ignoring the dynamics of the site. The plan places one bedroom to the exterior surface of the roof and terrace edge, where it acted as an arbiter between public and private. The sun, the view and neighbourly privacy commanded full aesthetic response. While the Willamson house evolved directly from the site, the Sussman house was a pure academic exercise. Obviously a predecessor of the Exhibition House, the Sussman house at Kurrajong Heights, N.S.W., was designed in 1950 and completed in 1951 (**104** and **105**). It is the essential Seidler:[47] two enclosing walls, large expanses of glass in public areas, small windows set into wood or stucco planes, boldly cantilevered terrace off entertaining area, exposed constructional pieces, neat little eyebrows for sun protection, high windows to the street, planes extended not only at floor level but the ceiling/roof through the carport/entry canopy, a wood and glass box perched on a stone base of small mass, bedroom cantilevered and a gentle (but obvious) slope to the roof. It sounds so familiar, yet Breuer would not, perhaps could not, design a house to such an aesthetic: reducibly severed to the most essential, effectual statement, yet full of complement and contrast and interest and finesse—a superb schooled piece of work.

That word finesse suggests what is probably the most important aspect of Seidler's architecture; or perhaps sophistication or perhaps, as critic Peter Blake has said, an architecture of flawless taste.[48] The fact remains that in the idioms of his limited palette and within the circumscribed influences which he carefully nurtured, he was a better architect than most of his contemporaries at Boston or Manitoba or London or Melbourne. With the exception of faltering attempts when developing the peculiar apartment buildings, Seidler's architecture at mid-century, although it appeared diverse was in fact constrained by the knowledge of his capabilities. And it must be added that those capabilities have expanded with responsible experience as followers of Seidler will attest. But at mid-century, and to reiterate, Seidler saw his role most clearly: 'The pioneering days of modern architecture are over. We are now in a period of consolidation and development.'[49]

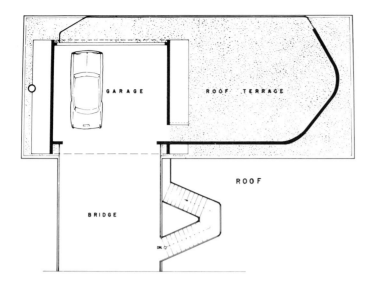

102 Williamson House, Mosman, N.S.W. Harry Seidler, architect. 1950. (Courtesy the architect)

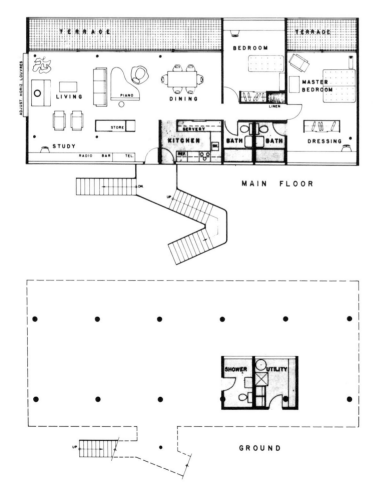

103 Williamson House, Mosman, N.S.W. Harry Seidler, architect. 1950. (Courtesy the architect)

In 1952 Seidler won the Sir John Sulman Medal and Diploma for his R. Seidler House. The period under consideration by the jury was the three years ending in December 1951. The acknowledgement contained not only the profession's nod but, and most importantly, a nod to an acceptance of the ideas and forms of another modern architecture. It must be clear that the award in the past was often a compromise. This was not the case in 1952. The triumph should have been a mandate for modern architecture to stand at least side-by-side with traditional architecture, but there was some hesitancy.

By 1951 or 1952 the tremors of reaction to the now modified International Style were such as to be full arguments. Under the guise of regionalism and in fact many other titles or 'isms', the issue architecturally was how should the accepted functional building *appear*. All schools of thought conceded that for the mere survival of the art and profession of architecture, buildings must work, must have rationally organized plans, walls responding

195

to needs of light, fenestration, etc. But what was not conceded was the expression, one might say, of the architectural entity. The titular head of the more romantic trends or styles was, of course, Frank Lloyd Wright. There were many who seemed to rise only momentarily to be mentor of the Internationalists, yet always the debt was to Le Corbusier, Gropius or Mies van der Rohe.

Robin Boyd exemplified the search for true expression when he pieced together an argument that both sides were more similar than not and that semantics may have been the problem.

The difficulty, of course, is to define the difference and to find suitable sub-classifications for each building. One undoubtedly, is Organic; but it could be also ... Regionalistic, Empirical, Humanistic, Romantic, Irrational or merely Cottage Style. The other is, of course, Functional; but some may prefer Rational, Geometric, Post Cubist, Mechanistic or merely International Style.[50]

The difficulty was, of course, that Organic was Wright's term for Functional back in 1908, that Irrational may not be the antonym of Rational, that Regionalistic is not like Empirical (in a prose series or otherwise) and one could go on. But the difficulty of nomenclature did not originate with Boyd. If he did not effectively argue for a more rational (if the word can now be used in a proper reference) set of definitions or classifications he at least avoided further complications by using *A* and *B*. He was highlighting the issues in 1950–1 by presenting two Australian houses to an international audience in the London architectural magazine *Architectural Review*. The houses were by Seidler (*B*) and Roy Grounds (*A*).

A basks beneath a clear sky in the porous shade of a great blue eucalypt.
B has little time for its environment.
A may be more Organic, Regionalistic and even Empirical than *B*, but is it more Romantic or less Rational?
The living-room floor and gravelled outdoors are level in *A*; but *B* is on stilts, the better to watch a view.

Finally Boyd reasoned that 'the terms become meaningless'. He urged one interpretation 'which always holds: *A* is bound to nature; *B* is divorced from nature'. Yet further along he found this not entirely satisfactory. If his arguments lacked a sense of structural cohesion, his final dismissal of similarities and semantics resolved the issue.

Here are two buildings of strong character, each confident and valid according to its lights, at opposite ends [we now observe] of a regrettably nameless scale of architectural quality. It seems probable that

Opposite:
104 Sussman House, Kurrajong Heights, N.S.W. Harry Seidler, architect. 1950–1. (Courtesy the architect)

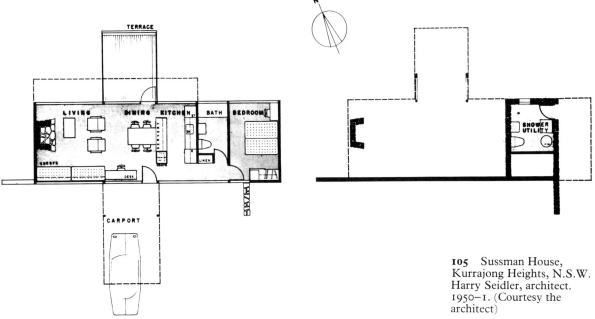

105 Sussman House, Kurrajong Heights, N.S.W. Harry Seidler, architect. 1950–1. (Courtesy the architect)

this scale will be destroyed in a natural leavening to the average. . . .

Might not an architect select, in a new era of vital eclecticism, the mood best suited to the time, the place and the purpose?[51]

Who to copy? Was this the issue? It was certainly one issue to consider. Or was the issue more isolated? In England, in another journal, the observation of events in Australia was directed to the international discussion:

Bearing in mind this prevalent desire for the evolution of a national style, one is tempted to ask what type of building now receives official blessing. Such a building is . . . a house in Turramurra, New South Wales, designed by Harry Seidler, who . . . has just won the John Sulman medal, one of Australia's most important architectural prizes. Is it typical of Australia's idea of a 'truly national architecture'? It is unlikely that even architects 'down under' could answer that question yet. It will be interesting to see whether something really indigenous grows up as a result of shortage of materials in a country which has always had to build quicker than it thinks.[52]

Admittedly it was a rather snobbish criticism. But it exemplified both England's attitude and the architectural debate. Also, it was a criticism the profession was willing to level against itself particularly just after the war. Seidler showed in explicit terms that good design was the result of working within given means: materials were innocent of vulgarity or virtue.

Part of the problem of the Australian, both the professional architect and others, was a view that Seidler was a rather myopic eclectic. We have seen that he was a student.

Part of the problem of the Australian, both the professional architect and others, was a fear of lost identity. Seidler arrived at a moment in Australia's history when an attitude and position of nationalism seemed threatened by an obvious dependency on other nations and an involvement in another war on other shores. In architecture, a search for a so-called national style had been without reward since 1901, except momentarily in the 1920s, but that is arguable if we disregard Griffin's domestic work. The seeds of affluence were only suggested as following World War II. Materials and equipment were extremely difficult to get on antipodean shores (even in the early 1950s). Architects searched for a style which would evoke a national identity when that affluence did in fact arrive. The underlying arguments were not directed wholly or even in large measure to the more inter-national issue of architectural style containing a moral base. They were directed to encouraging, to supporting an Australian architecture for Australians. They were, therefore, part of the worldwide issue whether by intent or otherwise. Seidler's

106 Stanhill, Melbourne, Victoria. F. Romberg, architect. (1942) 1948–50. (Photograph courtesy W. Seivers)

architecture was uncompromising. It was exact, precise, finely cut and expertly detailed. The appearance was white, cubic, geometric. It was homeless. Yet, Seidler argued that his architecture was not only a total response to Australia but in complete sympathy, that it was an architecture created out of the needs of Australians (society) and for a site (environment), that it was logical (rational) in its approach, therefore it must be suitable. Logical, perhaps, but it did not look logical. It looked different, not Australian. It looked very much like North American and European models that were being published in overseas and occasionally in Australian journals. The word 'occasionally' is used because the outward appearance of the building (or published excerpts) often looked deceptively like the modern genre, especially the massing characteristics of W. Dudok in the 1930s. The internal organism—the plan—belied traditional thinking. And this led to a further problem for Seidler's acceptance. Many architects had, and many were, engaged in designing in a similar vein to

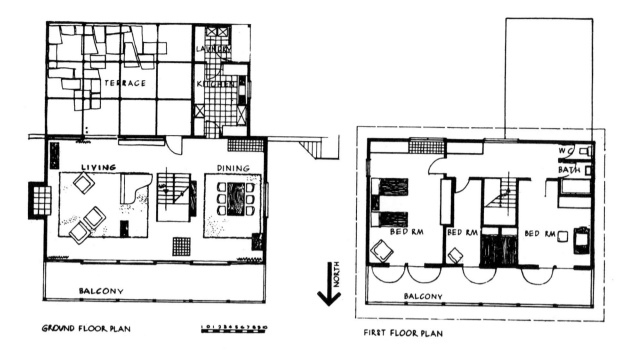

GROUND FLOOR PLAN   FIRST FLOOR PLAN

that of Seidler. Obviously, the need was for some form of arbitration, not in determination of which style should be most acceptable, *A* or *B*, but that the disciple's architecture might *also* be acceptable. The Sulman Award did just that.

The Sir John Sulman Medal Award is for New South Wales buildings only. Over the years it gained a reputation for sound judgement through its selections, although in retrospect they appear to be judgements for compromise. There were five categories: 1) public and monumental, 2) educational and ecclesiastical, 3) commercial and industrial, 4) recreational, 5) domestic and residential.[53] The categories rotate each year and the category in 1951 was 5. Beginning with 1934 it was the fifth time the category was to be considered. The jury for that category was composed of four architects, A. E. Stafford, J. C. Fowell, N. A. Ashton, G. H. B. McDonell (who won the domestic award in 1940), as well as the Director of the New South Wales National Art Gallery, Mr Hal Missingham, the painter William Dobell and the sculptor, G. F. Lewers. In making the award to Seidler this group must have known it would provoke controversy, or rather more controversy.[54] The Sulman Award also acknowledged that by accepting a style of architecture (and it would have then been recognized as a style) which had its origins elsewhere and which was international in every sense of the word, that architecture could be whatever the architects might wish. Australian

107 'Iluka' House, Mornington, Victoria. Roy Grounds, architect, in association with Mussen, MacKay, Mirams and Potter. 1950.

108 'Iluka' House, Mornington, Victoria. Roy Grounds, architect, in association with Mussen, MacKay, Mirams and Potter. 1950. (Courtesy the architect)

architecture matured by transcending parochial attitudes and accepting a position in the international community. Perhaps it might be distasteful to consider, but implied was the acceptance of a position where a willingness to compete in and with international standards was required.

Some of the early pioneers in the faltering, unsure years prior to 1940 continued to design in modern idioms but with an obvious expansive freedom. If the 1930s were characterized by a certain temerity, then the post-war decade was one of experimentation. Even the now older pioneers were enthralled by the liberation. The robust, masculine and chunky massing of the 'Stanhill' apartment building in Melbourne of 1948 by Frederick Romberg

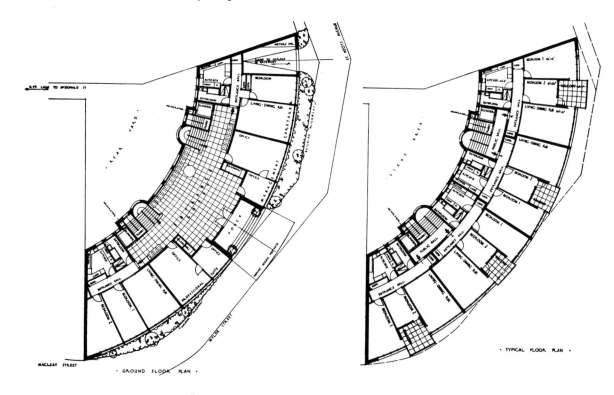

· GROUND FLOOR PLAN ·

· TYPICAL FLOOR PLAN ·

(106) was reminiscent in many aspects of the 1930s, particularly his Newburn flats of 1939, yet Stanhill received attention overseas in the California publication *Architect and Engineer*.[55] Romberg's Hillstan Flats at Brighton, Victoria of 1950 were much more restrained and more in keeping with the brick genre developed by Roy Grounds and others in the Melbourne area. The site plan was notable for a deep set back and extensive open ground space about the similar units. Yet, both flat buildings were contrasted by the discreet, rather delicately contrived geometry of an equilateral triangle plan of Roy Grounds in a house for a professional couple, overlooking Port Phillip, or his sophisticated Iluka residence at Beleura Hill, Mornington, Victoria.[56] Iluka had a completely open ground floor with a kitchen as nearly a separate building. A stair divided living and dining in a unified single space. With a terrace to the rear and balconies full width, it was an excellent house (107 and 108). Arthur Baldwinson's small house for D. Wilkinson at Church Point near Sydney was contrasted with the power of horizontality in the north elevation and the strong verticals of the south elevation of the Nurses' Home for the Heatherton Sanatorium, Victoria. Hospitals continued to receive a modern aesthetic for modern needs—in a very real sense, client-generated. The Sulman Award in 1950 in the Commercial and Industrial

109 Urban Co-operative Multi-Home Units, Potts Point, Sydney. A. M. Bolot, architect. 1948-50.

110 Urban Co-operative Multi-Home Units, Potts Point, Sydney. A. M. Bolot, architect. 1948–50. (Courtesy the architect)

Class (ending in December of that year) went to Top Dog Men's Wear Production Centre, located at Dee Why, by the architects Spencer, Spencer and Blomfield. The gentle massing first used by Dudok and the Scandinavians continued to sway and influence design and here it was employed with care.

In 1949 at St Ives, New South Wales, overlooking the Pymble golf links, Sydney Ancher completed a finely organized and carefully detailed house which fulfilled the promise of his proposals of the late 1930s. It is almost a textbook example of post-war California modern. Basking in the light, warmth and humidity of Mackay, Queensland, was the new Nurses' Quarters by the architects Prangley and Crofts: precisely modulated bays identifying living cubicles, each of which opened to ground or balcony with a full sliding glass wall. If borrowing from the balcony schemes of Stephenson in the 1930s and especially his Darwin Hotel, the reasons in the Mackay building seem to have had stronger logic, if only climate was considered. The alternating large and small structural supports provided subtle secondary rhythms, broken only in the hesitancy of an open dining space where the smaller members do not continue to ground level. Arthur Baldwinson designed a small studio/house at Clareville, New South Wales, for Elaine Haxton, which perched on the side of a hill, turned itself to view and away from the sun and which was a fine architectural statement and one of Baldwinson's finest works.

Some architects were new to the belatedly new ideas. Architect A. M. Bolot designed a series of flats at Potts Point, Sydney in 1948 (**109** and **110**) which were in the tradition of Yule House and of Eric Mendolsohn in his department stores for the German firm Shocken in the late 1920s. Bolot's flats were the first 'tenant-ownership' for high-rise flats in Sydney.[57] Restricted by a difficult triangular site, Bolot's solution was a direct response. Each of nine floors had four two-bedroom flats with one-bedroom flats at entry level and parking below. The sweeping lines of glass and spandrel, accentuated by exposed columns and deep balcony recesses, relieved the surface, yet emphasized the vertical against the stronger horizontal. It was a significant moment in the development of a high-rise aesthetic matched only by Seidler's proposals. In 1949–50, Douglas Snelling designed a house for Newport, New South Wales, looking like Southern California modern, in particular the Gordon Drake modular designs and some Frank Lloyd Wright influence, especially in the flow of the plan. Snelling studied under Wright[58] but he was not, if this design was an indication, wholly converted to the Wrightian forms of the 1940s. A design blend was skilfully developed in the Newport house.

The established School of Architecture at Sydney University and the new school at Melbourne were at full swing and the staff and students were enthusiastic.[59] The course at the University of Queensland was just beginning under R. P. Cummings. The various institutes continued to train architects but their influence began to wane before the more prestigious degree courses. A contemporary reflected on the enthusiasm of the time: 'It was the European revolution happening all over again, a generation later. What sensations. What excitement. What inexperience!'[60]

One could go on selecting buildings and projects at mid-century which reflect a growing awareness of trends, but that is not the purpose of this book. We have been concerned with identifying the consummation of a process that was part of Australia's history: the migration of ideas on the art of architecture and their adoption in the Australian environment. The selections above should be sufficient to indicate an interest in contemporary ideas, in the stabilization of not only trends begun in the 1920s and 1930s, but of the people—of the architects who attempted to sway a resisting lay group. That lay group, even before the flush of prosperity in the late 1950s was willing to invest thought and engagement in a contemporary society. In many ways Griffin, Romberg and Seidler exemplified not only Australian history (in fact the experience of most people during the decades just prior to mid-century), not only the Australian dream of success in a free society that acknowledges enterprise and initiative, but more particularly, they exemplified the architect.

The arts were perhaps slow to respond to external influences and especially concomitant intellectual forces in the initial stages of development in this century. Painting, dance, theatre, sculpture in particular, and architecture were all imbued with parochial, insular rigidity. The art of architecture became Australian by the mature act of accepting any form or style without prejudice. If, in the future, we wish a national architecture, it will evolve with ease and grace out of such an open commitment. Let us pray it will not continue to be an architecture belonging to the market place.

NOTES TO CHAPTER FIVE

1. George Nelson (ed.), *Living Spaces*, New York 1952, p. 4.
2. The best reference on the life and work of Breuer before 1948 is Peter Blake, *Marcel Breuer. Architect and Designer*, New York 1949.
3. Gilbert Herbert, *The Synthetic Vision of Walter Gropius*, Johannesburg 1959, p. 3, a book favoured by Gropius (see American Association of Architectural Bibliographers, *Papers*, 3 (1966), p. 47n.), and described by Gropius as 'the essence of my thinking and doing' (Herbert, p. vii).
4. Blake, *Marcel Breuer*, p. 16, Blake's emphasis.
5. Interview with Mies, 1966.
6. The author is aware of the problem of exclusion and its inference. The

discussion is about one aspect of 1930s architecture as it related to future events.

7. S. Giedion, *Walter Gropius. Work and Teamwork*, Zurich 1954, p. 186.
8. Interview, 1973.
9. Some of the other graduate students at Harvard with Seidler were I. M. Pei, Paul Rudolph, Ulrich Franzen, Henry Cobb, Don Olsen and John Parkin (interview, 1973).
10. Interview, 1973.
11. Blake, *Marcel Breuer*, p. 86.
12. Ibid., p. 91.
13. Ibid., pp. 96–7. Interiors of Breuer and Seidler are illustrated in Nelson, *Living Spaces*.
14. Seidler's parents arrived in Australia in 1946.
15. Interview, 1973.
16. Ibid.
17. 'Hirschfeld Mack', National Gallery Society of Victoria, *Bulletin* (A), (October 1974), pp. 5–7, and cf. L. Hirschfeld-Mack, *The Bauhaus*, Melbourne 1963.
18. Harry Seidler, *Houses, Interiors and Projects*, Sydney 1954 (reprinted 1959), where all of the houses under discussion are found without owners' names. See also, Harry Seidler, 'Painting Toward Architecture', *Architecture* (A), 37 (October 1949), pp. 119–24.
19. Paul Rudolph, 'Regionalism in Architecture', *Perspecta. The Yale Architectural Journal* (US), (4, 1957), p. 13. Also, illustrated were two Miesian-type buildings which were built for different purposes and different locations.
20. Ibid. Perhaps Rudolph's attitude would have been tempered by a recollection of all of his GSD colleagues, such as the review of the clan, so to speak, in *Architectural Forum* in June 1951 where the work of Twitchell, Rudolph, Scully (a Yale man!), Franzen, Barnes, Warnecke, and Kennedy was given full display. It reveals some similarities one to the other as well as some differences.
21. 'House in Foxborough, Massachusetts', *Royal Architectural Institute of Canada Journal*, 25 (April 1948), pp. 117–19, and 'Project', *Arts and Architecture* (US), 64 (January 1948), pp. 32–3. The house was obviously designed prior to 1948.
22. The R. Seidler house was widely published after winning the Sulman Award, nationally and internationally.
23. See also, Peter Barttlelot, 'Living Gracefully on the Rocks', *Australian Home Beautiful*, 28 (August 1949), pp. 26–7, 44, and 'Suburban House in Sydney Australia', *Arts and Architecture* (US), 68 (November 1951), p. 28.
24. See also, 'Proposed House in Australia . . .', *Arts and Architecture* (US), 67 (May 1950), pp. 26–7, and 'House at Sydney', *The Architectural Review* (B), 115 (May 1954), pp. 317–21.
25. Interview, 1973.
26. 'Harry Seidler', *Art and Australia*, 9 (June 1971), p. 34.
27. See also, John Wentworth, 'Designed to Cost Less', *Australian Home Beautiful*, 29 (March 1950), pp. 18, 74.
28. Seidler, *Houses*, p. 70.
29. The list is too extensive to note here. The articles mentioned in these notes for each house or building are usually only suggestions.
30. 'House Near Sydney', *The Architectural Review* (B), 112 (November 1952), pp. 337–8.
31. Not widely published, see Seidler, *Houses*, p. 52.
32. Not widely published, ibid., pp. 112–18.
33. Ibid., p. 27.
34. Ibid., pp. 129–30.

35. See also, John Wentworth, 'House on Two Levels', *Australian Home Beautiful*, 29 (May 1950), pp. 38–9.
36. Seidler, *Houses*, pp. 100–2, and Blake, *Marcel Breuer*, p. 91.
37. Giedion, *Walter Gropius*, pp. 79–83 and illustrations.
38. Seidler, *Houses*, pp. 135–7.
39. The word 'pilotis' is a Le Corbusier word for the exposed compressive structural elements, or legs, on which the bulk of a building sits.
40. Construction on the apartment block was begun but not completed by Seidler.
41. The Paris hostel was commissioned in 1952, begun in 1957 and completed in 1959.
42. Widely published when complete, Blake, *Marcel Breuer*, pp. 110–15.
43. See 'Staff Houses by Harry Seidler', *Architecture and Arts* (A), 29 (April 1956), pp. 23–5, and Harry Seidler, *Harry Seidler, 1955/63*, Sydney 1963, pp. 84–7.
44. See also, 'Model House—Harry Seidler', *Arts and Architecture* (US), 72 (May 1955), pp. 18–19.
45. Seidler, *Houses*, pp. 82–3.
46. Ibid., p. 82.
47. See also, 'Casa per Weekend in Australia', *Domus* (Italy), 228 (November 1953), p. 16, and 'Two Small Houses in Australia', *Arts and Architecture* (US), 70 (February 1953), pp. 21–2. The similarity with Breuer's Cape Cod Cottage project of 1945 must be noted (Blake, *Marcel Breuer*, p. 100).
48. Peter Blake, *Architecture for the New World. The Work of Harry Seidler*, Sydney 1973, p. 9.
49. Seidler, *Houses*, p. ix.
50. Robin Boyd, 'A New Electicism?', *The Architectural Review* (B), 110 (September 1951), p. 151. Cf. 'House ... ', *The Architectural Review* (B), 110 (November 1951), pp. 306–9.
51. Boyd, 'A New Eclecticism', pp. 151–2. The problem sorting the cross currents of theory during this period is very complex. The essay herein is meant to simplify but not, it is believed, to the point of oversimplification. The rise of a new rationalism countered both the Wrightian and Miesian modes and this can be best exemplified not only by the books published about sun, wind and rain as design determinants, but by some provocative articles in journals and three are suggested. First is Victor G. Olgyay, 'The Temperate House', *Architectural Forum* (US), 94 (March 1951), pp. 8off. Olgyay was a Hungarian emigrant. 'Testing Design ... ', *Architectural Forum* (US), 94 (May 1951), pp. 170–8, and 'House Design Competition ... ', *Architectural Forum* (US), 94 (March 1951), pp. 93ff. The *Forum* seems to have supported the rationalists' view.
52. 'National Architecture?', *The Architects' Journal* (B), 116 (September 1952), p. 274.
53. 'Sulman Medal Award to "Ultra-modern" Type House', *Construction* (A), (6 August 1952), p. 6. There are many articles discussing the award, but this is recommended for its completeness and brevity.
54. One of the more sensitive responses was by Dr Karl Langer in 'Contemporary Renaissance', *Architecture* (A), 41 (October/December 1953), pp. 100, 105.
55. John Loughlin, 'Ultra Modern Australian Apartment Building', *Architect and Engineer* (US), 188 (February 1952), pp. 10–14. See also 'Newburn Flats in South Melbourne', *Art in Australia* (A), 1 (March 1941), pp. 73–4.
56. Associated architects were Mussen, MacKay, Mirams and Potter.
57. 'Co-operative Home Apartments', *Building and Engineering* (A), 84 (May 1948), p. 19. The building was completed in 1950.
58. John Wentworth, 'Less Housework—Better Views', *Australian Home Beautiful* (A), 29 (February 1950), pp. 36–7, 49.

59. Hilary Lewis, 'Planning with Models', *Australian Home Beautiful* (A), 29 (March 1950), pp. 22–5, displays a series of residential designs, and more particularly, Robin Boyd, 'Modern Home Exhibition Melbourne', *Architecture* (A), 38 (January 1950), pp. 18–28. See also, 'Students' Designs . . . ', *Architecture* (A), 39 (October-December 1951), pp. 114–17.
60. Robin Boyd, 'The State of Australian Architecture', *Architecture in Australia* (A), 56 (June 1967), p. 459, and for visual information see Boyd, 'Modern Home Exhibition'.

Epilogue: The Sydney Opera House

Comparison of people's acts is always difficult, especially when time intervenes. Yet, one is tempted. . . .

Seidler was quite different from Griffin in all aspects except two—both believed in the supremacy of the individual to respond to design and to create architecture, and both were foreign born and trained. The designer of the Sydney Opera House, Jørn Utzon, combined many of the traits and ideals of his two predecessors. Like Griffin (who was an expatriate), Utzon was also invited to the antipodean continent. He was foreign trained, very much an individual and totally and completely devoted to the profession of architecture as well as the art. Griffin was totally involved with the art and less with the profession. Yet, parallels exist between the two men. They both won international competitions. They both were welcomed with open arms, they were both encouraged to continue with their ideas, they were both met with hostility and harassment by politicians and their bureaucrats (the people who invited the architects), they were both the object of disquiet and jealousy by fellow professionals, they both went overseas for assistance and after approximately the same period of time both were relieved (in one way or another) of their jobs. Bureaucrats replaced them. Griffin stayed in Australia and Utzon, the wiser, returned to his native Denmark.

The Canberra plan was a very stable, reasonable document and not the object of controversy except in detail. The Opera House was from its announcement the object of a great deal of controversy yet the New South Wales government, the sponsor through its gambling receipts, was willing to see the design through to completion, if modified. The Federal government was also willing to see Griffin's plan through. But neither agency was willing to continue with the people who created those important moments and monuments in Australian history. Between 1901 and 1961, no two acts had more impact on the intellectual, artistic, and aspects of the political life of this country and certainly no two acts have received more attention outside this country. During those sixty years the *only* Australian architects to receive international attention were Griffin, Seidler and Utzon. Stephenson was received only in England while Robin Boyd was recognized for his critical writing. Is it a peculiar twist of fate that there are so many comparisons between Griffin and Utzon or is it that they were both working for the same people? Or, did Seidler's professional independence free him of the trials and tribulations brought to bear on the other two men? Was he therefore outside the causes?

The Opera House as a piece of architecture was, in 1957, part of the international reaction to the box or International Style architecture of the 1950s which we noted in Chapter 5. Utzon's initial design was very vague in its structural means. The platform and the canopies were organized about a rather simple (if physically difficult) circulation scheme on an impossible (if dramatically beautiful) site. But other than to tentatively compare the artists and to suggest a place for the building in an historical context, there would be a loss of objectivity to attempt to delve deeply into the situation. The construction, societal reactions and political ramifications have been discussed elsewhere (see Bibliography) with an obvious lack of perspective if with verve and passion.

Those who lived through the 1950s remember: the architect continued to absorb European and North American influences, continued to travel, in particular to Italy (for the hill towns), to Scandinavia (for excellent commercial design and gentle architecture), to Great Britain (more or less home) and to the U.S.A. And he continued to demand practical means, not theoretical inspiration. He was a modern eclectic.

Select Bibliography

The bibliography is divided into two parts: one, those publications contemporary with 1901–51, and the other, histories and evaluations of the period since 1951. Within those two parts are three further subdivisions: first, sources of information issued from Australia, second, sources published in Britain and North America, and third, sources published in Europe. The works mentioned are probably not found in architectural surveys of the past twenty years for they tended, and only tended, to be chronicles rather than histories: and the books and articles they mention are rather well known to most readers so are not repeated herein.

There are two bibliographies of any assistance; only one includes the 1901–51 period and it is not a true bibliographic work. David Saunders has produced 'An Author-List of Those Works on Architecture With a Bearing on Domestic Buildings Published in the Nineteenth Century . . . ' (typescript, Sydney 1969) which contains some information on aspects of domestic architecture around the turn of the century. The type of information varies dramatically and most entries lack a place of publication. My own 'Australian Architectural Histories, 1848–1968' (*Journal of the Society of Architectural Historians*, 31, December 1972, pp. 323–32) is about historical studies but because of the scarcity of such work it includes other helpful material. Maureen Fallon and I have collaborated on '18th and 19th Century Architecture Books and Serials in South Australia: a Bibliography and Research Guide', which we hope will be published by the Libraries Board of South Australia. Also, my *Canberra and Walter Burley Griffin. A bibliography of 1876 to 1976 and a guide to published sources* is to be published by Oxford University Press, 1980. There is an obvious and serious lack of bibliographic work on the subject of twentieth-century architecture in Australia.

Books or monographs of a general nature concerned with the period are few and even fewer are useful or reliable enough to recommend. Robin Boyd's *Victorian Modern* of 1947 is short but of value on certain Melbourne architects. His study of *Australia's Home* (1952) includes the first survey of domestic architecture of this or the past century. In some respects it amplifies his very useful 1947 book. J. M. Freeland in *Architecture in Australia: a History*, first published in 1968, presents the first survey of Australian architecture between boards and includes a portion on the present century. His study of some of the architectonic techniques of the art—materials, manufactures, sizes, etc.—is very helpful up to about 1930. To emphasize a point, none of the above books contain useful notes or bibliographies.

A very significant number of the books mentioned in this bibliography were located in the State Library of Victoria on Swanston Street in Melbourne. The library's collection of late nineteenth-century architecture books is exemplary and raises an interesting question about the relationship between this collection and the obvious fact that Melbourne's architecture of the same period was strides ahead and shoulders above the architecture of other urban centres in Australia. It might be suggested that the books provided a source of design information but this must not be the case. Surely the desire for the books is part of the unique cultural milieu which would invoke a general attitude about the arts and include good architecture and fine books.

While the discussion in the essays in this book was on development in Australia as a whole, the author admits to a deficiency in relation to Western Australia, Queensland and to some extent, South Australia, and especially the urban centres of Perth and Brisbane. There are two reasons for this unhappy circumstance. First, the role of those states (perhaps less true of Queensland domestic) in relation to the rest of Australia appears to parallel in a micro-condition the role of Australia to the rest of the Western world. Second, there is virtually no information available on twentieth-century architecture in those states. The information which has come to light more often than not confirms the first point: those states tended to follow the example of the cultural, economic and political centres of Sydney and Melbourne. Perhaps the lamentable lack of information will be corrected in the near future and the suggested theories of an imitative role and of an architecture of conformity will prove to be incorrect.

Sources of information related to each chapter and to specific architects are contained in the notes. The following is a selected bibliography of monographs, some theses and articles which are generally in addition to the chapter notes.

CONTEMPORARY 1901–51

Australia

Adams, John R. P. (comp.), *Distinctive Australian Homes*, Sydney 1925.

Australia, Ministry of National Development, *Australian Housing*, Bulletins of the Housing Division. Those of the late 1940s and early 1950s are pertinent.

[Allen, G. P. (ed.)], 'Historical Sketch of The Society of Arts & Crafts of N.S.W.', typed and machine copied, Sydney, August 1931. The Society started in 1906.

Baker, R. T., *Building and Ornamental Stones of Australia*, Sydney 1915.

Beiers, George, *Houses of Australia*, Sydney 1948.

Boyd, Robin, *Victorian Modern*, Melbourne 1947.

Briggs, Martin S., 'British Colonial Architecture. 8—Australia', *The Builder* (London), 173, October 1947, pp. 425–9.

Clark, A. Lanyou, *Fifty Modern Homes*, Sydney 1940. 2nd edn 1946.

Dowling, Edward, *Australia and America in 1892 : a Contrast*, Government Printer, Sydney 1893 (pamphlet). Also in New South Wales Commissioners for the World's Columbian Exposition, Chicago, *Pamphlets issued by ...* , Government Printer, Sydney 1893, Vol. 2, pp. 1–172. Dowling concentrates on N.S.W., California and Canada.

Haddon, R. J., *Australian Architecture*, Melbourne 1908 (?).

Hanson, Brian, 'Rhapsody in Black Glass', *The Architectural Review* (London), 162, July 1977, pp. 58–64. Interview with Raymond McGrath.

[MacDonald, J. S.], *Australian Homes. Volume number 1*. Melbourne 1927.

Moore, William, *Story of Australian Art*, 2 vols, Sydney 1934. Vol. 2 has a biographical dictionary.

Nicholson, C. A., 'Notes on Australian Architecture: specially sketched and written for "The Review"', *The Architectural Review* (London), 3, 1897–8, pp. 100–9.

Prevost, Reginald A., *Australian Bungalows and Cottage Homes Design*, [Sydney? 1912?]. Reviewed by 'R. T.' in *Home and Garden Beautiful* (Melbourne), October 1912, pp. 60–5.

Sulman, John, *An Introduction to the Study of Town Planning in Australia*, Sydney 1921.

Taylor, George A., *Town Planning for Australia*, Sydney 1914.

——, *Town Planning with Common Sense*, 2nd edn, Sydney 1918.

Ure Smith, S. and Stevens, Bertram (eds), with Wilson, W. Hardy (collab.), *Domestic Architecture in Australia*, Sydney 1919.

Walling, Edith, *Cottages and Gardens in Australia*, Oxford 1947.

Wigmore, Lionel, *The Long View*, Melbourne 1963.

Britain and North America

Abercrombie, Patrick, *The Book of the Modern House*, London 1939.

American Institute of Architects, *A Symposium on Contemporary Architecture With Other Papers*, Washington 1931.

——, *The Significance of the Fine Arts*, Boston 1923.

Architect and Building News (London), 'The Colonies and Colonial Architecture', 75, 5 January 1906, pp. 18–23; 12 January 1906, pp. 33–6; 19 January 1906, pp. 49–50; 2 February 1906, pp. 81–2.

Architectural Essays from the Chicago School, Chicago 1967 reprint.

The Architectural Forum (New York), *The Book of Small Houses*, 1940.

——, 'House Design Competition', 94, March 1951.

——, *The House for Modern Living*, New York 1935.

——, 'Houses. . . .', November 1938, April 1939, October 1939. In each issue the major portion of the contents is about houses. See 1940 book immediately above.

——, [Modern Dutch Architecture], February 1929. Illustrations and plates, most of the issue.

The Architectural Record (New York), 'Marcel Breuer Builds for Himself', October 1948, pp. 92–8.

——, 'A New Appreciation of "Greene and Green"', May 1948, pp. 138–40.

The Architectural Review (London), 'British Empire Exhibition Wembley', 55, June 1924. Australia begins p. 248.

Ashbee, C. R., *A Book of Cottages and Little Houses*, [London 1906].

Ashworth, H. Ingham, *Flats. Design and Equipment*, London 1936.

Atkinson, William, *Views of Picturesque Cottages With Plans*, London 1905.

Beeson, E. W., *Port Sunlight. The Model Village of England*, New York 1905.

Bevier, Isabel, *The House. Its Plan, Decoration and Care*, American School of Home Economics, Chicago 1911.

Bicknell's Village Builder . . . , rev. edn, New York 1872.

Bidlake, W. H. *et al.*, *The Modern Home*, London [1906?]. (Ed. Walter Shaw Sparrow.)

Blake, Peter, *Marcel Breuer. Architect and Designer*, New York 1949.

The Book of a Hundred Houses, Chicago 1902.

Briggs, R. A., *Bungalows and Country Residences*, London 1891.

Cheney, Sheldon, *The New World Architecture*, New York 1929.

Dow, Alden B., 'Planning the Contemporary House', *The Architectural Record*, November 1947, pp. 89–114. An interesting parallel to events in Australia.

Elwood, P. H., Jr (ed.), *American Landscape Architecture*, New York 1924.

Ford, James and Ford, Katherine Morrow, *The Modern House in America*, New York 1940. A good survey.

Gibson, Louis H., *Convenient Houses*, New York 1889.

Ham, W. H. 'Prefabrication and the Small House', *Architecture* (New York), 65, April 1932, pp. 187–99.

Harbeson, John F., 'Design in Modern Architecture'. A series in *Pencil Points* (New York) that began in January 1930, pp. 3–10, and continued through the year.

Hastings, H. de C., *Recent English Domestic Architecture*, London 1929. Very good.

Hering, Oswald C., *Concrete and Stucco Houses*, New York 1912.

Hitchcock, Henry-Russell and Drexler, Arthur, *Built in USA : Postwar Architecture*, New York [1953].

Hitchcock, Henry-Russell and Johnson, Philip, *The International Style*, New York 1966 edn.

Holden, McLaughlin & Associates, 'American Houses, Inc.', *The Architectural Forum* (New York), April 1934, pp. 277–82.

Howard, Ebenezer (ed. R. J. Osborn), *Garden Cities of Tomorrow*, London 1945 edn.

Howe, George, 'Square Shadows, Whitemarsh, Pa.', *The Architectural Forum* (New York), 1936, pp. 193–206. An impeccable house by architect Howe.

Lake, Frances (ed.), *Daily Mail Ideal Home Book 1953–54*, [London 1954?]. Includes Australia.

Lowenstein, Milton D., 'Germany's Bauhaus Experiment', *Architecture* (New York), July 1929, pp. 1–6.

McDonald, John R. H., *Modern Housing*, London 1931.

McGrath, Raymond, *Twentieth-Century Houses*, London 1934.

Mumford, Lewis, 'Form in Modern Architecture', *Architecture* (New York). A series that began with September 1929, pp. 125–8, and continued through 1930.

——, 'Mass-production and the Modern House', *The Architectural Record* (New York), 67, January 1930, pp. 13–20; (Part 2), 67, February 1930, pp. 110–16.

Nelson, George (ed.), *Living Spaces*, New York 1952.

Newcomb, Rexford, *The Spanish House for America. Its Design, Furnishing and Garden*, Philadelphia 1927. Standard text of the period.

[Richardson, H. H.], *The Ames Memorial Buildings, North Easton, Mass.*, monograph of *American Architecture*, Boston 1866 (?).

Saylor, Henry H., *Bungalows : Their design, construction and furnishing with suggestions also for camps, summer homes and cottages of similar character*, New York 1911 and later editions.

Scott, M. H. Baillie, *Houses and Gardens*, London 1906.

Stevens, John Calvin and Cobb, A. W., *Examples of American Domestic Architecture*, New York 1889.

Summerson, John, 'The London Suburban Villa', *The Architectural Review* (London), 104, August 1948, pp. 63–72.

Vogelgesang, Shepard, 'Architect versus Engineer', *The Architectural Forum* (New York), September 1929, pp. 373–86.

von Holst, H. V., *Modern American Houses*, Chicago 1912.

Weaver, Lawrence, *The 'Country Life' Book of Cottages Costing from £150 to £600*, London 1913.

Yerbury, F. R., 'A Pictorial Review of Modern Architecture in Europe'. A series that ran in *Architecture* (New York) for most of 1929–31.

——, *Small Modern English Houses*, London 1929.

Yorke, F. R. S., *The Modern House in England*, London 1937.

Europe

Gut, Albert, *Der Wohnungsbau in Deutschland nach dem Wellkriege*, München 1928.

Muthesius, Hermann, *Das Englische Haus*, 3 vols, Berlin 1904. Excellent.

Vogel, F. Rud., *Das Amerikanische Haus*, Berlin 1910. Excellent.

Wattjes, J. G., *Moderne Nederlandsche villa's en Landhuizen*, Amsterdam 1929 (?).

Wendingen [no. 6], ... *Architect W. M. Dudok* ..., H. Th. Wijdeveld, Amsterdam, n.d. (received 1935 in Australia).

POST-1952

Australia

Anderson, Douglas, *Alexander Stewart Jolly, His Life and Works*, BArch thesis, University of New South Wales, 1969.

Apperly, Richard Eric, *Sydney Houses 1914–1939*, 2 vols, MArch thesis, University of New South Wales, 1973.

Baume, Michael, *The Sydney Opera House Affair*, Sydney 1967.

Berry, Jennifer, *Australian Cinema Architecture 1929–1940*, Honours thesis, Fine Arts Department, University of Sydney, 1973. (Held by Prof. Ross Thorne—for some reason.)

Birrell, James, *Walter Burley Griffin*, Brisbane 1964.

Blake, Peter, *Architecture for the New World. The Work of Harry Seidler*, Sydney 1973.

Boyd, Robin, *The Australian Ugliness*, Ringwood 1963 and later editions.

——, *Australia's Home. Its Origins, Builders and Occupiers*, Melbourne 1952 and later editions.

Brown, A. J., Sherrard, H. M. and Shaw, J. H., *An Introduction to Town and Country Planning*, 2nd edn, New York 1969.

Burchell, Lawrence Edward, *Government School Architecture in Colonial Victoria*, 2 vols, MA thesis, University of Melbourne, 1975.

Burnley, I. H. (ed.), *Urbanization in Australia: Aspects of the Post-war Experience*, Cambridge 1974.

Freeland, J. M., *Architect Extraordinary. The Life and Work of John Horbury Hunt: 1838–1904*, North Melbourne 1970.

——, *Architecture in Australia: a History*, Melbourne 1968 and later editions.

[Galbally, Ann and Plant, Margaret (eds)], *Studies in Australian Art*, Melbourne [1978].

Herman, Morton E., *The Architecture of Victorian Sydney*, 2 vols, MArch thesis, University of Sydney, 1960.

——, *The Architecture of Victorian Sydney*, Sydney 1956 and 2nd edn 1964.

——, *The Blackets, an Era of Australian Architecture*, Sydney 1962.

Johnson, Donald Leslie, *The Architecture of Walter Burley Griffin*, Melbourne 1977.

——, 'Australian Architectural Histories: 1848–1968', *Journal of the Society of Architectural Historians*, 31, December 1972, pp. 323–32.

——, 'Bauhaus, Breuer, Seidler: An Australian Synthesis', *Australian Journal of Art*, 1, 1977, pp. 65–81.

——, 'An Expatriate Planner at Canberra', *Journal of the American Institute of Planners*, 39, September 1973, pp. 326–36.

——, 'The Griffin/REICo Incinerators', *Architectural Association Quarterly*, 3, October 1971, pp. 46–55.

——, 'Sources of Modernism in Australian Architecture,' Art Association of Australia, *Architectural Papers 1976*, Sydney 1977.

——, 'Walter Burley Griffin, Architect, Landscape Architect and Community Planner' in H. Tanner (ed.), *Architects of Australia*, Melbourne, to be published in 1980.

——, 'Walter Burley Griffin in India', *Architecture Australia*, 66, May 1977, pp. 36–9.

Kooyman, Brian R., *William Hardy Wilson*, BArch thesis, University of New South Wales, 1971.

Orth, Myra Dickman, 'The Influence of the "American Romanesque" in Australia', *Journal of the Society of Architectural Historians*, 34, March 1975, pp. 3–18.

Queensland State Chapter, R.A.I.A., *Buildings of Queensland*, Brisbane 1959. Out of date.

Reynolds, Peter Leggett, *The Evolution of the Government Architect's Branch of the New South Wales Department of Public Works, 1788–1911*, 2 vols, Phd thesis, University of New South Wales, 1972.

Ruddock, Grenfell, 'Town and Country Planning in Great Britain, Part II', *The Regional Development Journal*, Canberra (Ministry of National Development, Division of Regional Development), 1, February 1950, pp. 2–31.

Sandercock, Leonie, *Property, Politics and Power: A History of City Planning in Adelaide, Melbourne and Sydney since 1900*, Phd thesis, Australian National University, 1974.

Saunders, David, 'Retrospective Robin Boyd', *Architecture in Australia*, February 1972, pp. 92–7.

——, ' . . . So I decided to go Overseas', *Architecture Australia*, 66, February 1977, pp. 22–8. Responses in letters, June and August 1977.

Seidler, Harry, *Houses, Interiors and Projects*, Sydney 1954.

——, *Harry Seidler, 1955/63*, Sydney 1963.

Serle, Geoffrey, *From Deserts the Prophets Come*, Melbourne 1973.

Smith, Bernard, *European Vision and the South Pacific, 1768–1850. A Study in the History of Art and Ideas*, Oxford 1960.

Smith, Bernard and Smith, Kate, *The Architectural Character of Glebe, Sydney*, Sydney 1973.

Spearritt, Peter, *An Urban History of Sydney 1920–1950*, Phd thesis, Australian National University, 1976. The pre-World War II period is well documented and discussed. Excellent bibliography.

Stevens, Clive William, *The Development of the Nineteenth Century Terrace House in Sydney*, MArch thesis, University of New South Wales, 1968.

Sumner, Ray, 'The Tropical Bungalow—the Search for an Indigenous Australian Architecture', *Australian Journal of Art*, 1, 1977, pp. 27–39.

Taylor, Jennifer, *An Australian Identity. Houses for Sydney 1953–63*, Sydney 1972.

Thorne, Ross, *Picture Palace Architecture in Australia*, South Melbourne 1976.

Wallace, Richard Ian, *Studies on the Natural Building Stones of New South Wales*, 2 vols, Phd thesis, University of New South Wales, 1972.

Wille, Peter, 'Frank Lloyd Wright in Victoria; one hundred years after his birth he still practises vicariously in Melbourne', *Architect* (Melbourne), 3, November 1969, pp. 24 ff.

Woffenden, H. G., *Architecture in New South Wales 1840–1900*, 2 vols, Phd thesis, University of Sydney, 1966.

Britain and North America

Andrews, Wayne, *Architecture, Ambitions and Americans*, Glencoe 1964.

Breuer, Marcel, *Buildings and Projects 1921–1961*, New York 1962.

Briggs, Asa, *Victorian Cities*, Middlesex 1968.

Brooks, H. Allen, *The Prairie School. Frank Lloyd Wright and His Midwest Contemporaries*, Toronto 1972.

Current, K. and Current, W. R., *Greene and Greene. Architects in the Residential Style*, Fort Worth 1974.

Gebhard, David (comp.), *Charles F. A. Voysey, Architect*, Santa Barbara 1970.

Greenberg, Allan, 'Lutyens' Architecture Restudied', *Perspecta* [12]: *the Yale Architectural Journal*, 1969, pp. 129–52.

Greif, Martin, *Depression Modern. The Thirties Style in America*, New York [1975].

Girouard, Mark, *Sweetness and Light. The 'Queen Anne' Movement 1860–1900*, Oxford 1977.

Gould, Jeremy, *Modern Houses in Britain, 1919–1939*, London 1977.

Gowans, Alan, *Images of American Living*, Philadelphia 1964.

Herbert, Gilbert, *Pioneers of Prefabrication. The British Contribution in the Nineteenth Century*, Baltimore 1978. Includes colonial work.

Hitchcock, Henry-Russell, *Architecture Nineteenth and Twentieth Centuries*, Baltimore 1958 and later editions. Good bibliography.

——, *The Architecture of H. H. Richardson and His Times*, 2nd edn, M.I.T., 1966.

Jackson, Anthony, *The Politics of Architecture. A History of Modern Architecture in Britain*, London 1970.

Jordy, William H., 'The Aftermath of the Bauhaus in America; Gropius, Mies and Breuer', *Perspectives in American History*, 2, Harvard University, 1968, pp. 485–543. Devoted to 'The Intellectual Migration'.

——, *American Buildings and Their Architects. The Impact of European Modernism in the Mid-Twentieth Century*, New York 1972.

——, *American Buildings and Their Architects. Progressive and Academic Ideals at the Turn of the Twentieth Century*, New York 1972.

Kronwolf, James D., *M. H. Baillie Scott and the Arts and Crafts Movement. Pioneers of Modern Design*, Baltimore 1972.

Macleod, Robert, *Style and Society. Architectural Ideology in Britain 1835–1914*, London 1971.

McCoy, Elizabeth, *Five California Architects*, New York 1960 (?).

Manson, Grant C., *Frank Lloyd Wright to 1910*, New York 1958.

Naylor, Gillian, *The Arts and Crafts Movement*, London 1971.

Nilsson, Sten, *European Architecture in India 1750–1850*, London 1968.

O'Gorman, James F., *H. H. Richardson and His Office*, Boston 1976.

Peisch, Mark L., *The Chicago School. Early Followers of Sullivan and Wright*, New York 1965.

Pommer, Richard, 'The Architecture of Urban Housing in the United States during the Early 1930s', *Journal of the Society of Architectural Historians*, 37, December 1974, pp. 235–64.

Richards, J. M. (ed.), *New Buildings in the [British] Commonwealth*, London 1961.

Robinson, Cervin and Bletter, Rosemarie Haag, *Skyscraper Style. Art Deco New York*, Oxford 1975.

Rykwert, Joseph, *On Adam's House in Paradise. The Idea of the Primitive Hut in Architectural History*, New York 1972.

Service, Alastair (ed.), *Edwardian Architecture and its Origins*, London 1975. Select bibliography.

——, *Edwardian Architecture. A Handbook to Building Design in Britain 1890–1914*, London 1977.

Scully, Vincent J. Jr, *The Shingle Style and the Stick Style*, rev. edn, New Haven 1971.

Stein, Clarence S., *Toward New Towns for America*, New York 1957.

Watkin, David, *Morality and Architecture. The Development of a Theme in Architectural History and Theory from the Gothic Revival to the Modern Movement*, Oxford 1977. Read carefully.

Whiffen, Marcus, *American Architecture Since 1780. A Guide to the Styles*, Cambridge, Mass. 1969. Good primer to styles.

Wrightson, Priscilla (ed.), *The small English house. A Catalogue of Books*, B. Weinreb cat. 35, London 1977.

European

Boesiger, W. and Birsberger, H., *Le Corbusier. 1910–1965*, London 1967.

Conrads, Ulrich (ed.), *Programmes and Manifestoes on Twentieth-Century Architecture*, London 1970.

Giedion, S., *Walter Gropius. Work and Teamwork*, Zurich 1954.

Herbert, Gilbert, *The Synthetic Vision of Walter Gropius*, Johannesburg 1959.

Le Corbusier, *Oeuvre Complete*, 7 vols, Zurich 1957–65.

Pehnt, Wolfgang, *Expressionist Architecture*, London 1973, New York 1975.

Rykwert, Joseph, 'Figini and Pollini', *The Architectural Design* (London), 37, August 1967, pp. 369–78.

Vickery, Robert, 'Bijvoet and Duiker', *Perspecta Thirteen Perspecta Fourteen* (The Yale Architectural Journal), 1971, pp. 131–61.

Index

PEOPLE, PLACES, BUILDINGS

ABBREVIATIONS

A.C.T.	Australian Capital Territory	MICH.	Michigan
ADEL.	Adelaide	N.J.	New Jersey
BRISB.	Brisbane	N.S.W.	New South Wales
BUCKS.	Buckinghamshire	N.T.	Northern Territory
CALIF.	California	N.Y.	New York
CONN.	Connecticut	N.Z.	New Zealand
ENG.	England	QLD	Queensland
FLA	Florida	S.A.	South Australia
HERTS.	Hertfordshire	SYD.	Sydney
IA	Iowa	TAS.	Tasmania
ILL.	Illinois	VIC.	Victoria
MASS.	Massachusetts	W.A.	Western Australia
MELB.	Melbourne	WISC.	Wisconsin

Page numbers in bold type refer to illustrations of buildings and designs